MapReduce Design Patterns

Vikram,
thanks!

Donald Miner and Adam Shook

O'REILLY®

Beijing · Cambridge · Farnham · Köln · Sebastopol · Tokyo

MapReduce Design Patterns

by Donald Miner and Adam Shook

Published by O'Reilly Media, Inc., 1005 Gravenstein Highway North, Sebastopol, CA 95472.

O'Reilly books may be purchased for educational, business, or sales promotional use. Online editions are also available for most titles (*http://my.safaribooksonline.com*). For more information, contact our corporate/institutional sales department: 800-998-9938 or *corporate@oreilly.com*.

Editors: Andy Oram and Mike Hendrickson	**Cover Designer:** Karen Montgomery
Production Editor: Christopher Hearse	**Interior Designer:** David Futato
Proofreader: Dawn Carelli	**Illustrator:** Rebecca Demarest

October 2012:   First Edition.

Revision History for the First Edition:
   2012-10-01   First release
See *http://oreilly.com/catalog/errata.csp?isbn=9781449358556* for release details.

ISBN: 978-1-449-35855-6

[LSI]

1349117903

Table of Contents

Preface

Welcome to *MapReduce Design Patterns*! This book will be unique in some ways and familiar in others. First and foremost, this book is obviously about design patterns, which are templates or general guides to solving problems. We took a look at other design patterns books that have been written in the past, particularly *Design Patterns: Elements of Reusable Object-Oriented Software*, by Gamma et al., which is commonly referred to as "The Gang of Four" book. For each pattern, you'll see a template that we reuse over and over that we loosely based off of their book. Repeatedly seeing a similar template will help you get to the specific information you need. This will be especially useful in the future when using this book as a reference.

This book is a bit more open-ended than a book in the "cookbook" series of texts as we don't call out specific problems. However, similarly to the cookbooks, the lessons in this book are short and categorized. You'll have to go a bit further than just copying and pasting our code to solve your problems, but we hope that you will find a pattern to get you at least 90% of the way for just about all of your challenges.

This book is mostly about the analytics side of Hadoop or MapReduce. We intentionally try not to dive into too much detail on how Hadoop or MapReduce works or talk too long about the APIs that we are using. These topics have been written about quite a few times, both online and in print, so we decided to focus on analytics.

In this preface, we'll talk about how to read this book since its format might be a bit different than most books you've read.

Intended Audience

The motivation for us to write this book was to fill a missing gap we saw in a lot of new MapReduce developers. They had learned how to use the system, got comfortable with writing MapReduce, but were lacking the experience to understand how to do things right or well. The intent of this book is to make up for having to make some of your own mistakes by educating you on how experts have figured out how to solve problems with MapReduce. So, in some ways, this book can be viewed as an intermediate or advanced MapReduce developer resource, but we think early beginners and gurus will find use out of it.

This book is also intended for anyone wanting to learn more about the MapReduce paradigm. The book goes deeply into the technical side of MapReduce with code examples and detailed explanations of the inner workings of a MapReduce system, which will help software engineers develop MapReduce analytics. However, quite a bit of time is spent discussing the motivation of some patterns and the common use cases for these patterns, which could be interesting to someone who just wants to know what a system like Hadoop can do.

To get the most out of this book, we suggest you have some knowledge of Hadoop, as all of the code examples are written for Hadoop and many of the patterns are discussed in a Hadoop context. A brief refresher will be given in the first chapter, along with some suggestions for additional reading material.

Pattern Format

The patterns in this book follow a single template format so they are easier to read in succession. Some patterns will omit some of the sections if they don't make sense in the context of that pattern.

Intent
> This section is a quick description of the problem the pattern is intended to solve.

Motivation
> This section explains why you would want to solve this problem or where it would appear. Some use cases are typically discussed in brief.

Applicability
> This section contains a set of criteria that must be true to be able to apply this pattern to a problem. Sometimes these are limitations in the design of the pattern and sometimes they help you make sure this pattern will work in your situation.

Structure
> This section explains the layout of the MapReduce job itself. It'll explain what the map phase does, what the reduce phase does, and also lets you know if it'll be using any custom partitioners, combiners, or input formats. This is the meat of the pattern and explains how to solve the problem.

Consequences
> This section is pretty short and just explains what the output of the pattern will be. This is the end goal of the output this pattern produces.

Resemblances
> For readers that have some experience with SQL or Pig, this section will show analogies of how this problem would be solved with these other languages. You

may even find yourself reading this section first as it gets straight to the point of what this pattern does.

Sometimes, SQL, Pig, or both are omitted if what we are doing with MapReduce is truly unique.

Known Uses

This section outlines some common use cases for this pattern.

Performance Analysis

This section explains the performance profile of the analytic produced by the pattern. Understanding this is important because every MapReduce analytic needs to be tweaked and configured properly to maximize performance. Without the knowledge of what resources it is using on your cluster, it would be difficult to do this.

The Examples in This Book

All of the examples in this book are written for Hadoop version 1.0.3. MapReduce is a paradigm that is seen in a number of open source and commercial systems these days, but we had to pick one to make our examples consistent and easy to follow, so we picked Hadoop. Hadoop was a logical choice since it a widely used system, but we hope that users of MongoDB's MapReduce and other MapReduce implementations will be able to extrapolate the examples in this text to their particular system of choice.

 In general, we try to use the newer mapreduce API for all of our examples, not the deprecated mapred API. Just be careful when mixing code from this book with other sources, as plenty of people still use mapred and their APIs are not compatible.

Our examples generally omit any sort of error handling, mostly to make the code more terse. In real-world big data systems, you can expect your data to be malformed and you'll want to be proactive in handling those situations in your analytics.

We use the same data set throughout this text: a dump of StackOverflow's databases. StackOverflow is a popular website in which software developers can go to ask and answer questions about any coding topic (including Hadoop). This data set was chosen because it is reasonable in size, yet not so big that you can't use it on a single node. This data set also contains human-generated natural language text as well as "structured" elements like usernames and dates.

Throughout the examples in this book, we try to break out parsing logic of this data set into helper functions to clearly distinguish what code is specific to this data set and which code is general and part of the pattern. Since the XML is pretty simple, we usually avoid using a full-blown XML parser and just parse it with some string operations in our Java code.

The data set contains five tables, of which we only use three: comments, posts, and users. All of the data is in well-formed XML, with one record per line.

We use the following three StackOverflow tables in this book:

comments

```
<row Id="2579740" PostId="2573882" Text="Are you getting any results? What
are you specifying as the command text?" CreationDate="2010-04-04T08:48:51.347"
UserId="95437" />
```

Comments are follow-up questions or suggestions users of the site can leave on posts (i.e., questions or answers).

posts

```
<row Id="6939296" PostTypeId="2" ParentId="6939137"
CreationDate="2011-08-04T09:50:25.043" Score="4" ViewCount=""
Body="&lt;p&gt;You should have imported Poll with &lt;code&gt;
from polls.models import Poll&lt;/code&gt;&lt;/p&gt;&#xA;"
OwnerUserId="634150" LastActivityDate="2011-08-04T09:50:25.043"
CommentCount="1" />
```

```
<row Id="6939304" PostTypeId="1" AcceptedAnswerId="6939433"
CreationDate="2011-08-04T09:50:58.910" Score="1" ViewCount="26"
Body="&lt;p&gt;Is it possible to gzip a single asp.net 3.5 page? my
site is hosted on IIS7 and for technical reasons I cannot enable gzip
compression site wide. does IIS7 have an option to gzip individual pages or
will I have to override OnPreRender and write some code to compress the
output?&lt;/p&gt;&#xA;" OwnerUserId="743184"
LastActivityDate="2011-08-04T10:19:04.107" Title="gzip a single asp.net page"
Tags="&lt;asp.net&gt;&lt;iis7&gt;&lt;gzip&gt;"
AnswerCount="2" />
```

Posts contain the questions and answers on the site. A user will post a question, and then other users are free to post answers to that question. Questions and answers can be upvoted and downvoted depending on if you think the post is constructive or not. In order to help categorize the questions, the creator of the question can specify a number of "tags," which say what the post is about. In the example above, we see that this post is about asp.net, iis, and gzip.

One thing to notice is that the body of the post is escaped HTML. This makes parsing it a bit more challenging, but it's not too bad with all the tools available. Most of the questions and many of the answers can get to be pretty long!

Posts are a bit more challenging because they contain both answers and questions intermixed. Questions have a PostTypeId of 1, while answers have a PostTypeId of 2. Answers point to their related question via the ParentId, a field that questions do not have. Questions, however, have a Title and Tags.

users

```
<row Id="352268" Reputation="3313" CreationDate="2010-05-27T18:34:45.817"
DisplayName="orangeoctopus" EmailHash="93fc5e3d9451bcd3fdb552423ceb52cd"
```

```
LastAccessDate="2011-09-01T13:55:02.013" Location="Maryland" Age="26"
Views="48" UpVotes="294" DownVotes="4" />
```

The users table contains all of the data about the account holders on StackOverflow. Most of this information shows up in the user's profile.

Users of StackOverflow have a reputation score, which goes up as other users upvote questions or answers that user has submitted to the website.

To learn more about the data set, refer to the documentation included with the download in *README.txt*.

In the examples, we parse the data set with a helper function that we wrote. This function takes in a line of StackOverflow data and returns a HashMap. This HashMap stores the labels as the keys and the actual data as the value.

```java
package mrdp.utils;

import java.util.HashMap;
import java.util.Map;

public class MRDPUtils {

    // This helper function parses the stackoverflow into a Map for us.
    public static Map<String, String> transformXmlToMap(String xml) {
        Map<String, String> map = new HashMap<String, String>();
        try {
            // exploit the fact that splitting on double quote
            //  tokenizes the data nicely for us
            String[] tokens = xml.trim().substring(5, xml.trim().length() - 3)
                .split("\"");

            for (int i = 0; i < tokens.length - 1; i += 2) {
                String key = tokens[i].trim();
                String val = tokens[i + 1];

                map.put(key.substring(0, key.length() - 1), val);
            }
        } catch (StringIndexOutOfBoundsException e) {
            System.err.println(xml);
        }

        return map;
    }
}
```

Conventions Used in This Book

The following typographical conventions are used in this book:

Italic
    Indicates new terms, URLs, email addresses, filenames, and file extensions.

Constant width

> Used for program listings, as well as within paragraphs to refer to program elements such as variable or function names, databases, data types, environment variables, statements, and keywords.

Constant width bold

> Shows commands or other text that should be typed literally by the user.

Constant width italic

> Shows text that should be replaced with user-supplied values or by values determined by context.

 This icon signifies a tip, suggestion, or general note.

 This icon indicates a warning or caution.

Using Code Examples

This book is here to help you get your job done. In general, you may use the code in this book in your programs and documentation. You do not need to contact us for permission unless you're reproducing a significant portion of the code. For example, writing a program that uses several chunks of code from this book does not require permission. Selling or distributing a CD-ROM of examples from O'Reilly books does require permission. Answering a question by citing this book and quoting example code does not require permission. Incorporating a significant amount of example code from this book into your product's documentation does require permission.

We appreciate, but do not require, attribution. An attribution usually includes the title, author, publisher, and ISBN. For example: "*MapReduce Design Patterns* by Donald Miner and Adam Shook (O'Reilly). Copyright 2013 Donald Miner and Adam Shook, 978-1-449-35855-6."

If you feel your use of code examples falls outside fair use or the permission given above, feel free to contact us at *permissions@oreilly.com*.

Safari® Books Online

Safari Books Online (*www.safaribooksonline.com*) is an on-demand digital library that delivers expert content in both book and video form from the world's leading authors in technology and business.

Technology professionals, software developers, web designers, and business and creative professionals use Safari Books Online as their primary resource for research, problem solving, learning, and certification training.

Safari Books Online offers a range of product mixes and pricing programs for organizations, government agencies, and individuals. Subscribers have access to thousands of books, training videos, and prepublication manuscripts in one fully searchable database from publishers like O'Reilly Media, Prentice Hall Professional, Addison-Wesley Professional, Microsoft Press, Sams, Que, Peachpit Press, Focal Press, Cisco Press, John Wiley & Sons, Syngress, Morgan Kaufmann, IBM Redbooks, Packt, Adobe Press, FT Press, Apress, Manning, New Riders, McGraw-Hill, Jones & Bartlett, Course Technology, and dozens more. For more information about Safari Books Online, please visit us online.

How to Contact Us

Please address comments and questions concerning this book to the publisher:

O'Reilly Media, Inc.
1005 Gravenstein Highway North
Sebastopol, CA 95472
800-998-9938 (in the United States or Canada)
707-829-0515 (international or local)
707-829-0104 (fax)

We have a web page for this book, where we list errata, examples, and any additional information. You can access this page at *http://oreil.ly/mapreduce-design-patterns*.

To comment or ask technical questions about this book, send email to *bookquestions@oreilly.com*.

For more information about our books, courses, conferences, and news, see our website at *http://www.oreilly.com*.

Find us on Facebook: *http://facebook.com/oreilly*

Follow us on Twitter: *http://twitter.com/oreillymedia*

Watch us on YouTube: *http://www.youtube.com/oreillymedia*

Acknowledgements

Books published by O'Reilly are always top notch and now we know why first hand. The support staff, especially our editor Andy Oram, has been extremely helpful in guiding us through this process. They give freedom to the authors to convey the message while supporting us in any way we need.

A special thanks goes out to those that read our book and provided useful commentary and reviews: Tom Wheeler, Patrick Angeles, Tom Kulish, and Lance Byrd. Thanks to Jeff Gold for providing some early encouragement and comments. We appreciate Eric Sammer's help in finding reviewers and wish him luck with his book *Hadoop Operations* (*http://shop.oreilly.com/product/0636920025085.do*).

The StackOverflow data set, which is used throughout this book, is freely available under the Creative Commons license. It's great that people are willing to spend the time to release the data set so that projects like this can make use of the content. What a truly wonderful contribution.

Don would like to thank the support he got from coworkers at Greenplum, who provided slack in my schedule to work on this project, moral support, and technical suggestions. These folks from Greenplum have helped in one way or another, whether they realize it or not: Ian Andrews, Dan Baskette, Nick Cayou, Paul Cegielski, Will Davis, Andrew Ettinger, Mike Goddard, Jacque Istok, Mike Maxey, Michael Parks, and Parham Parvizi. Also, thanks to Andy O'Brien for contributing the chapter on Postgres.

Adam would like to thank caffeine.

CHAPTER 1

Design Patterns and MapReduce

MapReduce is a computing paradigm for processing data that resides on hundreds of computers, which has been popularized recently by Google, Hadoop, and many others. The paradigm is extraordinarily powerful, but it does not provide a general solution to what many are calling "big data," so while it works particularly well on some problems, some are more challenging. This book will teach you what problems are amenable to the MapReduce paradigm, as well as how to use it effectively.

At first glance, many people do not realize that MapReduce is more of a framework than a tool. You have to fit your solution into the framework of map and reduce, which in some situations might be challenging. MapReduce is not a feature, but rather a constraint.

This makes problem solving easier and harder. It provides clear boundaries for what you can and cannot do, making the number of options you have to consider fewer than you may be used to. At the same time, figuring out how to solve a problem with constraints requires cleverness and a change in thinking.

Learning MapReduce is a lot like learning recursion for the first time: it is challenging to find the recursive solution to the problem, but when it comes to you, it is clear, concise, and elegant. In many situations you have to be conscious of system resources being used by the MapReduce job, especially inter-cluster network utilization. The tradeoff of being confined to the MapReduce framework is the ability to process your data with distributed computing, without having to deal with concurrency, robustness, scale, and other common challenges. But with a unique system and a unique way of problem solving, come unique design patterns.

What is a MapReduce design pattern? It is a template for solving a common and general data manipulation problem with MapReduce. A pattern is not specific to a domain such as text processing or graph analysis, but it is a general approach to solving a problem. Using design patterns is all about using tried and true design principles to build better software.

Designing good software is challenging for a number of reasons, and similar challenges face those who want to achieve good design in MapReduce. Just as good programmers can produce bad software due to poor design, good programmers can produce bad MapReduce algorithms. With MapReduce we're not only battling with clean and maintainable code, but also with the performance of a job that will be distributed across hundreds of nodes to compute over terabytes and even petabytes of data. In addition, this job is potentially competing with hundreds of others on a shared cluster of machines. This makes choosing the right design to solve your problem with MapReduce extremely important and can yield performance gains of several orders of magnitude. Before we dive into some design patterns in the chapters following this one, we'll talk a bit about how and why design patterns and MapReduce together make sense, and a bit of a history lesson of how we got here.

Design Patterns

Design patterns have been making developers' lives easier for years. They are tools for solving problems in a reusable and general way so that the developer can spend less time figuring out how he's going to overcome a hurdle and move onto the next one. They are also a way for veteran problem solvers to pass down their knowledge in a concise way to younger generations.

One of the major milestones in the field of design patterns in software engineering is the book *Design Patterns: Elements of Reusable Object-Oriented Software*, by Gamma et al. (the "Gang of Four"). None of the patterns in this very popular book were new and many had been in use for several years. The reason why it was and still is so influential is the authors took the time to document the most important design patterns across the field of object-oriented programming. Since the book was published in 1994, most individuals interested in good design heard about patterns from word of mouth or had to root around conferences, journals, and a barely existent World Wide Web.

Design patterns have stood the test of time and have shown the right level of abstraction: not too specific that there are too many of them to remember and too hard to tailor to a problem, yet not too general that tons of work has to be poured into a pattern to get things working. This level of abstraction also has the major benefit of providing developers with a common language in which to communicate verbally and through code. Simply saying "abstract factory" is easier than explaining what an abstract factory is over and over. Also, when looking at a stranger's code that implements an abstract factory, you already have a general understanding of what the code is trying to accomplish.

MapReduce design patterns fill this same role in a smaller space of problems and solutions. They provide a general framework for solving your data computation issues, without being specific to the problem domain. Experienced MapReduce developers can pass on knowledge of how to solve a general problem to more novice MapReduce developers. This is extremely important because MapReduce is a new technology with a fast adoption rate and there are new developers joining the community every day. MapReduce design patterns also provide a common language for teams working together on MapReduce problems. Suggesting to someone that they should use a "reduce-side join" instead of a "map-side replicated join" is more concise than explaining the low-level mechanics of each.

The MapReduce world is in a state similar to the object-oriented world before 1994. Patterns today are scattered across blogs, websites such as StackOverflow, deep inside other books, and inside very advanced technology teams at organizations across the world. The intent of this book is not to provide some groundbreaking new ways to solve problems with MapReduce that nobody has seen before, but instead to collect patterns that have been developed by veterans in the field so that they can be shared with everyone else.

 Even provided with some design patterns, genuine experience with the MapReduce paradigm is still necessary to understand when to apply them. When you are trying to solve a new problem with a pattern you saw in this book or elsewhere, be very careful that the pattern fits the problem by paying close attention to its "Applicability" section.

For the most part, the MapReduce design patterns in this book are intended to be platform independent. MapReduce, being a paradigm published by Google without any actual source code, has been reimplemented a number of times, both as a stand-alone system (e.g., Hadoop, Disco, Amazon Elastic MapReduce) and as a query language within a larger system (e.g., MongoDB, Greenplum DB, Aster Data). Even if design patterns are intended to be general, we write this book with a Hadoop perspective. Many of these patterns can be applied in other systems, such as MongoDB, because they conform to the same conceptual architecture. However, some technical details may be different from implementation to implementation. The Gang of Four's book on design patterns was written with a C++ perspective, but developers have found the concepts conveyed in the book useful in modern languages such as Ruby and Python. The patterns in this book should be usable with systems other than Hadoop. You'll just have to use the code examples as a guide to developing your own code.

MapReduce History

How did we get to the point where a MapReduce design patterns book is a good idea? At a certain point, the community's momentum and widespread use of the paradigm reaches a critical mass where it is possible to write a comprehensive list of design patterns to be shared with developers everywhere. Several years ago, when Hadoop was still in its infancy, not enough had been done with the system to figure out what it is capable of. But the speed at which MapReduce has been adopted is remarkable. It went from an interesting paper from Google in 2004 to a widely adopted industry standard in distributed data processing in 2012.

The actual origins of MapReduce are arguable, but the paper that most cite as the one that started us down this journey is "MapReduce: Simplified Data Processing on Large Clusters" (*http://research.google.com/archive/mapreduce.html*) by Jeffrey Dean and Sanjay Ghemawat in 2004. This paper described how Google split, processed, and aggregated their data set of mind-boggling size.

Shortly after the release of the paper, a free and open source software pioneer by the name of Doug Cutting started working on a MapReduce implementation to solve scalability in another project he was working on called Nutch, an effort to build an open source search engine. Over time and with some investment by Yahoo!, Hadoop split out as its own project and eventually became a top-level Apache Foundation project. Today, numerous independent people and organizations contribute to Hadoop. Every new release adds functionality and boosts performance.

Several other open source projects have been built with Hadoop at their core, and this list is continually growing. Some of the more popular ones include Pig, Hive, HBase, Mahout, and ZooKeeper. Doug Cutting and other Hadoop experts have mentioned several times that Hadoop is becoming the kernel of a distributed operating system in which distributed applications can be built. In this book, we'll be explaining the examples with the least common denominator in the Hadoop ecosystem, Java MapReduce. In the resemblance sections of each pattern in some chapters, we'll typically outline a parallel for Pig and SQL that could be used in Hive.

MapReduce and Hadoop Refresher

The point of this section is to provide a quick refresher on MapReduce in the Hadoop context, since the code examples in this book are written in Hadoop. Some beginners might want to refer to a more in-depth resource such as Tom White's excellent *Hadoop: The Definitive Guide* (*http://shop.oreilly.com/product/0636920021773.do*) or the Apache Hadoop website (*http://hadoop.apache.org/*). These resources will help you get started in setting up a development or fully productionalized environment that will allow you to follow along the code examples in this book.

Hadoop MapReduce jobs are divided into a set of *map tasks* and *reduce tasks* that run in a distributed fashion on a cluster of computers. Each task works on the small subset of the data it has been assigned so that the load is spread across the cluster. The map tasks generally load, parse, transform, and filter data. Each reduce task is responsible for handling a subset of the map task output. Intermediate data is then copied from mapper tasks by the reducer tasks in order to group and aggregate the data. It is incredible what a wide range of problems can be solved with such a straightforward paradigm, from simple numerical aggregations to complex join operations and Cartesian products.

The input to a MapReduce job is a set of files in the data store that are spread out over the *Hadoop Distributed File System* (HDFS). In Hadoop, these files are split with an *input format*, which defines how to separate a file into *input splits*. An input split is a byte-oriented view of a chunk of the file to be loaded by a map task.

Each map task in Hadoop is broken into the following phases: *record reader, mapper, combiner*, and *partitioner*. The output of the map tasks, called the intermediate keys and values, are sent to the reducers. The reduce tasks are broken into the following phases: *shuffle, sort, reducer*, and *output format*. The nodes in which the map tasks run are optimally on the nodes in which the data rests. This way, the data typically does not have to move over the network and can be computed on the local machine.

record reader
> The record reader translates an input split generated by input format into records. The purpose of the record reader is to parse the data into records, but not parse the record itself. It passes the data to the mapper in the form of a key/value pair. Usually the key in this context is positional information and the value is the chunk of data that composes a record. Customized record readers are outside the scope of this book. We generally assume you have an appropriate record reader for your data.

map
> In the mapper, user-provided code is executed on each key/value pair from the record reader to produce zero or more new key/value pairs, called the intermediate pairs. The decision of what is the key and value here is not arbitrary and is very important to what the MapReduce job is accomplishing. The key is what the data will be grouped on and the value is the information pertinent to the analysis in the reducer. Plenty of detail will be provided in the design patterns in this book to explain what and why the particular key/value is chosen. One major differentiator between MapReduce design patterns is the semantics of this pair.

combiner
> The combiner, an optional localized reducer, can group data in the map phase. It takes the intermediate keys from the mapper and applies a user-provided method to aggregate values in the small scope of that one mapper. For example, because the count of an aggregation is the sum of the counts of each part, you can produce an intermediate count and then sum those intermediate counts for the final result. In many situations, this significantly reduces the amount of data that has to move over the network. Sending (`hello world, 3`) requires fewer bytes than sending (`hello world, 1`) three times over the network. Combiners will be covered in more depth with the patterns that use them extensively. Many new Hadoop developers ignore combiners, but they often provide extreme performance gains with no downside. We will point out which patterns benefit from using a combiner, and which ones cannot use a combiner. A combiner is not guaranteed to execute, so it cannot be a part of the overall algorithm.

partitioner
> The partitioner takes the intermediate key/value pairs from the mapper (or combiner if it is being used) and splits them up into shards, one shard per reducer.

By default, the partitioner interrogates the object for its hash code, which is typically an md5sum. Then, the partitioner performs a modulus operation by the number of reducers: `key.hashCode() % (number of reducers)`. This randomly distributes the keyspace evenly over the reducers, but still ensures that keys with the same value in different mappers end up at the same reducer. The default behavior of the partitioner can be customized, and will be in some more advanced patterns, such as sorting. However, changing the partitioner is rarely necessary. The partitioned data is written to the local file system for each map task and waits to be pulled by its respective reducer.

shuffle and sort

The reduce task starts with the *shuffle and sort* step. This step takes the output files written by all of the partitioners and downloads them to the local machine in which the reducer is running. These individual data pieces are then sorted by key into one larger data list. The purpose of this sort is to group equivalent keys together so that their values can be iterated over easily in the reduce task. This phase is not customizable and the framework handles everything automatically. The only control a developer has is how the keys are sorted and grouped by specifying a custom `Comparator` object.

reduce

The reducer takes the grouped data as input and runs a `reduce` function once per key grouping. The function is passed the key and an iterator over all of the values associated with that key. A wide range of processing can happen in this function, as we'll see in many of our patterns. The data can be aggregated, filtered, and combined in a number of ways. Once the `reduce` function is done, it sends zero or more key/value pair to the final step, the output format. Like the `map` function, the `reduce` function will change from job to job since it is a core piece of logic in the solution.

output format

The output format translates the final key/value pair from the `reduce` function and writes it out to a file by a record writer. By default, it will separate the key and value with a tab and separate records with a newline character. This can typically be customized to provide richer output formats, but in the end, the data is written out to HDFS, regardless of format. Like the record reader, customizing your own output format is outside of the scope of this book, since it simply deals with I/O.

Hadoop Example: Word Count

Now that you're refreshed on the steps of the whole MapReduce process, let's dive into a quick and simple example. The "Word Count" program is the canonical example in MapReduce, and for good reason. It is a straightforward application of MapReduce and MapReduce can handle it extremely efficiently. Many people complain about the

"Word Count" program being overused as an example, but hopefully the rest of the book makes up for that!

In this particular example, we're going to be doing a word count over user-submitted comments on StackOverflow. The content of the Text field will be pulled out and pre-processed a bit, and then we'll count up how many times we see each word. An example record from this data set is:

```
<row Id="8189677" PostId="6881722" Text="Have you looked at Hadoop?" Creation
Date="2011-07-30T07:29:33.343" UserId="831878" />
```

This record is the 8,189,677th comment on Stack Overflow, and is associated with post number 6,881,722 by user number 831,878. The number of the PostId and the UserId are foreign keys to other portions of the data set. We'll show how to join these datasets together in the chapter on join patterns.

The first chunk of code we'll look at is the driver. The driver takes all of the components that we've built for our MapReduce job and pieces them together to be submitted to execution. This code is usually pretty generic and considered "boiler plate." You'll find that in all of our patterns the driver stays the same for the most part.

This code is derived from the "Word Count" example that ships with Hadoop Core:

```
import java.io.IOException;
import java.util.StringTokenizer;
import java.util.Map;
import java.util.HashMap;

import org.apache.hadoop.conf.Configuration;
import org.apache.hadoop.fs.Path;
import org.apache.hadoop.io.IntWritable;
import org.apache.hadoop.io.Text;
import org.apache.hadoop.mapreduce.Job;
import org.apache.hadoop.mapreduce.Mapper;
import org.apache.hadoop.mapreduce.Reducer;
import org.apache.hadoop.mapreduce.lib.input.FileInputFormat;
import org.apache.hadoop.mapreduce.lib.output.FileOutputFormat;
import org.apache.hadoop.util.GenericOptionsParser;

import org.apache.commons.lang.StringEscapeUtils;

public class CommentWordCount {

  public static Map<String, String> transformXmlToMap(String xml) {
        ...
  }

  public static class WordCountMapper
      extends Mapper<Object, Text, Text, IntWritable> {
        ...
  }

  public static class IntSumReducer
      extends Reducer<Text, IntWritable, Text, IntWritable> {
```

```
        ...
    }

    public static void main(String[] args) throws Exception {
      Configuration conf = new Configuration();
      String[] otherArgs =
          new GenericOptionsParser(conf, args).getRemainingArgs();
      if (otherArgs.length != 2) {
        System.err.println("Usage: CommentWordCount <in> <out>");
        System.exit(2);
      }

      Job job = new Job(conf, "StackOverflow Comment Word Count");
      job.setJarByClass(CommentWordCount.class);
      job.setMapperClass(WordCountMapper.class);
      job.setCombinerClass(IntSumReducer.class);
      job.setReducerClass(IntSumReducer.class);
      job.setOutputKeyClass(Text.class);
      job.setOutputValueClass(IntWritable.class);
      FileInputFormat.addInputPath(job, new Path(otherArgs[0]));
      FileOutputFormat.setOutputPath(job, new Path(otherArgs[1]));
      System.exit(job.waitForCompletion(true) ? 0 : 1);
    }
  }
```

The purpose of the driver is to orchestrate the jobs. The first few lines of main are all about parsing command line arguments. Then we start setting up the job object by telling it what classes to use for computations and what input paths and output paths to use. That's about it! It's just important to make sure the class names match up with the classes you wrote and that the output key and value types match up with the output types of the mapper.

One way you'll see this code change from pattern to pattern is the usage of job.setCombinerClass. In some cases, the combiner simply cannot be used due to the nature of the reducer. In other cases, the combiner class will be different from the reducer class. The combiner is very effective in the "Word Count" program and is quite simple to activate.

Next is the mapper code that parses and prepares the text. Once some of the punctuation and random text is cleaned up, the text string is split up into a list of words. Then the intermediate key produced is the word and the value produced is simply "1." This means we've seen this word once. Even if we see the same word twice in one line, we'll output the word and "1" twice and it'll be taken care of in the end. Eventually, all of these ones will be summed together into the global count of that word.

```
    public static class WordCountMapper
        extends Mapper<Object, Text, Text, IntWritable> {

      private final static IntWritable one = new IntWritable(1);
      private Text word = new Text();

      public void map(Object key, Text value, Context context)
```

```
            throws IOException, InterruptedException {

        // Parse the input string into a nice map
        Map<String, String> parsed = MRDPUtils.transformXmlToMap(value.toString());

        // Grab the "Text" field, since that is what we are counting over
        String txt = parsed.get("Text");

        // .get will return null if the key is not there
        if (txt == null) {
          // skip this record
            return;
        }

        // Unescape the HTML because the data is escaped.
        txt = StringEscapeUtils.unescapeHtml(txt.toLowerCase());

        // Remove some annoying punctuation
        txt = txt.replaceAll("'", ""); // remove single quotes (e.g., can't)
        txt = txt.replaceAll("[^a-zA-Z]", " "); // replace the rest with a space

        // Tokenize the string by splitting it up on whitespace into
        //   something we can iterate over,
        //   then send the tokens away
        StringTokenizer itr = new StringTokenizer(txt);
        while (itr.hasMoreTokens()) {
          word.set(itr.nextToken());
          context.write(word, one);
        }
      }
    }
}
```

The first function, `MRDP.transformXmlToMap`, is a helper function to parse a line of Stack Overflow data in a generic manner. You'll see it used in a number of our examples. It basically takes a line of the StackOverflow XML (which has a very predictable format) and matches up the XML attributes with the values into a `Map`.

Next, turn your attention to the `WordCountMapper` class. This code is a bit more complicated than the driver (for good reason!). The mapper is where we'll see most of the work done. The first major thing to notice is the type of the parent class:

```
Mapper<Object, Text, Text, IntWritable>
```

They map to the types of the input key, input value, output key, and output value, respectively. We don't care about the key of the input in this case, so that's why we use `Object`. The data coming in is `Text` (Hadoop's special `String` type) because we are reading the data as a line-by-line text document. Our output key and value are `Text` and `IntWritable` because we will be using the word as the key and the count as the value.

The mapper input key and value data types are dictated by the job's configured FileInputFormat. The default implementation is the TextInputFormat, which provides the number of bytes read so far in the file as the key in a LongWritable object and the line of text as the value in a Text object. These key/value data types are likely to change if you are using different input formats.

Up until we start using the StringTokenizer towards the bottom of the code, we're just cleaning up the string. We unescape the data because the string was stored in an escaped manner so that it wouldn't mess up XML parsing. Next, we remove any stray punctuation so that the literal string Hadoop! is considered the same word as Hadoop? and Hadoop. Finally, for each token (i.e., word) we emit the word with the number 1, which means we saw the word once. The framework then takes over to shuffle and sorts the key/value pairs to reduce tasks.

Finally comes the reducer code, which is relatively simple. The reduce function gets called once per key grouping, in this case each word. We'll iterate through the values, which will be numbers, and take a running sum. The final value of this running sum will be the sum of the ones.

```
public static class IntSumReducer
        extends Reducer<Text, IntWritable, Text, IntWritable> {
    private IntWritable result = new IntWritable();

    public void reduce(Text key, Iterable<IntWritable> values,
            Context context) throws IOException, InterruptedException {
        int sum = 0;
        for (IntWritable val : values) {
            sum += val.get();
        }

        result.set(sum);
        context.write(key, result);
    }
}
```

As in the mapper, we specify the input and output types via the template parent class. Also like the mapper, the types correspond to the same things: input key, input value, output key, and output value. The input key and input value data types must match the output key/value types from the mapper. The output key and output value data types must match the types that the job's configured FileOutputFormat is expecting. In this case, we are using the default TextOutputFormat, which can take any two Writable objects as output.

The reduce function has a different signature from map, though: it gives you an Iterator over values instead of just a single value. This is because you are now iterating over all values that have that key, instead of just one at a time. The key is very important in the reducer of pretty much every MapReduce job, unlike the input key in the map.

Anything we pass to `context.write` will get written out to a file. Each reducer will create one file, so if you want to coalesce them together you'll have to write a post-processing step to concatenate them.

Now that we've gotten a straightforward example out of the way, let's dive into some design patterns!

Pig and Hive

There is less need for MapReduce design patterns in a ecosystem with Hive and Pig. However, we would like to take this opportunity early in the book to explain why MapReduce design patterns are still important.

Pig and Hive are higher-level abstractions of MapReduce. They provide an interface that has nothing to do with "map" or "reduce," but the systems interpret the higher-level language into a series of MapReduce jobs. Much like how a query planner in an RDBMS translates SQL into actual operations on data, Hive and Pig translate their respective languages into MapReduce operations.

As will be seen throughout this book in the resemblances sections, Pig and SQL (or HiveQL) can be significantly more terse than the raw Hadoop implementations in Java. For example, it will take several pages to explain total order sorting, while Pig is able to get the job done in a few lines.

So why should we use Java MapReduce in Hadoop at all when we have options like Pig and Hive? What was the point in the authors of this book spending time explaining how to implement something in hundreds of lines of code when the same can be accomplished in a couple lines? There are two core reasons.

First, there is conceptual value in understanding the lower-level workings of a system like MapReduce. The developer that understands how Pig actually performs a reduce-side join will make smarter decisions. Using Pig or Hive without understanding Map-Reduce can lead to some dangerous situations. Just because you're benefiting from a higher-level interface doesn't mean you can ignore the details. Large MapReduce clusters are heavy machinery and need to be respected as such.

Second, Pig and Hive aren't there yet in terms of full functionality and maturity (as of 2012). It is obvious that they haven't reached their full potential yet. Right now, they simply can't tackle all of the problems in the ways that Java MapReduce can. This will surely change over time and with every major release, major features, and bux fixes are added. Speaking hypothetically, say that at Pig version 0.6, your organization could write 50% of their analytics in Pig. At version 0.9, now you are at 90%. With every release, more and more can be done at a higher-level of abstraction. The funny thing about trends things like this in software engineering is that the last 10% of problems that can't be solved with a higher-level of abstraction are also likely to be the most critical and most challenging. This is when something like Java is going to be the best tool for the job. Some still use assembly language when they really have to!

When you can, write your MapReduce in Pig or Hive. Some of the major benefits of using these higher-level of abstractions include readability, maintainability, development time, and automatic optimization. Rarely is the often-cited performance hit due to indirection a serious consideration. These analytics are running in batch and are taking several minutes already, so what does a minute or two more really matter? In some cases, the query plan optimizer in Pig or Hive will be better at optimizing your code than you are! In a small fraction of situations, the extra few minutes added by Pig or Hive will matter, in which case you should use Java MapReduce.

Pig and Hive are likely to influence MapReduce design patterns more than anything else. New feature requests in Pig and Hive will likely translate down into something that could be a design pattern in MapReduce. Likewise, as more design patterns are developed for MapReduce, some of the more popular ones will become first-class operations at a higher level of abstraction.

Pig and Hive have patterns of their own and experts will start documenting more as they solve more problems. Hive has the benefit of building off of decades of SQL patterns, but not all patterns in SQL are smart in Hive and vice versa. Perhaps as these platforms gain more popularity, cookbook and design pattern books will be written for them.

CHAPTER 2

Summarization Patterns

Your data is large and vast, with more data coming into the system every day. This chapter focuses on design patterns that produce a top-level, summarized view of your data so you can glean insights not available from looking at a localized set of records alone. Summarization analytics are all about grouping similar data together and then performing an operation such as calculating a statistic, building an index, or just simply counting.

Calculating some sort of aggregate over groups in your data set is a great way to easily extract value right away. For example, you might want to calculate the total amount of money your stores have made by state or the average amount of time someone spends logged into your website by demographic. Typically, with a new data set, you'll start with these types of analyses to help you gauge what is interesting or unique in your data and what needs a closer look.

The patterns in this chapter are *numerical summarizations*, *inverted index*, and *counting with counters*. They are more straightforward applications of MapReduce than some of the other patterns in this book. This is because grouping data together by a key is the core function of the MapReduce paradigm: all of the keys are grouped together and collected in the reducers. If you emit the fields in the mapper you want to group on as your key, the grouping is all handled by the MapReduce framework for free.

Numerical Summarizations

Pattern Description

The *numerical summarizations* pattern is a general pattern for calculating aggregate statistical values over your data is discussed in detail. Be careful of how deceptively simple this pattern is! It is extremely important to use the combiner properly and to understand the calculation you are performing.

Intent

Group records together by a key field and calculate a numerical aggregate per group to get a top-level view of the larger data set.

Consider θ to be a generic numerical summarization function we wish to execute over some list of values $(v_1, v_2, v_3, ..., v_n)$ to find a value λ, i.e. $\lambda = \theta(v_1, v_2, v_3, ..., v_n)$. Examples of θ include a minimum, maximum, average, median, and standard deviation.

Motivation

Many data sets these days are too large for a human to get any real meaning out it by reading through it manually. For example, if your website logs each time a user logs onto the website, enters a query, or performs any other notable action, it would be extremely difficult to notice any real usage patterns just by reading through terabytes of log files with a text reader. If you group logins by the hour of the day and perform a count of the number of records in each group, you can plot these counts on a histogram and recognize times when your website is more active. Similarly, if you group advertisements by types, you can determine how affective your ads are for better targeting. Maybe you want to cycle ads based on how effective they are at the time of day. All of these types of questions can be answered through numerical summarizations to get a top-level view of your data.

Applicability

Numerical summarizations should be used when both of the following are true:

- You are dealing with numerical data or counting.
- The data can be grouped by specific fields.

Structure

Figure 2-1 shows the general structure of how a numerical summarization is executed in MapReduce. The breakdown of each MapReduce component is described in detail:

- The mapper outputs keys that consist of each field to group by, and values consisting of any pertinent numerical items. Imagine the mapper setting up a relational table, where the columns relate to the fields which the function θ will be executed over and each row contains an individual record output from the mapper. The output value of the mapper contains the values of each column and the output key determines the table as a whole, as each table is created by MapReduce's grouping functionality.

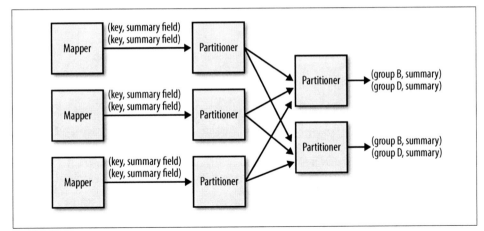

Figure 2-1. The structure of the numerical summarizations pattern

 Grouping typically involves sending a large subset of the input data down to finally be reduced. Each input record is most likely going to be output from the map phase. Make sure to reduce the amount of data being sent to the reducers by choosing only the fields that are necessary to the analytic and handling any bad input conditions properly.

- The combiner can greatly reduce the number of intermediate key/value pairs to be sent across the network to the reducers for some numerical summarization functions. If the function θ is an associative and commutative operation, it can be used for this purpose. That is, if you can arbitrarily change the order of the values and you can group the computation arbitrarily, you can use a combiner here. Discussions of such combiners are given in the examples following this section.

- Numerical summaries can benefit from a custom partitioner to better distribute key/value pairs across n number of reduce tasks. The need for this is rare, but can be done if job execution time is critical, the amount of data is huge, and there is severe data skew.

  A custom partitioner is often overlooked, but taking the time to understand the distribution of output keys and partitioning based on this distribution will improve performance when grouping (and everything else, for that matter). Starting a hundred reduce tasks, only to have eighty of them complete in thirty seconds and the others in twenty-five minutes, is not efficient.

- The reducer receives a set of numerical values $(v_1, v_2, v_3, ..., v_n)$ associated with a group-by key records to perform the function $\lambda = \theta(v_1, v_2, v_3, ..., v_n)$. The value of λ is output with the given input key.

Consequences

The output of the job will be a set of part files containing a single record per reducer input group. Each record will consist of the key and all aggregate values.

Known uses

Word count

The "Hello World" of MapReduce. The application outputs each word of a document as the key and "1" as the value, thus grouping by words. The reduce phase then adds up the integers and outputs each unique word with the sum. An example of a word count application can be seen in Chapter 1.

Record count

A very common analytic to get a heartbeat of your data flow rate on a particular interval (weekly, daily, hourly, etc.).

Min/Max/Count

An analytic to determine the minimum, maximum, and count of a particular event, such as the first time a user posted, the last time a user posted, and the number of times they posted in between that time period. You don't have to collect all three of these aggreagtes at the same time, or any of the other use cases listed here if you are only interested in one of them.

Average/Median/Standard deviation

Similar to Min/Max/Count, but not as straightforward of an implementation because these operations are not associative. A combiner can be used for all three, but requires a more complex approach than just reusing the reducer implementation.

Resemblances

SQL

The Numerical Aggregation pattern is analogous to using aggregates after a GROUP BY in SQL:

```
SELECT MIN(numericalcol1), MAX(numericalcol1),
       COUNT(*) FROM table GROUP BY groupcol2;
```

Pig

The GROUP … BY expression, followed by a FOREACH … GENERATE:

```
b = GROUP a BY groupcol2;
c = FOREACH b GENERATE group, MIN(a.numericalcol1),
       MAX(a.numericalcol1), COUNT_STAR(a);
```

Performance analysis

Aggregations performed by jobs using this pattern typically perform well when the combiner is properly used. These types of operations are what MapReduce was built for. Like most of the patterns in this book, developers need to be concerned about the appropriate number of reducers and take into account any data skew that may be present in the reduce groups. That is, if there are going to be many more intermediate key/value pairs with a specific key than other keys, one reducer is going to have a lot more work to do than others.

Numerical Summarization Examples

Minimum, maximum, and count example

Calculating the minimum, maximum, and count of a given field are all excellent applications of the numerical summarization pattern. After a grouping operation, the reducer simply iterates through all the values associated with the group and finds the min and max, as well as counts the number of members in the key grouping. Due to the associative and commutative properties, a combiner can be used to vastly cut down on the number of intermediate key/value pairs that need to be shuffled to the reducers. If implemented correctly, the code used for your reducer can be identical to that of a combiner.

The following descriptions of each code section explain the solution to the problem.

Problem: Given a list of user's comments, determine the first and last time a user commented for each hour and the total number of comments in each hour.

MinMaxCountTuple code. The MinMaxCountTuple is a Writable object that stores three values. This class is used as the output value from the mapper. While these values can be crammed into a Text object with some delimiter, it is typically a better practice to create a custom Writable. Not only is it cleaner, but you won't have to worry about any string parsing when it comes time to grab these values from the reduce phase. These custom writable objects are used throughout other examples in this pattern. Below is the implementation of the MinMaxCountTuple writable object. Other writables used in this chapter are very similar to this and are ommitted for brevity.

```
public class MinMaxCountTuple implements Writable {
    private Date min = new Date();
    private Date max = new Date();
    private long count = 0;

    private final static SimpleDateFormat frmt = new SimpleDateFormat(
            "yyyy-MM-dd'T'HH:mm:ss.SSS");

    public Date getMin() {
        return min;
    }

    public void setMin(Date min) {
        this.min = min;
    }
```

```
        public Date getMax() {
            return max;
        }

        public void setMax(Date max) {
            this.max = max;
        }

        public long getCount() {
            return count;
        }

        public void setCount(long count) {
            this.count = count;
        }

        public void readFields(DataInput in) throws IOException {
            // Read the data out in the order it is written,
            // creating new Date objects from the UNIX timestamp
            min = new Date(in.readLong());
            max = new Date(in.readLong());
            count = in.readLong();
        }

        public void write(DataOutput out) throws IOException {
            // Write the data out in the order it is read,
            // using the UNIX timestamp to represent the Date
            out.writeLong(min.getTime());
            out.writeLong(max.getTime());
            out.writeLong(count);
        }

        public String toString() {
            return frmt.format(min) + "\t" + frmt.format(max) + "\t" + count;
        }
    }
```

Mapper code. The mapper will preprocess our input values by extracting the XML attributes from each input record: the creation data and the user identifier. The input key is ignored. The creation date is parsed into a Java `Date` object for ease of comparison in the combiner and reducer. The output key is the user ID and the value is three columns of our future output: the minimum date, the maximum date, and the number of comments this user has created. These three fields are stored in a custom `Writable` object of type `MinMaxCountTuple`, which stores the first two columns as `Date` objects and the final column as a `long`. These names are accurate for the reducer but don't really reflect how the fields are used in the mapper, but we wanted to use the same data type for both the mapper and the reducer. In the mapper, we'll set both min and max to the comment creation date. The date is output twice so that we can take advantage of the combiner optimization that is described later. The third column will be a count of 1, to indicate that we know this user posted one comment. Eventually, all of these counts are going to be summed together and the minimum and maximum date will be determined in the reducer.

```
public static class MinMaxCountMapper extends
        Mapper<Object, Text, Text, MinMaxCountTuple> {

    // Our output key and value Writables
    private Text outUserId = new Text();
    private MinMaxCountTuple outTuple = new MinMaxCountTuple();

    // This object will format the creation date string into a Date object
    private final static SimpleDateFormat frmt =
                    new SimpleDateFormat("yyyy-MM-dd'T'HH:mm:ss.SSS");

    public void map(Object key, Text value, Context context)
            throws IOException, InterruptedException {

        Map<String, String> parsed = transformXmlToMap(value.toString());

        // Grab the "CreationDate" field since it is what we are finding
        // the min and max value of
        String strDate = parsed.get("CreationDate");

        // Grab the "UserID" since it is what we are grouping by
        String userId = parsed.get("UserId");
        // Parse the string into a Date object
        Date creationDate = frmt.parse(strDate);

        // Set the minimum and maximum date values to the creationDate
        outTuple.setMin(creationDate);
        outTuple.setMax(creationDate);

        // Set the comment count to 1
        outTuple.setCount(1);

        // Set our user ID as the output key
        outUserId.set(userId);

        // Write out the user ID with min max dates and count
        context.write(outUserId, outTuple);
    }
}
```

Reducer code. The reducer iterates through the values to find the minimum and maximum dates, and sums the counts. We start by initializing the output result for each input group. For each value in this group, if the output result's minimum is not yet set, or the value's minimum is less than result's current minimum, we set the result's minimum to the input value. The same logic applies to the maximum, except using a greater than operator. Each value's count is added to a running sum, similar to the word count example in the introductory chapter. After determining the minimum and maximum dates from all input values, the final count is set to our output value. The input key is then written to the file system along with the output value.

```
public static class MinMaxCountReducer extends
        Reducer<Text, MinMaxCountTuple, Text, MinMaxCountTuple> {

    // Our output value Writable
```

```
        private MinMaxCountTuple result = new MinMaxCountTuple();

        public void reduce(Text key, Iterable<MinMaxCountTuple> values,
                Context context) throws IOException, InterruptedException {

            // Initialize our result
            result.setMin(null);
            result.setMax(null);
            result.setCount(0);
            int sum = 0;

            // Iterate through all input values for this key
            for (MinMaxCountTuple val : values) {
                // If the value's min is less than the result's min
                // Set the result's min to value's
                if (result.getMin() == null ||
                        val.getMin().compareTo(result.getMin()) < 0) {
                    result.setMin(val.getMin());
                }

                // If the value's max is less than the result's max
                // Set the result's max to value's
                if (result.getMax() == null ||
                        val.getMax().compareTo(result.getMax()) > 0) {
                    result.setMax(val.getMax());
                }

                // Add to our sum the count for value
                sum += val.getCount();
            }

            // Set our count to the number of input values
            result.setCount(sum);
            context.write(key, result);
        }
    }
```

Combiner optimization. The reducer implementation just shown can be used as the job's combiner. As we are only interested in the count, minimum date, and maximum date, multiple comments from the same user do not have to be sent to the reducer. The minimum and maximum comment dates can be calculated for each local map task without having an effect on the final minimum and maximum. The counting operation is an associative and commutative operation and won't be harmed by using a combiner.

Data flow diagram. Figure 2-2 shows the flow between the mapper, combiner, and reducer to help describe their interactions. Numbers are used rather than dates for simplicity, but the concept is the same. A combiner possibly executes over each of the highlighted output groups from a mapper, determining the minimum and maximum values in the first two columns and adding up the number of rows in the "table" (group). The combiner then outputs the minimum and maximum along with the new count. If a combiner does not execute over any rows, they will still be accounted for in the reduce phase.

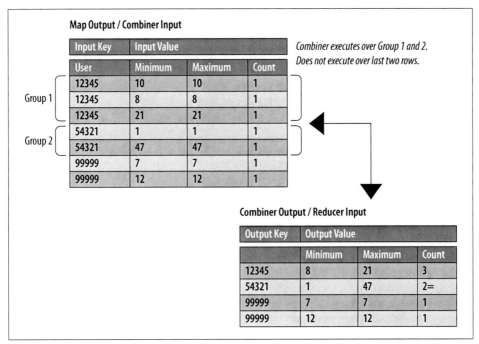

Figure 2-2. The Min/Max/Count MapReduce data flow through the combiner

Average example

To calculate an average, we need two values for each group: the sum of the values that we want to average and the number of values that went into the sum. These two values can be calculated on the reduce side very trivially, by iterating through each value in the set and adding to a running sum while keeping a count. After the iteration, simply divide the sum by the count and output the average. However, if we do it this way we cannot use this same reducer implementation as a combiner, because calculating an average is not an associative operation. Instead, our mapper will output two "columns" of data, count and average. For each input record, this will simply be "1" and the value of the field. The reducer will multiply the "count" field by the "average" field to add to a running sum, and add the "count" field to a running count. It will then divide the running sum with the running count and output the count with the calculated average. With this more round-about algorithm, the reducer code can be used as a combiner as associativity is preserved.

The following descriptions of each code section explain the solution to the problem.

Problem: Given a list of user's comments, determine the average comment length per hour of day.

Mapper code. The mapper will process each input record to calculate the average comment length based on the time of day. The output key is the hour of day, which is parsed from the creation date XML attribute. The output value is two columns, the comment count and the average length of the comments for that hour. Because the mapper operates on one record at a time, the count is simply 1 and the average length is equivalent to the comment length. These two values are output in a custom `Writable`, a `CountAverageTuple`. This type contains two float values, a count, and an average.

```
public static class AverageMapper extends
        Mapper<Object, Text, IntWritable, CountAverageTuple> {

    private IntWritable outHour = new IntWritable();
    private CountAverageTuple outCountAverage = new CountAverageTuple();
    private final static SimpleDateFormat frmt = new SimpleDateFormat(
            "yyyy-MM-dd'T'HH:mm:ss.SSS");

    public void map(Object key, Text value, Context context)
            throws IOException, InterruptedException {

        Map<String, String> parsed = transformXmlToMap(value.toString());

        // Grab the "CreationDate" field,
        // since it is what we are grouping by
        String strDate = parsed.get("CreationDate");

        // Grab the comment to find the length
        String text = parsed.get("Text");

        // get the hour this comment was posted in
        Date creationDate = frmt.parse(strDate);
        outHour.set(creationDate.getHours());

        // get the comment length
        outCountAverage.setCount(1);
        outCountAverage.setAverage(text.length());

        // write out the user ID with min max dates and count
        context.write(outHour, outCountAverage);
    }
}
```

Reducer code. The reducer code iterates through all given values for the hour and keeps two local variables: a running count and running sum. For each value, the count is multiplied by the average and added to the running sum. The count is simply added to the running count. After iteration, the input key is written to the file system with the count and average, calculated by dividing the running sum by the running count.

```
public static class AverageReducer extends
        Reducer<IntWritable, CountAverageTuple,
            IntWritable, CountAverageTuple> {

    private CountAverageTuple result = new CountAverageTuple();

    public void reduce(IntWritable key, Iterable<CountAverageTuple> values,
            Context context) throws IOException, InterruptedException {

        float sum = 0;
```

```
        float count = 0;

        // Iterate through all input values for this key
        for (CountAverageTuple val : values) {
            sum += val.getCount() * val.getAverage();
            count += val.getCount();
        }

        result.setCount(count);
        result.setAverage(sum / count);

        context.write(key, result);
    }
}
```

Combiner optimization. When determining an average, the reducer code can be used as a combiner when outputting the count along with the average. An average is not an associative operation, but if the count is output from the reducer with the count, these two values can be multiplied to preserve the sum for the final reduce phase. Without outputting the count, a combiner cannot be used because taking an average of averages is not equivalent to the true average. Typically, writing the count along with the average to the file system is not an issue. However, if the count is impeding the analysis at hand, it can be omitted by making a combiner implementation nearly identical to the reducer implementation just shown. The only differentiation between the two classes is that the reducer does not write the count with the average.

Data flow diagram. Figure 2-3 shows the flow between the mapper, combiner, and reducer to help describe their interactions. A combiner possibly executes over each of the high-lighted output groups from a mapper, determining the average and outputting it with the count, which is the number of rows corresponding to the group. If a combiner does not execute over any rows, they will still be accounted for in the reduce phase.

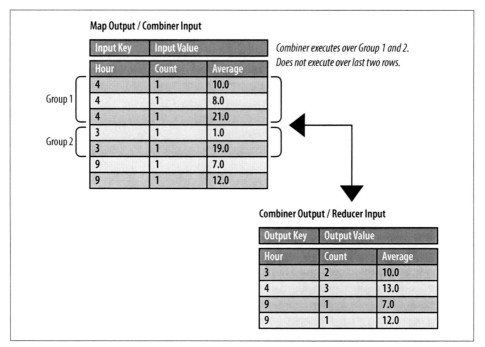

Map Output / Combiner Input

Combiner executes over Group 1 and 2.
Does not execute over last two rows.

Input Key	Input Value	
Hour	Count	Average
4	1	10.0
4	1	8.0
4	1	21.0
3	1	1.0
3	1	19.0
9	1	7.0
9	1	12.0

Combiner Output / Reducer Input

Output Key	Output Value	
Hour	Count	Average
3	2	10.0
4	3	13.0
9	1	7.0
9	1	12.0

Figure 2-3. Data flow for the average example

Median and standard deviation

Finding the median and standard deviation is a little more complex than the previous examples. Because these operations are not associative, they cannot benefit from a combiner as easily as their counterparts. A median is the numerical value separating the lower and higher halves of a data set. This requires the data set to be complete, which in turn requires it to be shuffled. The data must also be sorted, which can present a barrier because MapReduce does not sort values.

A standard deviation shows how much variation exists in the data from the average, thus requiring the average to be discovered prior to reduction. The easiest way to perform these operations involves copying the list of values into a temporary list in order to find the median or iterating over the set again to determine the standard deviation. With large data sets, this implementation may result in Java heap space issues, because each value is copied into memory for every input group. We'll address these issues in the next example.

The following descriptions of each code section explain the solution to the problem.

Problem: Given a list of user's comments, determine the median and standard deviation of comment lengths per hour of day.

Mapper code. The mapper will process each input record to calculate the median comment length within each hour of the day. The output key is the hour of day, which is parsed from the `CreationDate` XML attribute. The output value is a single value: the comment length.

```
public static class MedianStdDevMapper extends
        Mapper<Object, Text, IntWritable, IntWritable> {

    private IntWritable outHour = new IntWritable();
    private IntWritable outCommentLength = new IntWritable();

    private final static SimpleDateFormat frmt = new SimpleDateFormat(
            "yyyy-MM-dd'T'HH:mm:ss.SSS");

    public void map(Object key, Text value, Context context)
            throws IOException, InterruptedException {

        Map<String, String> parsed = transformXmlToMap(value.toString());

        // Grab the "CreationDate" field,
        // since it is what we are grouping by
        String strDate = parsed.get("CreationDate");

        // Grab the comment to find the length
        String text = parsed.get("Text");

        // get the hour this comment was posted in
        Date creationDate = frmt.parse(strDate);
        outHour.set(creationDate.getHours());

        // set the comment length
        outCommentLength.set(text.length());

        // write out the user ID with min max dates and count
        context.write(outHour, outCommentLength);
    }
}
```

Reducer code. The reducer code iterates through the given set of values and adds each value to an in-memory list. The iteration also calculates a running sum and count. After iteration, the comment lengths are sorted to find the median value. If the list has an odd number of entries, the median value is set to the middle value. If the number is even, the middle two values are averaged. Next, the standard deviation is calculated by iterating through our sorted list after finding the mean from our running sum and count. A running sum of deviations is calculated by squaring the difference between each comment length and the mean. The standard deviation is then calculated from this sum. Finally, the median and standard deviation are output along with the input key.

```
public static class MedianStdDevReducer extends
        Reducer<IntWritable, IntWritable,
            IntWritable, MedianStdDevTuple> {

    private MedianStdDevTuple result = new MedianStdDevTuple();
```

```
        private ArrayList<Float> commentLengths = new ArrayList<Float>();

        public void reduce(IntWritable key, Iterable<IntWritable> values,
                Context context) throws IOException, InterruptedException {

            float sum = 0;
            float count = 0;
            commentLengths.clear();
            result.setStdDev(0);

            // Iterate through all input values for this key
            for (IntWritable val : values) {
                commentLengths.add((float) val.get());
                sum += val.get();
                ++count;
            }

            // sort commentLengths to calculate median
            Collections.sort(commentLengths);

            // if commentLengths is an even value, average middle two elements
            if (count % 2 == 0) {
                result.setMedian((commentLengths.get((int) count / 2 - 1) +
                        commentLengths.get((int) count / 2)) / 2.0f);
            } else {
                // else, set median to middle value
                result.setMedian(commentLengths.get((int) count / 2));
            }

            // calculate standard deviation
            float mean = sum / count;
            float sumOfSquares = 0.0f;
            for (Float f : commentLengths) {
                sumOfSquares += (f - mean) * (f - mean);
            }

            result.setStdDev((float) Math.sqrt(sumOfSquares / (count - 1)));
            context.write(key, result);
        }
    }
```

Combiner optimization. A combiner cannot be used in this implementation. The reducer requires all the values associated with a key in order to find the median and standard deviation. Because a combiner runs only over a map's locally output intermediate key/value pairs, being able to calculate the full median and standard deviation is impossible. However, the next example describes aa more complex implementation that uses a custom combiner.

Memory-conscious median and standard deviation

The following implementation is differentiated from the previous median and standard deviation example by reducing the memory footprint. Inserting every value into a list will result in many duplicate elements. One way to get around this duplication is to keep a count of elements instead. For instance, instead of keeping a list of < 1, 1, 1, 1, 2, 2, 3, 4, 5, 5, 5 >, a sorted map of values to counts is kept: (1→4, 2→2, 3→1, 4→1, 5→3). The core concept is the same: all the values are iterated through in the reduce phase and stored in an in-memory data structure. The data structure and how it is searched are all that has changed. A map reduces the memory footprint drastically. Instead of having a list whose scaling is $O(n)$ where n = number of comments, the number of key/value pairs in our map is $O(\max(m))$ where m = maximum comment length. As an added bonus, a combiner can be used to help aggregate counts of comment lengths and output the map in a `Writable` object to be used later by the reducer.

The following descriptions of each code section explain the solution to the problem.

Problem: Given a list of user's comments, determine the median and standard deviation of comment lengths per hour of day.

Mapper code. The mapper processes each input record to calculate the median comment length based on the hour of the day during which the comment was posted. The output key is the hour of day, which is parsed from the creation date XML attribute. The output value is a `SortedMapWritable` object that contains one element: the comment length and a count of "1". This map is used more heavily in the combiner and reducer.

```
public static class MedianStdDevMapper extends
        Mapper<lObject, Text, IntWritable, SortedMapWritable> {

    private IntWritable commentLength = new IntWritable();
    private static final LongWritable ONE = new LongWritable(1);
    private IntWritable outHour = new IntWritable();

    private final static SimpleDateFormat frmt = new SimpleDateFormat(
        "yyyy-MM-dd'T'HH:mm:ss.SSS");

    public void map(Object key, Text value, Context context)
            throws IOException, InterruptedException {

        Map<String, String> parsed = transformXmlToMap(value.toString());

        // Grab the "CreationDate" field,
        // since it is what we are grouping by
        String strDate = parsed.get("CreationDate");

        // Grab the comment to find the length
        String text = parsed.get("Text");

        // Get the hour this comment was posted in
        Date creationDate = frmt.parse(strDate);
        outHour.set(creationDate.getHours());

        commentLength.set(text.length());
        SortedMapWritable outCommentLength = new SortedMapWritable();
        outCommentLength.put(commentLength, ONE);

        // Write out the user ID with min max dates and count
```

```
            context.write(outHour, outCommentLength);
        }
    }
```

Reducer code. The reducer code iterates through the given set of `SortedMapWritable` to aggregate all the maps together into a single `TreeMap`, which is a implementation of `SortedMap`. The key is the comment length and the value is the total count associated with the comment length.

After iteration, the median is calculated. The code finds the list index where the median would be by dividing the total number of comments by two. The entry set of the `TreeMap` is then iterated to find the keys that satisfy the condition `previousCommentCount` ≤ `medianIndex` < `commentCount`, adding the value of the tree map to `comments` at each step of the iteration. Once this condition is met, if there is an even number of comments and `medianIndex` is equivalent to `previousComment`, the median is reset to the average of the previous length and current length. Otherwise, the median is simply the current comment length.

Next, the standard deviation is calculated by iterating through the `TreeMap` again and finding the sum of squares, making sure to multiply by the count associated with the comment length. The standard deviation is then calculated from this sum. The median and standard deviation are output with the input key, the hour during which these comments were posted.

```
public static class MedianStdDevReducer extends
        Reducer<IntWritable, SortedMapWritable,
            IntWritable, MedianStdDevTuple> {

    private MedianStdDevTuple result = new MedianStdDevTuple();
    private TreeMap<Integer, Long> commentLengthCounts =
        new TreeMap<Integer, Long>();

    public void reduce(IntWritable key, Iterable<SortedMapWritable> values,
            Context context) throws IOException, InterruptedException {

        float sum = 0;
        long totalComments = 0;
        commentLengthCounts.clear();
        result.setMedian(0);
        result.setStdDev(0);

        for (SortedMapWritable v : values) {
            for (Entry<WritableComparable, Writable> entry : v.entrySet()) {
                int length = ((IntWritable) entry.getKey()).get();
                long count = ((LongWritable) entry.getValue()).get();

                totalComments += count;
                sum += length * count;

                Long storedCount = commentLengthCounts.get(length);
                if (storedCount == null) {
                    commentLengthCounts.put(length, count);
```

```
            } else {
                commentLengthCounts.put(length, storedCount + count);
            }
        }
    }

    long medianIndex = totalComments / 2L;
    long previousComments = 0;
    long comments = 0;
    int prevKey = 0;
    for (Entry<Integer, Long> entry : commentLengthCounts.entrySet()) {
        comments = previousComments + entry.getValue();

        if (previousComments ≤ medianIndex && medianIndex < comments) {
            if (totalComments % 2 == 0 && previousComments == medianIndex) {
                result.setMedian((float) (entry.getKey() + prevKey) / 2.0f);
            } else {
                result.setMedian(entry.getKey());
            }
            break;
        }

        previousComments = comments;
        prevKey = entry.getKey();
    }

    // calculate standard deviation
    float mean = sum / totalComments;

    float sumOfSquares = 0.0f;
    for (Entry<Integer, Long> entry : commentLengthCounts.entrySet()) {
        sumOfSquares += (entry.getKey() - mean) * (entry.getKey() - mean) *
                entry.getValue();
    }

    result.setStdDev((float) Math.sqrt(sumOfSquares / (totalComments - 1)));
    context.write(key, result);
    }
}
```

Combiner optimization. Unlike the previous examples, the combiner for this algorithm is different from the reducer. While the reducer actually calculates the median and standard deviation, the combiner aggregates the SortedMapWritable entries for each local map's intermediate key/value pairs. The code to parse through the entries and aggregate them in a local map is identical to the reducer code in the previous section. Here, a HashMap is used instead of a TreeMap, because sorting is unnecessary and a HashMap is typically faster. While the reducer uses this map to calculate the median and standard deviation, the combiner uses a SortedMapWritable in order to serialize it for the reduce phase.

```
public static class MedianStdDevCombiner extends
        Reducer<IntWritable, SortedMapWritable, IntWritable, SortedMapWritable> {

    protected void reduce(IntWritable key,
```

```
            Iterable<SortedMapWritable> values, Context context)
            throws IOException, InterruptedException {

    SortedMapWritable outValue = new SortedMapWritable();

    for (SortedMapWritable v : values) {
        for (Entry<WritableComparable, Writable> entry : v.entrySet()) {
            LongWritable count = (LongWritable) outValue.get(entry.getKey());

            if (count != null) {
                count.set(count.get()
                        + ((LongWritable) entry.getValue()).get());
            } else {
                outValue.put(entry.getKey(), new LongWritable(
                        ((LongWritable) entry.getValue()).get()));
            }
        }
    }

    context.write(key, outValue);
}
}
```

Data flow diagram. Figure 2-4 shows the flow between the mapper, combiner, and reducer to help describe their interactions. A combiner possibly executes over each of the highlighted output groups from a mapper. For each group, it builds the internal map of comment length to the count of comment lengths. The combiner then outputs the input key and the `SortedMapWritable` of length/count pairs, which it serializes from the map.

Inverted Index Summarizations

Pattern Description

The *inverted index* pattern is commonly used as an example for MapReduce analytics. We're going to discuss the general case where we want to build a map of some term to a list of identifiers.

Intent

Generate an index from a data set to allow for faster searches or data enrichment capabilities.

Motivation

It is often convenient to index large data sets on keywords, so that searches can trace terms back to records that contain specific values. While building an inverted index does require extra processing up front, taking the time to do so can greatly reduce the amount of time it takes to find something.

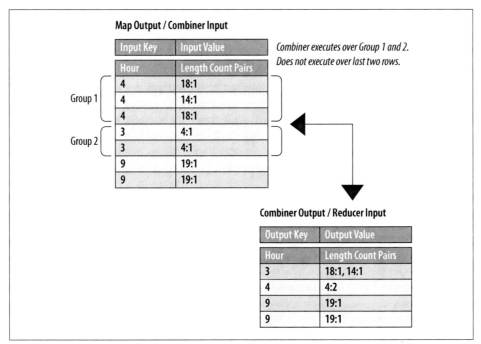

Map Output / Combiner Input

Input Key	Input Value
Hour	**Length Count Pairs**
4	18:1
4	14:1
4	18:1
3	4:1
3	4:1
9	19:1
9	19:1

Group 1 (first three rows), Group 2 (rows 4 and 5)

Combiner executes over Group 1 and 2. Does not execute over last two rows.

Combiner Output / Reducer Input

Output Key	Output Value
Hour	**Length Count Pairs**
3	18:1, 14:1
4	4:2
9	19:1
9	19:1

Figure 2-4. Data flow for the standard deviation example

Search engines build indexes to improve search performance. Imagine entering a keyword and letting the engine crawl the Internet and build a list of pages to return to you. Such a query would take an extremely long amount of time to complete. By building an inverted index, the search engine knows all the web pages related to a keyword ahead of time and these results are simply displayed to the user. These indexes are often ingested into a database for fast query responses. Building an inverted index is a fairly straightforward application of MapReduce because the framework handles a majority of the work.

Applicability

Inverted indexes should be used when quick search query responses are required. The results of such a query can be preprocessed and ingested into a database.

Structure

Figure 2-5 shows the general structure of how an inverted index is executed in MapReduce. The breakdown of each MapReduce component is described in detail below:

- The mapper outputs the desired fields for the index as the key and the unique identifier as the value.
- The combiner can be omitted if you are just using the *identity reducer*, because under those circumstances a combiner would just create unnecessary processing.

Some implementations concatenate the values associated with a group before outputting them to the file system. In this case, a combiner can be used. It won't have as beneficial an impact on byte count as the combiners in other patterns, but there will be an improvement.

- The partitioner is responsible for determining where values with the same key will eventually be copied by a reducer for final output. It can be customized for more efficient load balancing if the intermediate keys are not evenly distributed.

- The reducer will receive a set of unique record identifiers to map back to the input key. The identifiers can either be concatenated by some unique delimiter, leading to the output of one key/value pair per group, or each input value can be written with the input key, known as the identity reducer.

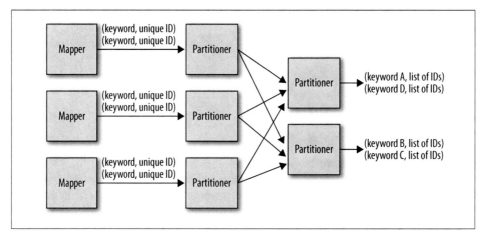

Figure 2-5. The structure of the inverted index pattern

Consequences

The final output of is a set of part files that contain a mapping of field value to a set of unique IDs of records containing the associated field value.

Performance analysis

The performance of building an inverted index depends mostly on the computational cost of parsing the content in the mapper, the cardinality of the index keys, and the number of content identifiers per key.

Parsing text or other types of content in the mapper can sometimes be the most computationally intense operation in a MapReduce job. This is especially true for semi-structured data, such as XML or JSON, since these typically require parsing arbitrary quantities of information into usable objects. It's important to parse the incoming records as efficiently as possible to improve your overall job performance.

If the number of unique keys and the number of identifiers is large, more data will be sent to the reducers. If more data is going to the reducers, you should increase the number of reducers to increase parallelism during the reduce phase.

Inverted indexes are particularly susceptible to hot spots in the index keys, since the index keys are rarely evenly distributed. For example, the reducer that handles the word "the" in a text search application is going to be particularly busy since "the" is seen in so much text. This can slow down your entire job since a few reducers will take much longer than the others. To avoid this problem, you might need to implement a custom partitioner, or omit common index keys that add no value to your end goal.

Inverted Index Example

Wikipedia reference inverted index

Building an inverted index is a straightforward MapReduce application and is often the second example newcomers to MapReduce experience after the word count application. Much like the word count application, the bulk of the operation is a group and is therefore handled entirely by the MapReduce framework.

Suppose we want to add StackOverflow links to each Wikipedia page that is referenced in a StackOverflow comment. The following example analyzes each comment in Stack-Overflow to find hyperlinks to Wikipedia. If there is one, the link is output with the comment ID to generate the inverted index. When it comes to the reduce phase, all the comment IDs that reference the same hyperlink will be grouped together. These groups are then concatenated together into a white space delimited `String` and directly output to the file system. From here, this data file can be used to update the Wikipedia page with all the comments that reference it.

The following descriptions of each code section explain the solution to the problem.

Problem: Given a set of user's comments, build an inverted index of answer post ID to a set of Wikipedia URLs.

Mapper code. The mapper parses the posts from StackOverflow to output the row IDs of all answer posts that contain a particular Wikipedia URL. First, the XML attributes for the text, post type, and row ID are extracted. If the post type is not an answer, identified by a post type of "2", we parse the text to find a Wikipedia URL. This is done using the `getWikipediaURL` method, which takes in a `String` of unescaped HTML and returns a Wikipedia URL if found, or `null` otherwise. The method is omitted for brevity. If a URL is found, the URL is output as the key and the row ID is output as the value.

```
public static class WikipediaExtractor extends
        Mapper<Object, Text, Text, Text> {

    private Text link = new Text();
    private Text outkey = new Text();
```

```
public void map(Object key, Text value, Context context)
        throws IOException, InterruptedException {

    Map<String, String> parsed = MRDPUtils.transformXmlToMap(value
            .toString());

    // Grab the necessary XML attributes
    String txt = parsed.get("Body");
    String posttype = parsed.get("PostTypeId");
    String row_id = parsed.get("Id");

    // if the body is null, or the post is a question (1), skip
    if (txt == null || (posttype != null && posttype.equals("1"))) {
        return;
    }

    // Unescape the HTML because the SO data is escaped.
    txt = StringEscapeUtils.unescapeHtml(txt.toLowerCase());

    link.set(getWikipediaURL(txt));
    outkey.set(row_id);
    context.write(link, outkey);
    }
}
```

Reducer code. The reducer iterates through the set of input values and appends each row ID to a `String`, delimited by a space character. The input key is output along with this concatenation.

```
public static class Concatenator extends Reducer<Text,Text,Text,Text> {
    private Text result = new Text();

    public void reduce(Text key, Iterable<Text> values, Context context)
            throws IOException, InterruptedException {

        StringBuilder sb = new StringBuilder();
        boolean first = true;
        for (Text id : values) {
            if (first) {
                first = false;
            } else {
                sb.append(" ");
            }
            sb.append(id.toString());
        }

        result.set(sb.toString());
        context.write(key, result);
    }
}
```

Combiner optimization. The combiner can be used to do some concatenation prior to the reduce phase. Because all row IDs are simply concatenated together, the number of bytes that need to be copied by the reducer is more than in a numerical summarization pattern. The same code for the reducer class is used as the combiner.

Counting with Counters

Pattern Description

This pattern utilizes the MapReduce framework's counters utility to calculate a global sum entirely on the map side without producing any output.

Intent

An efficient means to retrieve count summarizations of large data sets.

Motivation

A count or summation can tell you a lot about particular fields of data, or your data as a whole. Hourly ingest record counts can be post procesed to generate helpful histograms. This can be executed in a simple "word count" manner, in that for each input record, you output the same key, say the hour of data being processed, and a count of 1. The single reduce will sum all the input values and output the final record count with the hour. This works very well, but it can be done more efficiently using counters. Instead of writing any key value pairs at all, simply use the framework's counting mechanism to keep track of the number of input records. This requires no reduce phase and no summation! The framework handles monitoring the names of the counters and their associated values, aggregating them across all tasks, as well as taking into account any failed task attempts.

Say you want to find the number of times your employees log into your heavily used public website every day. Assuming you have a few dozen employees, you can apply filter conditions while parsing through your web logs. Rather than outputting the employee's user name with a count of '1', you can simply create a counter with the employee's ID and increment it by 1. At the end of the job, simply grab the counters from the framework and save them wherever your heart desires—the log, local file system, HDFS, etc.

Some counters come built into the framework, such as number of input/output records and bytes. Hadoop allows for programmers to create their own custom counters for whatever their needs may be. This pattern describes how to utilize these custom counters to gather count or summation metrics from your data sets. The major benefit of using counters is all the counting can be done during the map phase.

The caveat to using counters is they are all stored in-memory by the JobTracker. The counters are serialized by each map task and sent with status updates. In order to play nice and not bog down the JobTracker, the number of counters should be in the tens -- a hundred at most... and thats a big "at most"! Counters are definitely not meant to aggregate lots of statistics about your MapReduce job! Newer versions of Hadoop actually limit the number of counters a job can create to prevent any permanent damage to the JobTracker. The last thing you want is to have your analytic take down the JobTracker because you created a few hundred custom counters!

Applicability

Counting with counters should be used when:

- You have a desire to gather counts or summations over large data sets.
- The number of counters you are going to create is small—in the double digits.

Structure

Figure 2-6 shows the general structure of how this pattern works in MapReduce.

- The mapper processes each input record at a time to increment counters based on certain criteria. The counter is either incremented by one if counting a single instance, or incremented by some number if executing a summation. These counters are then aggregated by the TaskTrackers running the tasks and incrementally reported to the JobTracker for overall aggregation upon job success. The counters from any failed tasks are disregarded by the JobTracker in the final summation.
- As this job is map only, there is no combiner, partitioner, or reducer required.

Consequences

The final output is a set of counters grabbed from the job framework. There is no actual output from the analytic itself. However, the job requires an output directory to execute. This directory will exist and contain a number of empty part files equivalent to the number of map tasks. This directory should be deleted on job completion.

Known uses

Count number of records
> Simply counting the number of records over a given time period is very common. It's typically a counter provided by the framework, among other common things.

Count a small number of unique instances
> Counters can also be created on the fly by using a string variable. You might now know what the value is, but the counters don't have to be created ahead of time. Simply creating a counter using the value of a field and incrementing it is enough

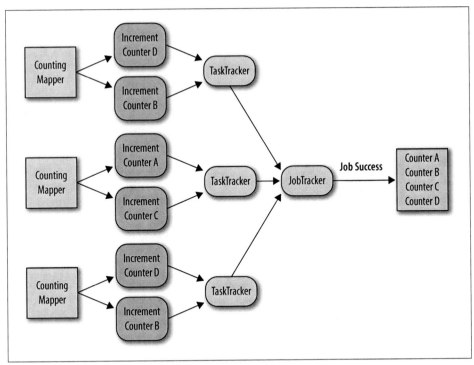

Figure 2-6. The structure of the counting with counters pattern

to solve this use case. Just be sure the number of counters you are creating is a small number!

Summations

Counters can be used to sum fields of data together. Rather than performing the sum on the reduce side, simply create a new counter and use it to sum the field values.

Performance analysis

Using counters is very fast, as data is simply read in through the mapper and no output is written. Performance depends largely on the number of map tasks being executed and how much time it takes to process each record.

Counting with Counters Example

Number of users per state

For this example, we use a map-only job to count the number of users in each state. The Location attribute is a user-entered value and doesn't have any concrete inputs. Because of this, there are a lot of null or empty fields, as well as made up locations. We need to account for this when processing each record to ensure we don't create a large number of counters. We verify each location contains a state abbreviation code prior to creating a counter. This will create at most 52 counters - 50 for the states and two for NullOrEmpty and Unknown. This is a manageable number of custom counters for the JobTracker, but your job should not have many more than this!

The following descriptions of each code section explain the solution to the problem.

Problem: Count the number of users from each state using Hadoop custom counters.

Mapper code. The mapper reads each user record and gets his or her location. The location is split on white space and searched for something that resembles a state. We keep a set of all the state abbreviations in-memory to prevent creating an excessive amount of counters, as the location is simply a string set by the user and nothing structured. If a state is recognized, the counter for the state is incremented by one and the loop is broken. Counters are identified by both a group and a name. Here, the group is "State" (identified by a public String variable) and the counter name is the state abbreviation code.

```java
public static class CountNumUsersByStateMapper extends
        Mapper<Object, Text, NullWritable, NullWritable> {

    public static final String STATE_COUNTER_GROUP = "State";
    public static final String UNKNOWN_COUNTER = "Unknown";
    public static final String NULL_OR_EMPTY_COUNTER = "Null or Empty";

    private String[] statesArray = new String[] { "AL", "AK", "AZ", "AR",
            "CA", "CO", "CT", "DE", "FL", "GA", "HI", "ID", "IL", "IN",
            "IA", "KS", "KY", "LA", "ME", "MD", "MA", "MI", "MN", "MS",
            "MO", "MT", "NE", "NV", "NH", "NJ", "NM", "NY", "NC", "ND",
            "OH", "OK", "OR", "PA", "RI", "SC", "SF", "TN", "TX", "UT",
            "VT", "VA", "WA", "WV", "WI", "WY" };

    private HashSet<String> states = new HashSet<String>(
            Arrays.asList(statesArray));

    public void map(Object key, Text value, Context context)
            throws IOException, InterruptedException {

        Map<String, String> parsed = MRDPUtils.transformXmlToMap(value
                .toString());

        // Get the value for the Location attribute
        String location = parsed.get("Location");

        // Look for a state abbreviation code if the
        // location is not null or empty
        if (location != null && !location.isEmpty()) {

            // Make location uppercase and split on white space
            String[] tokens = location.toUpperCase().split("\\s");

            // For each token
```

```
            boolean unknown = true;
            for (String state : tokens) {

                // Check if it is a state
                if (states.contains(state)) {
                    // If so, increment the state's counter by 1
                    // and flag it as not unknown
                    context.getCounter(STATE_COUNTER_GROUP, state)
                            .increment(1);
                    unknown = false;
                    break;
                }
            }

            // If the state is unknown, increment the UNKNOWN_COUNTER counter
            if (unknown) {
                context.getCounter(STATE_COUNTER_GROUP, UNKNOWN_COUNTER)
                        .increment(1);
            }
        } else {
            // If it is empty or null, increment the
            // NULL_OR_EMPTY_COUNTER counter by 1
            context.getCounter(STATE_COUNTER_GROUP,
                    NULL_OR_EMPTY_COUNTER).increment(1);
        }
    }
}
```

Driver code. The driver code is mostly boilerplate, with the exception of grabbing the counters after the job completes. If the job completed succesfully, we get the "States" counter group and write out the counter name and value to stdout. These counter values are also output when the job completes, so writing to stdout may be redundant if you are obtaining these values by scraping log files. The output directory is then deleted, success or otherwise, as this job doesn't create any tangible output.

```
...

int code = job.waitForCompletion(true) ? 0 : 1;

if (code == 0) {
    for (Counter counter : job.getCounters().getGroup(
            CountNumUsersByStateMapper.STATE_COUNTER_GROUP)) {
        System.out.println(counter.getDisplayName() + "\t"
                + counter.getValue());
    }
}

// Clean up empty output directory
FileSystem.get(conf).delete(outputDir, true);

System.exit(code);
```

CHAPTER 3

Filtering Patterns

The patterns in this chapter all have one thing in common: they don't change the actual records. These patterns all find a subset of data, whether it be small, like a top-ten listing, or large, like the results of a deduplication. This differentiates filtering patterns from those in the previous chapter, which was all about summarizing and grouping data by similar fields to get a top-level view of the data. Filtering is more about understanding a smaller piece of your data, such as all records generated from a particular user, or the top ten most used verbs in a corpus of text. In short, filtering allows you to apply a microscope to your data. It can also be considered a form of search. If you are interested in finding all records that involve a particular piece of distinguishing information, you can filter out records that do not match the search criteria.

Sampling, one common application of filtering, is about pulling out a sample of the data, such as the highest values for a particular field or a few random records. Sampling can be used to get a smaller, yet representative, data set in which more analysis can be done without having to deal with the much larger data set. Many machine learning algorithms simply do not work efficiently over a large data set, so tools that build models need to be applied to a smaller subset.

A subsample can also be useful for development purposes. Simply grabbing the first thousand records typically is not the best sample since the records are bound to be similar and do not give a good overall picture of the entire data set. A well-distributed sample will hopefully provide a better view of the data set and will allow your application and analytic development to be done against more realistic data, even if it is much smaller.

Four patterns are presented in this chapter: *filtering, Bloom filtering, top ten*, and *distinct*. There are numerous ways to find a slice of your data. Each pattern has a slight nuance to distinguish it from the others, even if they all pretty much do the same thing.

We will see a few clever uses of MapReduce in this chapter. Filtering, Bloom filtering, and simple random sampling allow us to use *map-only jobs*, which means we don't need a reducer.

Filtering

Pattern Description

As the most basic pattern, *filtering* serves as an abstract pattern for some of the other patterns. Filtering simply evaluates each record separately and decides, based on some condition, whether it should stay or go.

Intent

Filter out records that are not of interest and keep ones that are.

Consider an evaluation function *f* that takes a record and returns a Boolean value of *true* or *false*. If this function returns *true*, keep the record; otherwise, toss it out.

Motivation

Your data set is large and you want to take a subset of this data to focus in on it and perhaps do follow-on analysis. The subset might be a significant portion of the data set or just a needle in the haystack. Either way, you need to use the parallelism of Map-Reduce to wade through all of your data and find the keepers.

For example, you might be interested only in records that have something to do with Hadoop: Hadoop is either mentioned in the raw text or the event is tagged by a "Hadoop" tag. Filtering can be used to keep records that meet the "something to do with Hadoop" criteria and keep them, while tossing out the rest of the records.

Big data and processing systems like Hadoop, in general, are about bringing all of your organization's data to one location. Filtering is the way to pull subsets back out and deliver them to analysis shops that are interested in just that subset. Filtering is also used to zoom in on a particular set of records that match your criteria that you are more curious about. The exploration of a subset of data may lead to more valuable and complex analytics that are based on the behavior that was observed in the small subset.

Applicability

Filtering is very widely applicable. The only requirement is that the data can be parsed into "records" that can be categorized through some well-specified criterion determining whether they are to be kept.

Structure

The structure of the filter pattern is perhaps the simplest of all the patterns we'll see in this book. Figure 3-1 shows this pattern.

```
map(key, record):
    if we want to keep record then
        emit key,value
```

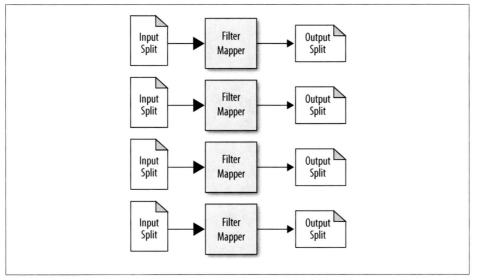

Figure 3-1. The structure of the filter pattern

Filtering is unique in not requiring the "reduce" part of MapReduce. This is because it doesn't produce an aggregation. Each record is looked at individually and the evaluation of whether or not to keep that record does not depend on anything else in the data set.

The mapper applies the evaluation function to each record it receives. Typically, the mapper outputs the same key/value type as the types of the input, since the record is left unchanged. If the evaluation function returns true, the mapper simply output the key and value verbatim.

Consequences

The output of the job will be a subset of the records that pass the selection criteria. If the format was kept the same, any job that ran over the larger data set should be able to run over this filtered data set, as well.

Known uses

Closer view of data

Prepare a particular subset of data, where the records have something in common or something of interest, for more examination. For example, a local office in Maryland may only care about records originating in Maryland from your international dataset.

Tracking a thread of events

Extract a thread of consecutive events as a case study from a larger data set. For example, you may be interested in how a particular user interacts with your website by analyzing Apache web server logs. The events for a particular user are interspersed with all the other events, so it's hard to figure out what happened. By filtering for that user's IP address, you are able to get a good view of that particular user's activities.

Distributed grep

Grep, a very powerful tool that uses regular expressions for finding lines of text of interest, is easily parallelized by applying a regular expression match against each line of input and only outputting lines that match.

Data cleansing

Data sometimes is dirty, whether it be malformed, incomplete, or in the wrong format. The data could have missing fields, a date could be not formatted as a date, or random bytes of binary data could be present. Filtering can be used to validate that each record is well-formed and remove any junk that does occur.

Simple random sampling

If you want a simple random sampling of your data set, you can use filtering where the evaluation function randomly returns true or false. A simple random sample is a sample of the larger data set in which each item has the same probability of being selected. You can tweak the number of records that make it through by having the evaluation function return true a smaller percentage of the time. For example, if your data set contains one trillion records and you want a sample size of about one million, have the evaluation function return true once in a million (because there are a million millions in a trillion).

Removing low scoring data

If you can score your data with some sort of scalar value, you can filter out records that don't meet a certain threshold. If you know ahead of time that certain types of records are not useful for analysis, you can assign those records a small score and they will get filtered out. This effectively has the same purpose as the top ten pattern discussed later, except that you do not know how many records you will get.

Resemblances

SQL

The filter pattern is synonymous to using the WHERE clause in a SELECT * statement. The records stay the same, but some are simply filtered out. For example:

```
SELECT * FROM table WHERE value < 3;
```

Pig

The FILTER keyword.

```
b = FILTER a BY value < 3;
```

Performance analysis

This pattern is basically as efficient as MapReduce can get because the job is map-only. There are a couple of reasons why map-only jobs are efficient.

- Since no reducers are needed, data never has to be transmitted between the map and reduce phase. Most of the map tasks pull data off of their locally attached disks and then write back out to that node.

- Since there are no reducers, both the sort phase and the reduce phase are cut out. This usually doesn't take very long, but every little bit helps.

One thing to be aware of is the size and number of the output files. Since this job is running with mappers only, you will get one output file per mapper with the prefix part-m- (note the m instead of the r). You may find that these files will be tiny if you filter out a lot of data, which can cause problems with scalability limitations of the NameNode further down the road.

If you are worried about the number of small files and do not mind if your job runs just a little bit longer, you can use an identity reducer to collect the results without doing anything with them. This will have the mapper send the reducer all of the data, but the reducer does nothing other than just output them to one file per reducer. The appropriate number of reducers depends on the amount of data that will be written to the file system and just how many small files you want to deal with.

Filtering Examples

Distributed grep

Grep is a popular text filtering utility that dates back to Unix and is available on most Unix-like systems. It scans through a file line-by-line and only outputs lines that match a specific pattern. We'd like to parallelize the regular expression search across a larger body of text. In this example, we'll show how to apply a regular expression to every line in MapReduce.

Mapper code. The mapper is pretty straightforward since we use the Java built-in libraries for regular expressions. If the text line matches the pattern, we'll output the line. Otherwise we do nothing and the line is effectively ignored. We use the setup function to retrieve the map regex from the job configuration.

```
public static class GrepMapper
        extends Mapper<Object, Text, NullWritable, Text> {

    private String mapRegex = null;

    public void setup(Context context) throws IOException,
        InterruptedException {

        mapRegex = context.getConfiguration().get("mapregex");
    }
```

```
    public void map(Object key, Text value, Context context)
        throws IOException, InterruptedException {

        if (value.toString().matches(mapRegex)) {
            context.write(NullWritable.get(), value);
        }
    }
}
```

As this is a map-only job, there is no combiner or reducer. All output records will be written directly to the file system.

Simple Random Sampling

In simple random sampling (SRS), we want to grab a subset of our larger data set in which each record has an equal probability of being selected. Typically this is useful for sizing down a data set to be able to do representative analysis on a more manageable set of data.

Implementing SRS as a filter operation is not a direct application of the filtering pattern, but the structure is the same. Instead of some filter criteria function that bears some relationship to the content of the record, a random number generator will produce a value, and if the value is below a threshold, keep the record. Otherwise, toss it out.

Mapper Code. In the mapper code, the setup function is used to pull the filter_percent age configuration value so we can use it in the map function.

In the map function, a simple check against the next random number is done. The random number will be anywhere between 0 and 1, so by comparing against the specified threshold, we can keep or throw out the record.

```
    public static class SRSMapper
            extends Mapper<Object, Text, NullWritable, Text> {

        private Random rands = new Random();
        private Double percentage;

        protected void setup(Context context) throws IOException,
                InterruptedException {
            // Retrieve the percentage that is passed in via the configuration
            //      like this: conf.set("filter_percentage", .5);
            //          for .5%
            String strPercentage = context.getConfiguration()
                    .get("filter_percentage");
            percentage = Double.parseDouble(strPercentage) / 100.0;
        }

        public void map(Object key, Text value, Context context)
                throws IOException, InterruptedException {

            if (rands.nextDouble() < percentage) {
                context.write(NullWritable.get(), value);
```

```
        }
    }
}
```

As this is a map-only job, there is no combiner or reducer. All output records will be written directly to the file system. When using a small percentage, you will find that the files will be tiny and plentiful. If this is the case, set the number of reducers to 1 without specifying a reducer class, which will tell the MapReduce framework to use a single identity reducer that simply collects the output into a single file. The other option would be to collect the files as a post-processing step using `hadoop fs -cat`.

Bloom Filtering

Pattern Description

Bloom filtering does the same thing as the previous pattern, but it has a unique evaluation function applied to each record.

Intent

Filter such that we keep records that are member of some predefined set of values. It is not a problem if the output is a bit inaccurate, because we plan to do further checking. The predetermined list of values will be called the set of `hot values`.

For each record, extract a feature of that record. If that feature is a member of a set of values represented by a Bloom filter, keep it; otherwise toss it out (or the reverse).

Motivation

Bloom filtering is similar to generic filtering in that it is looking at each record and deciding whether to keep or remove it. However, there are two major differences that set it apart from generic filtering. First, we want to filter the record based on some sort of set membership operation against the hot values. For example: keep or throw away this record if the value in the user field is a member of a predetermined list of users. Second, the set membership is going to be evaluated with a Bloom filter, described in the Appendix. In one sense, Bloom filtering is a join operation in which we don't care about the data values of the right side of the join.

This pattern is slightly related to the replicated join pattern covered later in Chapter 5. It is comparing one list to another and doing some sort of join logic, using only map tasks. Instead of replicating the hot list everywhere with the distributed cache, as in the replicated join, we will send a Bloom filter data object to the distributed cache. This allows a filter like operation with a Bloom filter instead of the list itself, which allows you to perform this operation across a much larger data set because the Bloom filter is much more compact. Instead of being constrained by the size of the list in memory, you are mostly confined by the feature limitations of Bloom filters.

Using a Bloom filter to calculate set membership in this situation has the consequence that sometimes you will get a false positive. That is, sometimes a value will return as a member of the set when it should not have. If the Bloom filter says a value is not in the Bloom filter, we can guarantee that it is indeed not in the set of values. For more information on why this happens, refer to Appendix. However, in some situations, this is not that big of a concern. In an example we'll show code for at the end of this chapter, we'll gather a rather large set of "interesting" words, in which when we see a record that contains one of those words, we'll keep the record, otherwise we'll toss it out. We want to do this because we want to filter down our data set significantly by removing uninteresting content. If we are using a Bloom filter to represent the list of watch words, sometimes a word will come back as a member of that list, even if it should not have. In this case, if we accidentally keep some records, we still achieved our goal of filtering out the majority of the garbage and keeping interesting stuff.

Applicability

The following criteria are necessary for Bloom filtering to be relevant:

- Data can be separated into records, as in filtering.
- A feature can be extracted from each record that could be in a set of hot values.
- There is a predetermined set of items for the hot values.
- Some false positives are acceptable (i.e., some records will get through when they should not have).

Structure

Figure 3-2 shows the structure of Bloom filtering and how it is split into two major components. First, the Bloom filter needs to be trained over the list of values. The resulting data object is stored in HDFS. Next is the filtering MapReduce job, which has the same structure as the previous filtering pattern in this chapter, except it will make use of the distributed cache as well. There are no reducers since the records are analyzed one-by-one and there is no aggregation done.

The first step of this job is to train the Bloom filter from the list of values. This is done by loading the data from where it is stored and adding each item to the Bloom filter. The trained Bloom filter is stored in HDFS at a known location.

The second step of this pattern is to do the actual filtering. When the map task starts, it loads the Bloom filter from the distributed cache. Then, in the map function, it iterates through the records and checks the Bloom filter for set membership in the hot values list. Each record is either forwarded or not based on the Bloom filter membership test.

The Bloom filter needs to be re-trained only when the data changes. Therefore, updating the Bloom filter in a lazy fashion (i.e., only updating it when it needs to be updated) is typically appropriate.

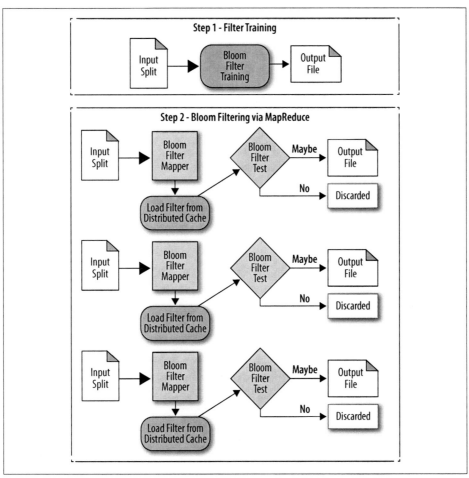

Figure 3-2. The structure of the Bloom filtering pattern

Consequences

The output of the job will be a subset of the records in that passed the Bloom filter membership test. You should expect that some records in this set may not actually be in the set of hot values, because Bloom filters have a chance of false positives.

Known uses

Removing most of the nonwatched values

> The most straightforward use case is cleaning out values that aren't hot. For example, you may be interested only in data that contains a word in a list of 10,000 words that deal with Hadoop, such as "map," "partitioning," etc. You take this list, train a Bloom filter on it, then check text as it is coming in to see whether you get a Bloom filter hit on any of the words. If you do, forward the record, and if not

don't do anything. The fact that you'll get some false positives isn't that big of a deal, since you still got rid of most of the data.

Prefiltering a data set for an expensive set membership check

Sometimes, checking whether some value is a member of a set is going to be expensive. For example, you might have to hit a webservice or an external database to check whether that value is in the set. The situations in which this may be the case are far and few between, but they do crop up in larger organizations. Instead of dumping this list periodically to your cluster, you can instead have the originating system produce a Bloom filter and ship that instead. Once you have the Bloom filter in place and filter out most of the data, you can do a second pass on the records that make it through to double check against the authoritative source. If the Bloom filter is able to remove over 95% of the data, you'll see the external resource hit only 5% as much as before! With this approach, you'll eventually have 100% accuracy but didn't have to hammer the external resource with tons of queries.

Later, in Chapter 5, we'll see a pattern called "Reduce Side Join with Bloom Filtering" where a Bloom filter is used to reduce the amount of data going to reducers. By determining whether a record will be relevant ahead of time, we can reduce network usage significantly.

Resemblances

Bloom filters are relatively new in the field of data analysis, likely because the properties of big data particularly benefit from such a thing in a way previous methodologies have not. In both SQL and Pig, Bloom filters can be implemented as user-defined functions, but as of the writing of this book, there is no native functionality out of the box.

Performance analysis

The performance for this pattern is going to be very similar to simple filtering from a performance perspective. Loading up the Bloom filter from the distributed cache is not that expensive since the file is relatively small. Checking a value against the Bloom filter is also a relatively cheap operation, as each test is executed in constant time.

Bloom Filtering Examples

Hot list

One of the most basic applications of a Bloom filter is what it was designed for: representing a data set. For this example, a Bloom filter is trained with a hot list of keywords. We use this Bloom filter to test whether each word in a comment is in the hot list. If the test returns true, the entire record is output. Otherwise, it is ignored. Here, we are not concerned with the inevitable false positives that are output due to the Bloom filter. The next example details how one way to verify a positive Bloom filter test using HBase.

The following descriptions of each code section explain the solution to the problem.

Problem: Given a list of user's comments, filter out a majority of the comments that do not contain a particular keyword.

Bloom filter training. To demonstrate how to use Hadoop Bloom filters, the following code segment generates a Bloom filter off a predetermined set of words. This is a generic application that takes in an input gzip file or directory of gzip files, the number of elements in the file, a desired false positive rate, and finally the output file name.

```java
public class BloomFilterDriver {
    public static void main(String[] args) throws Exception {
        // Parse command line arguments
        Path inputFile = new Path(args[0]);
        int numMembers = Integer.parseInt(args[1]);
        float falsePosRate = Float.parseFloat(args[2]);
        Path bfFile = new Path(args[3]);

        // Calculate our vector size and optimal K value based on approximations
        int vectorSize = getOptimalBloomFilterSize(numMembers, falsePosRate);
        int nbHash = getOptimalK(numMembers, vectorSize);

        // Create new Bloom filter
        BloomFilter filter = new BloomFilter(vectorSize, nbHash,
                Hash.MURMUR_HASH);

        System.out.println("Training Bloom filter of size " + vectorSize
                + " with " + nbHash + " hash functions, " + numMembers
                + " approximate number of records, and " + falsePosRate
                + " false positive rate");

        // Open file for read
        String line = null;
        int numElements = 0;
        FileSystem fs = FileSystem.get(new Configuration());

        for (FileStatus status : fs.listStatus(inputFile)) {
            BufferedReader rdr = new BufferedReader(new InputStreamReader(
                    new GZIPInputStream(fs.open(status.getPath()))));

            System.out.println("Reading " + status.getPath());
            while ((line = rdr.readLine()) != null) {
                filter.add(new Key(line.getBytes()));
                ++numElements;
            }

            rdr.close();
        }

        System.out.println("Trained Bloom filter with " + numElements
                + " entries.");

        System.out.println("Serializing Bloom filter to HDFS at " + bfFile);

        FSDataOutputStream strm = fs.create(bfFile);
```

```
            filter.write(strm);
            strm.flush();
            strm.close();

            System.exit(0);
        }
    }
```

A new `BloomFilter` object is constructed using the optimal vector size and optimal number of hash functions (*k*) based on the input parameters. Each file returned from `listStatus` is read line-by-line, and each line is used to train the Bloom filter. After all the input files are ready, the Bloom filter is serialized to the filename provided at the command line. Because a `BloomFilter` is also a `Writable` object, serializing it is fairly trivial. Simply use the `FileSystem` object to create a new `FSDataOutputStream`, pass the stream to the filter's `write` method, then just flush and close the stream!

This Bloom filter can later be deserialized from HDFS just as easily as it was written. Just open up the file using the `FileSystem` object and pass it to `BloomFilter.read Fields`. Deserialization of this Bloom filter is demonstrated in the `setup` method of the following Mapper code.

Mapper code. The `setup` method is called once for each mapper by the Hadoop framework prior to the many calls to `map`. Here, the Bloom filter is deserialized from the `DistributedCache` before being used in the map method. The `DistributedCache` is a Hadoop utility that ensures that a file in HDFS is present on the local file system of each task that requires that file. The Bloom filter was previously trained with a hot list of words.

In the map method, the comment is extracted from each input record. The comment is tokenized into words, and each word is cleaned of any extraneous characters. The clean words are testing against the Bloom filter. If the word is a member, the entire record is output to the file system.

 A Bloom filter is trained on the bytes of the word. The important thing of this is that the words "the" and "The" may look the same, but the bytes are different. Unless case sensitivity matters in you algorithm, it is best to trim the string and make the string all lower case when training and testing the filter.

```
public static class BloomFilteringMapper extends
    Mapper<Object, Text, Text, NullWritable> {

  private BloomFilter filter = new BloomFilter();

  protected void setup(Context context) throws IOException,
      InterruptedException {
    // Get file from the DistributedCache
    URI[] files = DistributedCache.getCacheFiles(context
      .getConfiguration());
    System.out.println("Reading Bloom filter from: "
```

```
        + files[0].getPath());

    // Open local file for read.
    DataInputStream strm = new DataInputStream(new FileInputStream(
        files[0].getPath()));

    // Read into our Bloom filter.
    filter.readFields(strm);
    strm.close();
}

public void map(Object key, Text value, Context context)
    throws IOException, InterruptedException {

    Map<String, String> parsed = transformXmlToMap(value.toString());

    // Get the value for the comment
    String comment = parsed.get("Text");
    StringTokenizer tokenizer = new StringTokenizer(comment);
    // For each word in the comment
    while (tokenizer.hasMoreTokens()) {
        // If the word is in the filter, output the record and break
        String word = tokenizer.nextToken();
        if (filter.membershipTest(new Key(word.getBytes()))) {
            context.write(value, NullWritable.get());
            break;
        }
    }
}
```

Because this is a map-only job, there is no combiner or reducer. All output records will be written directly to the file system.

HBase Query using a Bloom filter

Bloom filters can assist expensive operations by eliminating unnecessary ones. For the following example, a Bloom filter was previously trained with IDs of all users that have a reputation of at least 1,500. We use this Bloom filter to do an initial test before querying HBase to retrieve more information about each user. By eliminating unnecessary queries, we can speed up processing time.

The following descriptions of each code section explain the solution to the problem.

Problem: Given a list of users' comments, filter out comments from users with a reputation of less than 1,500.

Mapper Code. The setup method is called once for each mapper by the Hadoop framework prior to the many calls to the map method. Just like the previous example, the Bloom filter is deserialized from the DistributedCache before being used in the map method. This Bloom filter was trained with all user IDs that have a reputation of at least 1,500. This is a little over 1.5% of all users, so we will be filtering out a lot of unnecessary queries. In addition to the Bloom filter, a connection to the HBase table is obtained in **setup**.

In the map method, the user's ID is extracted from each record and checked against the Bloom filter. If the test is positive, HBase is queried with the user ID to get the rest of the data associated with that user. Here, we nullify the possibilities of outputing false positives by verifying that the user's actual reputation is at least 1,500. If it is, the record is output to the file system.

```java
public static class BloomFilteringMapper extends
        Mapper<Object, Text, Text, NullWritable> {

    private BloomFilter filter = new BloomFilter();
    private HTable table = null;

    protected void setup(Context context) throws IOException,
            InterruptedException {

        // Get file from the Distributed Cache
        URI[] files = DistributedCache.getCacheFiles(context
            .getConfiguration());
        System.out.println("Reading Bloom filter from: "
            + files[0].getPath());

        // Open local file for read.
        DataInputStream strm = new DataInputStream(new FileInputStream(
            files[0].getPath()));

        // Read into our Bloom filter.
        filter.readFields(strm);
        strm.close();

        // Get HBase table of user info
        Configuration hconf = HBaseConfiguration.create();
        table = new HTable(hconf, "user_table");
    }

    public void map(Object key, Text value, Context context)
            throws IOException, InterruptedException {

        Map<String, String> parsed = transformXmlToMap(value.toString());

        // Get the value for the comment
        String userid = parsed.get("UserId");

        // If this user ID is in the set
            if (filter.membershipTest(new Key(userid.getBytes()))) {
                // Get the reputation from the HBase table
                Result r = table.get(new Get(userid.getBytes()));
                int reputation = Integer.parseInt(new String(r.getValue(
                    "attr".getBytes(), "Reputation".getBytes())));

                // If the reputation is at least 1500,
                // write the record to the file system
```

```
            if (reputation >= 1500) {
                context.write(value, NullWritable.get());
            }
        }
    }
}
```

As this is a map-only job, there is no combiner or reducer. All output records will be
written directly to the file system.

Query Buffer Optimization

The previous example is a fairly naive way of querying HBase. It is meant
to show how to go about executing the pattern, but can be optimized
further. HBase supports batch queries, so it would be ideal to buffer all
the queries we want to execute up to some predetermined size. This
constant depends on how many records you can comfortably store in
memory before querying HBase. Then flush the queries to HBase and
perform the further processing with the returned results. If the expensive
operations can be buffered, it is recommended to do so. Just remember
to flush the buffer in the mapper or the reducer's `cleanup` method. The
`Context` object can be used to write output just like in the `map` or
`reduce` methods.

Top Ten

Pattern Description

The *top ten* pattern is a bit different than previous ones in that you know how many
records you want to get in the end, no matter what the input size. In generic filtering,
however, the amount of output depends on the data.

Intent

Retrieve a relatively small number of top *K* records, according to a ranking scheme in
your data set, no matter how large the data.

Motivation

Finding outliers is an important part of data analysis because these records are typically
the most interesting and unique pieces of data in the set. The point of this pattern is to
find the best records for a specific criterion so that you can take a look at them and
perhaps figure out what caused them to be so special. If you can define a ranking function or comparison function between two records that determines whether one is higher
than the other, you can apply this pattern to use MapReduce to find the records with
the highest value across your entire data set.

The reason why this pattern is particularly interesting springs from a comparison with how you might implement the top ten pattern outside of a MapReduce context. In SQL, you might be inclined to sort your data set by the ranking value, then take the top K records from that. In MapReduce, as we'll find out in the next chapter, total ordering is extremely involved and uses significant resources on your cluster. This pattern will instead go about finding the limited number of high-values records without having to sort the data.

Plus, seeing the top ten of something is always fun! What are the highest scoring posts on Stack Overflow? Who is the oldest member of your service? What is the largest single order made on your website? Which post has the word "meow" the most number of times?

Applicability

- This pattern requires a comparator function ability between two records. That is, we must be able to compare one record to another to determine which is "larger."
- The number of output records should be significantly fewer than the number of input records because at a certain point it just makes more sense to do a total ordering of the data set.

Structure

This pattern utilizes both the mapper and the reducer. The mappers will find their local top K, then all of the individual top K sets will compete for the final top K in the reducer. Since the number of records coming out of the mappers is at most K and K is relatively small, we'll only need one reducer. You can see the structure of this pattern in Figure 3-3.

```
class mapper:
    setup():
        initialize top ten sorted list

    map(key, record):
        insert record into top ten sorted list
        if length of array is greater-than 10 then
            truncate list to a length of 10

    cleanup():
        for record in top sorted ten list:
            emit null,record

class reducer:
    setup():
        initialize top ten sorted list

    reduce(key, records):
        sort records
        truncate records to top 10
```

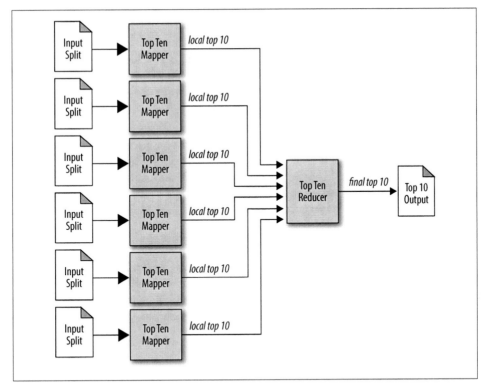

Figure 3-3. The structure of the top ten pattern

```
for record in records:
    emit record
```

The mapper reads each record and keeps an array object of size K that collects the largest K values. In the cleanup phase of the mapper (i.e., right before it exits), we'll finally emit the K records stored in the array as the value, with a null key. These are the lowest K for this particular map task.

We should expect $K * M$ records coming into the reducer under one key, null, where M is the number of map tasks. In the reduce function, we'll do what we did in the mapper: keep an array of K values and find the top K out of the values collected under the null key.

The reason we had to select the top K from every mapper is because it is conceivable that all of the top records came from one file split and that corner case needs to be accounted for.

Consequences

The top K records are returned.

Known uses

Outlier analysis

Outliers are usually interesting. They may be the users that are having difficulty using your system, or power users of your website. Outliers, like filtering and grouping, may give you another perspective from your data set.

Select interesting data

If you are able to score your records by some sort of value score, you can pull the "most valuable" data. This is particularly useful if you plan to submit data to follow-on processing, such as in a business intelligence tool or a SQL database, that cannot handle the scale of your original data set. Value scoring can be as complex as you make it by applying advanced algorithms, such as scoring text based on how grammatical it is and how accurate the spelling is so that you remove most of the junk.

Catchy dashboards

This isn't a psychology book, so who knows why top ten lists are interesting to consumers, but they are. This pattern could be used to publish some interesting top ten stats about your website and your data that will encourage users to think more about your data or even to instill some competition.

Resemblances

SQL

In a traditional and small SQL database, ordering may not be a big deal. In this case, you would retrieve data ordered by the criterion for which you want the top ten, then take a limit. You could follow this same approach in MapReduce, but as you will find out in later patterns, sorting is an expensive operation.

```
SELECT * FROM table ORDER BY col4 DESC LIMIT 10;
```

Pig

Pig will have issues performing this query in any sort of optimal way. The most straightforward pattern is to mirror the SQL query, but the ordering is expensive just to find a few records. This is a situation in which you'll find major gains in using Java MapReduce instead of Pig.

```
B = ORDER A BY col4 DESC;
C = LIMIT B 10;
```

Performance analysis

The performance of the top ten pattern is typically very good, but there are a number of important limitations and concerns to consider. Most of these limitations spring from the use of a single reducer, regardless of the number of records it is handling.

The number we need to pay attention to when using this pattern is how many records the reducer is getting. Each map task is going to output $O(K)$ records, and the job will consist of *M* map tasks, so the reducer is going to have to work through $O(K * M)$ records. This can be a lot.

A single reducer getting a lot of data is bad for a few reasons:

- The sort can become an expensive operation when it has too many records and has to do most of the sorting on local disk, instead of in memory.
- The host where the reducer is running will receive a lot of data over the network, which may create a network resource hot spot for that single host.
- Naturally, scanning through all the data in the reduce will take a long time if there are many records to look through.
- Any sort of memory growth in the reducer has the possibility of blowing through the Java virtual machine's memory. For example, if you are collecting all of the values into an ArrayList to perform a median, that ArrayList can get very big. This will not be a particular problem if you're really looking for the top ten items, but if you want to extract a very large number you may run into memory limits.
- Writes to the output file are not parallelized. Writing to the locally attached disk can be one of the more expensive operations in the reduce phase when we are dealing with a lot of data. Since there is only one reducer, we are not taking advantage of the parallelism involved in writing data to several hosts, or even several disks on the same host. Again, this is not an issue for the top ten, but becomes a factor when the data extracted is very large.

As *K* gets large, this pattern becomes less efficient. Consider the extreme case in which *K* is set at five million, when there are ten million records in the entire data set. Five million exceeds the number of records in any individual input split, so every mapper will send all of its records to the reducer. The single reducer will effectively have to handle all of the records in the entire dataset and the only thing that was parallelized was the data loading.

An optimization you could take if you have a large *K* and a large number of input splits is to prefilter some of the data, because you know what the top ten was last time and it hasn't changed much. Imagine your data has a value that can only increase with time (e.g., hits on web pages) and you want to find the top hundred records. If, in your previous MapReduce job, the hundredth record had a value of 52,485, then you know you can filter out all records that have a value of less than 52,485. There is no way that a record with a value with less than 52,845 can compete with the previous top hundred that are still in the data set.

For all these reasons, this pattern is intended only for pretty small values for *K*, in the tens or hundreds at most, though you can likely push it a bit further. There is a fuzzy line in which just doing a total ordering of the data set is likely more effective.

Top Ten Examples

Top ten users by reputation

Determining the top ten records of a data set is an interesting use of MapReduce. Each mapper determines the top ten records of its input split and outputs them to the reduce phase. The mappers are essentially filtering their input split to the top ten records, and the reducer is responsible for the final ten. Just remember to configure your job to only use one reducer! Multiple reducers would shard the data and would result in multiple "top ten" lists.

The following descriptions of each code section explain the solution to the problem.

Problem: Given a list of user information, output the information of the top ten users based on reputation.

Mapper code. The mapper processes all input records and stores them in a TreeMap. A TreeMap is a subclass of Map that sorts on key. The default ordering of Integers is ascending. Then, if there are more than ten records in our TreeMap, the first element (lowest value) can be removed. After all the records have been processed, the top ten records in the TreeMap are output to the reducers in the cleanup method. This method gets called once after all key/value pairs have been through map, just like how setup is called once before any calls to map.

```
public static class TopTenMapper extends
    Mapper<Object, Text, NullWritable, Text> {

  // Stores a map of user reputation to the record
  // Overloads the comparator to order the reputations in descending order
  private TreeMap<Integer, Text> repToRecordMap = new TreeMap<Integer, Text>();

  public void map(Object key, Text value, Context context)
      throws IOException, InterruptedException {
    Map<String, String> parsed = transformXmlToMap(value.toString());

    String userId = parsed.get("Id");
    String reputation = parsed.get("Reputation");

    // Add this record to our map with the reputation as the key
    repToRecordMap.put(Integer.parseInt(reputation), new Text(value));

    // If we have more than ten records, remove the one with the lowest rep
    // As this tree map is sorted in descending order, the user with
    // the lowest reputation is the last key.
    if (repToRecordMap.size() > 10) {
      repToRecordMap.remove(repToRecordMap.firstKey());
    }
  }

  protected void cleanup(Context context) throws IOException,
      InterruptedException {
    // Output our ten records to the reducers with a null key
```

```
    for (Text t : repToRecordMap.values()) {
      context.write(NullWritable.get(), t);
    }
  }
}
```

Reducer code. Overall, the reducer determines its top ten records in a way that's very similar to the mapper. Because we configured our job to have one reducer using `job.setNumReduceTasks(1)` and we used `NullWritable` as our key, there will be one input group for this reducer that contains all the potential top ten records. The reducer iterates through all these records and stores them in a `TreeMap`. If the `TreeMap`'s size is above ten, the first element (lowest value) is remove from the map. After all the values have been iterated over, the values contained in the `TreeMap` are flushed to the file system in descending order. This ordering is achieved by getting the descending map from the `TreeMap` prior to outputting the values. This can be done directly in the `reduce` method, because there will be only one input group, but doing it in the `cleanup` method would also work.

```
public static class TopTenReducer extends
    Reducer<NullWritable, Text, NullWritable, Text> {

  // Stores a map of user reputation to the record
  // Overloads the comparator to order the reputations in descending order
  private TreeMap<Integer, Text> repToRecordMap = new TreeMap<Integer, Text>();

  public void reduce(NullWritable key, Iterable<Text> values,
      Context context) throws IOException, InterruptedException {
    for (Text value : values) {
      Map<String, String> parsed = transformXmlToMap(value.toString());

      repToRecordMap.put(Integer.parseInt(parsed.get("Reputation")),
          new Text(value));

      // If we have more than ten records, remove the one with the lowest rep
      // As this tree map is sorted in descending order, the user with
      // the lowest reputation is the last key.
      if (repToRecordMap.size() > 10) {
        repToRecordMap.remove(repToRecordMap.firstKey());
      }
    }

    for (Text t : repToRecordMap.descendingMap().values()) {
      // Output our ten records to the file system with a null key
      context.write(NullWritable.get(), t);
    }
  }
}
```

There is no need for a combiner in this job, although the reducer code could technically be used. The combiner would simply output the same ten records and thus cause unnecessary processing. Also, this job is hardcoded to find the top ten records, but could easily be configured to find the top *K* records using a variable captured in the setup method. Just be sure to keep in mind the limitations discussed in the Performance Analysis section as *K* increases.

Distinct

Pattern Description

This pattern filters the whole set, but it's more challenging because you want to filter out records that look like another record in the data set. The final output of this filter application is a set of unique records.

Intent

You have data that contains similar records and you want to find a unique set of values.

Motivation

Reducing a data set to a unique set of values has several uses. One particular use case that can use this pattern is deduplication. In some large data sets, duplicate or extremely similar records can become a nagging problem. The duplicate records can take up a significant amount of space or skew top-level analysis results. For example, every time someone visits your website, you collect what web browser and device they are using for marketing analysis. If that user visits your website more than once, you'll log that information more than once. If you do some analysis to calculate the percentage of your users that are using a specific web browser, the number of times users have used your website will skew the results. Therefore, you should first deduplicate the data so that you have only one instance of each logged event with that device.

Records don't necessarily need to be exactly the same in the raw form. They just need to be able to be translated into a form in which they will be exactly the same. For example, if our web browser analysis done on HTTP server logs, extract only the user name, the device, and the browser that user is using. We don't care about the time stamp, the resource they were accessing, or what HTTP server it came from.

Applicability

The only major requirement is that you have duplicates values in your data set. This is not a requirement, but it would be silly to use this pattern otherwise!

Structure

This pattern is pretty slick in how it uses MapReduce. It's exploits MapReduce's ability to group keys together to remove duplicates. This pattern uses a mapper to transform the data and doesn't do much in the reducer. The combiner can always be utilized in this pattern and can help considerably if there are a large number of duplicates. Duplicate records are often located close to another in a data set, so a combiner will deduplicate them in the map phase.

```
map(key, record):
    emit record,null

reduce(key, records):
    emit key
```

The mapper takes each record and extracts the data fields for which we want unique values. In our HTTP logs example, this means extracting the user, the web browser, and the device values. The mapper outputs the record as the key, and null as the value.

The reducer groups the nulls together by key, so we'll have one null per key. We then simply output the key, since we don't care how many nulls we have. Because each key is grouped together, the output data set is guaranteed to be unique.

One nice feature of this pattern is that the number of reducers doesn't matter in terms of the calculation itself. Set the number of reducers relatively high, since the mappers will forward almost all their data to the reducers.

 This is a good time to resize your data file sizes. If you want your output files to be larger, reduce the number of reducers. If you want them smaller, increase the number of reducers. The files will come out to be about the same size thanks to the random hashing in the partitioner.

Consequences

The output data records are guaranteed to be unique, but any order has not been preserved due to the random partitioning of the records.

Known uses

Deduplicate data
    If you have a system with a number of collection sources that could see the same event twice, you can remove duplicates with this pattern.

Getting distinct values
    This is useful when your raw records may not be duplicates, but the extracted information is duplicated across records.

Protecting from an inner join explosion

If you are about to do an inner join between two data sets and your foreign keys are not unique, you risk retrieving a huge number of records. For example, if you have 3,000 of the same key in one data set, and 2,000 of the same key in the other data set, you'll end up with 6,000,000 records, all sent to one reducer! By runnning the distinct pattern, you can pair down your values to make sure they are unique and mitigate against this problem.

Resemblances

SQL

SELECT DISTINCT performs this operation for us in SQL.

```
SELECT DISTINCT * FROM table;
```

Pig

The DISTINCT operation.

```
b = DISTINCT a;
```

Performance analysis

Understanding this pattern's performance profile is important for effective use. The main consideration in determining how to set up the MapReduce job is the number of reducers you think you will need. The number of reducers is highly dependent on the total number of records and bytes coming out of the mappers, which is dependent on how much data the combiner is able to eliminate. Basically, if duplicates are very rare within an input split (and thus the combiner did almost nothing), pretty much all of the data is going to be sent to the reduce phase.

You can find the number of output bytes and records by looking at the JobTracker status of the job on a sample run. Take the number of output bytes and divide by the number of reducers you are thinking about using. That is about how many bytes each reducer will get, not accounting for skew. The number that a reducer can handle varies from deployment to deployment, but usually you shouldn't pass it more than a few hundred megabytes. You also don't want to pass too few records, because then your output files will be tiny and there will be unnecessary overhead in spinning up the reducers. Aim for each reducer to receive more than the block size of records (e.g., if your block size is 64MB, have at least 64MB sent to the reducer).

Since most of the data in the data set is going to be sent to the reducers, you will use a relatively large number of reducers to run this job. Anywhere from one reducer per hundred mappers, to one reducer per two mappers, will get the job done here. Start with the theoretical estimate based on the output records, but do additional testing to find the sweet spot. In general, with this pattern, if you want your reducers to run in half the time, double the number of reducers... Just be careful of the files getting too small.

Be conscious of how many reduce slots your cluster has when selecting the number of reducers of your job. A good start for the distinct pattern would be close to the number of reduce slots for reasonably sized data sets or twice the number of reduce slots for very large data sets.

Distinct Examples

Distinct user IDs

Finding a distinct set of values is a great example of MapReduce's power. Because each reducer is presented with a unique key and a set of values associated with that key, in order to produce a distinct value, we simply need to set our key to whatever we are trying to gather a distinct set of.

The following descriptions of each code section explain the solution to the problem.

Problem: Given a list of user's comments, determine the distinct set of user IDs.

Mapper code. The Mapper will get the user ID from each input record. This user ID will be output as the key with a null value.

```
public static class DistinctUserMapper extends
        Mapper<Object, Text, Text, NullWritable> {

    private Text outUserId = new Text();

    public void map(Object key, Text value, Context context)
        throws IOException, InterruptedException {

        Map<String, String> parsed = transformXmlToMap(value.toString());

        // Get the value for the UserId attribute
        String userId = parsed.get("UserId");

        // Set our output key to the user's id
        outUserId.set(userId);

        // Write the user's id with a null value
        context.write(outUserId, NullWritable.get());
    }
}
```

Reducer code. The grunt work of building a distinct set of user IDs is handled by the MapReduce framework. Each reducer is given a unique key and a set of null values. These values are ignored and the input key is written to the file system with a null value.

```
public static class DistinctUserReducer extends
        Reducer<Text, NullWritable, Text, NullWritable> {

    public void reduce(Text key, Iterable<NullWritable> values,
        Context context) throws IOException, InterruptedException {

        // Write the user's id with a null value
```

```
        context.write(key, NullWritable.get());
    }
}
```

Combiner optimization. A combiner can and should be used in the distinct pattern. Duplicate keys will be removed from each local map's output, thus reducing the amount of network I/O required. The same code for the reducer can be used in the combiner.

CHAPTER 4

Data Organization Patterns

In contrast to the previous chapter on sampling, this chapter is all about reorganizing data. The value of individual records is often multipled by the way they are partitioned, sharded, or sorted. This is especially true in distributed systems, where partitioning, sharding, and sorting can be exploited for performance.

In many organizations, Hadoop and other MapReduce solutions are only a piece in the larger data analysis platform. Data will typically have to be transformed in order to interface nicely with the other systems. Likewise, data might have to be transformed from its original state to a new state to make analysis in MapReduce easier.

This chapter contains several pattern subcategories as you will see in each pattern description:

- The *structured to hierarchical* pattern
- The *partitioning* and *binning* patterns
- The *total order sorting* and *shuffling* patterns
- The *generating data* pattern

The patterns in this chapter are often used together to solve data organization problems. For example, you may want to restructure your data to be hierarchical, bin the data, and then have the bins be sorted. See "Job Chaining" on page 131 in Chapter 6 for more details on how to tackle the problem of combining patterns together to solve more complex problems.

Structured to Hierarchical

Pattern Description

The *structured to hierarchical* pattern creates new records from data that started in a very different structure. Because of its importance, this pattern in many ways stands alone in the chapter.

Intent

Transform your row-based data to a hierarchical format, such as JSON or XML.

Motivation

When migrating data from an RDBMS to a Hadoop system, one of the first things you should consider doing is reformatting your data into a more conducive structure. Since Hadoop doesn't care what format your data is in, you should take advantage of hierarchical data to avoid doing joins.

For example, our StackOverflow data contains a table about comments, a table about posts, etc. It is pretty obvious that the data is stored in an normalized SQL database. When you visit a post on StackOverflow, all the different pieces need to be coalesced into one view. This gets even more complicated when you are trying to do analytics at the level of individual posts. Imagine trying to perform correlate the length of the post with the length of the comments. This requires you to first do a join, an expensive operation, then extract the data that allows you to do your real work. If instead you group the data by post so that the comments are colocated with the posts and the edit revisions (i.e., denormalizing the tables), this type of analysis will be much easier and more intuitive. Keeping the data in a normalized form in this case serves little purpose.

Unfortunately, data doesn't always come grouped together. When someone posts an answer to a StackOverflow question, Hadoop can't insert that record into the hierarchy immediately. Therefore, creating the denormalized records for MapReduce has to be done in a batch fashion periodically.

Another way to deal with a steady stream of updates is HBase. HBase is able to store data in a semi-structured and hierarchical fashion well. MongoDB would also be a good candidate for storing this types of data.

Applicability

The following should be true for this pattern to be appropriate:

* You have data sources that are linked by some set of foreign keys.
* Your data is structured and row-based.

Structure

Figure 4-1 shows the structure for this pattern. The description of each component is as follows:

* If you wish to combine multiple data sources into a hierarchical data structure, a Hadoop class called `MultipleInputs` from `org.apache.hadoop.mapre duce.lib.input` is extremely valuable. `MultipleInputs` allows you to specify different input paths and different mapper classes for each input. The configuration is

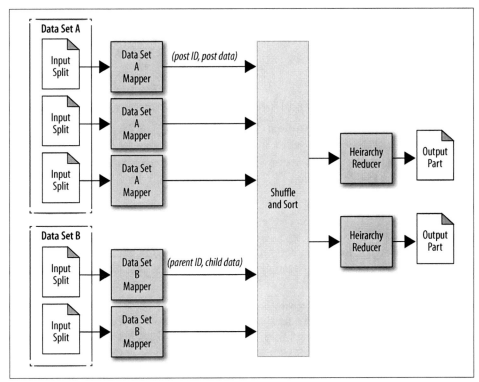

Figure 4-1. The structure of the structured to hierarchical pattern

done in the driver. If you are loading data from only one source in this pattern, you don't need this step.

- The mappers load the data and parse the records into one cohesive format so that your work in the reducers is easier. The output key should reflect how you want to identify the root of each hierarchical record. For example, in our StackOverflow example, the root would be the post ID. You also need to give each piece of data some context about its source. You need to identify whether this output record is a post or a comment. To do this, you can simply concatenate some sort of label to the output value text.

- In general, a combiner isn't going to help you too much here. You could hypo-thetically group items with the same key and send them over together, but this has no major compression gains since all you would be doing is concatenating strings, so the size of the resulting string would be the same as the inputs.

- The reducer receives the data from all the different sources key by key. All of the data for a particular grouping is going to be provided for you in one iterator, so all that is left for you to do is build the hierarchical data structure from the list of data items. With XML or JSON, you'll build a single object and then write it out as output. The examples in this section show XML, which provides several convenient methods for constructing data structures. If you are using some other format, such as a custom format, you'll just need to use the proper object building and serialization methods.

Consequences

The output will be in a hierarchical form, grouped by the key that you specified.

However, be careful that many formats such as XML and JSON have some sort of top-level root element that encompasses all of the records. If you actually need the document to be well-formed top-to-bottom, it's usually easier to add this header and footer text as some post-processing step.

Known uses

Pre-joining data
> Data arrives in disjointed structured data sets, and for analytical purposes it would be easier to bring the data together into more complex objects. By doing this, you are setting up your data to take advantage of the NoSQL model of analysis.

Preparing data for HBase or MongoDB
> HBase is a natural way to store this data, so you can use this method to bring the data together in preparation for loading into HBase or MongoDB. Creating a new table and then executing a bulk import via MapReduce is particularly effective. The alternative is to do several rounds of inserts, which might be less efficient.

Resemblances

SQL
> It's rare that you would want to do something like this in a relational database, since storing data in this way is not conducive to analysis with SQL. However, the way you would solve a similar problem in an RDBMS is to join the data and then perform analysis on the result.

Pig
> Pig has reasonable support for hierarchical data structures. You can have hierarchical bags and tuples, which make it easy to represent hierarchical structures and lists of objects in a single record. The COGROUP method in Pig does a great job of bringing data together while preserving the original structure. However, using the predefined keywords to do any sort of real analysis on a complex record is more challenging out of the box. For this, a user-defined function is the right way to go. Basically, you would use Pig to build and group the records, then a UDF to make sense of the data.
>
> ```
> data_a = LOAD '/data/comments/' AS PigStorage('|');
> data_b = LOAD '/data/posts/' as PigStorage(',');
>
> grouped = COGROUP data_a BY $2, data_b BY $1;
> ```

```
analyzed = FOREACH grouped GENERATE udfs.analyze(group, $1, $2);

...
```

Performance analysis

There are two performance concerns that you need to pay attention to when using this pattern. First, you need to be aware of how much data is being sent to the reducers from the mappers, and second you need to be aware of the memory footprint of the object that the reducer builds.

Since records with the grouping key can be scattered anywhere in the data set, pretty much all of data is going to move across the network. For this reason, you will need to pay particular attention to having an adequate number of reducers. The same strategies apply here that are employed in other patterns that shuffle everything over the network.

The next major concern is the possibility of hot spots in the data that could result in an obscenely large record. With large data sets, it is conceivable that a particular output record is going to have a lot of data associated with it. Imagine that for some reason a post on StackOverflow has a million comments associated with it. That would be extremely rare and unlikely, but not in the realm of the impossible. If you are building some sort of XML object, all of those comments at one point might be stored in memory before writing the object out. This can cause you to blow out the heap of the Java Virtual Machine, which obviously should be avoided.

Another problem with hot spots is a skew in how much data each reducer is handling. This is going to be a similar problem in just about any MapReduce job. In many cases the skew can be ignored, but if it really matters you can write a custom partitioner to split the data up more evenly.

Structured to Hierarchical Examples

Post/comment building on StackOverflow

In this example, we will take the posts and comments of the StackOverflow data and group them together. A hierarchy will look something like:

```
Posts
    Post
        Comment
        Comment
    Post
        Comment
        Comment
        Comment
```

The following descriptions of each code section explain the solution to the problem.

Problem: Given a list of posts and comments, create a structured XML hierarchy to nest comments with their related post.

Driver code. We don't usually describe the code for the driver, but in this case we are doing something exotic with `MultipleInputs`. All we do differently is create a `MultipleInputs` object and add the comments path and the posts path with their respective mappers. The paths for the posts and comments data are provided via the command line, and the program retrieves them from the `args` array.

```java
public static void main(String[] args) throws Exception {
    Configuration conf = new Configuration();
    Job job = new Job(conf, "PostCommentHierarchy");
    job.setJarByClass(PostCommentBuildingDriver.class);

    MultipleInputs.addInputPath(job, new Path(args[0]),
            TextInputFormat.class, PostMapper.class);

    MultipleInputs.addInputPath(job, new Path(args[1]),
            TextInputFormat.class, CommentMapper.class);

    job.setReducerClass(UserJoinReducer.class);

    job.setOutputFormatClass(TextOutputFormat.class);
    TextOutputFormat.setOutputPath(job, new Path(args[2]));

    job.setOutputKeyClass(Text.class);
    job.setOutputValueClass(Text.class);

    System.exit(job.waitForCompletion(true) ? 0 : 2);
}
```

Mapper code. In this case, there are two mapper classes, one for comments and one for posts. In both, we extract the post ID to use it as the output key. We output the input value prepended with a character ("P" for a post or "C" for a comment) so we know which data set the record came from during the reduce phase.

```java
public static class PostMapper extends Mapper<Object, Text, Text, Text> {

    private Text outkey = new Text();
    private Text outvalue = new Text();

    public void map(Object key, Text value, Context context)
            throws IOException, InterruptedException {

        Map<String, String> parsed = MRDPUtils.transformXmlToMap(value
                .toString());

        // The foreign join key is the post ID
        outkey.set(parsed.get("Id"));

        // Flag this record for the reducer and then output
        outvalue.set("P" + value.toString());
        context.write(outkey, outvalue);
    }
```

```
        }

    public static class CommentMapper extends Mapper<Object, Text, Text, Text> {
        private Text outkey = new Text();
        private Text outvalue = new Text();

        public void map(Object key, Text value, Context context)
                throws IOException, InterruptedException {

            Map<String, String> parsed = MRDPUtils.transformXmlToMap(value
                    .toString());

            // The foreign join key is the post ID
            outkey.set(parsed.get("PostId"));

            // Flag this record for the reducer and then output
            outvalue.set("C" + value.toString());
            context.write(outkey, outvalue);
        }
    }
```

Reducer code. The reducer builds the hierarchical XML object. All the values are iterated to get the post record and collect a list of comments. We know which record is which by the flag we added to the value. These flags are removed when assigning post or adding the list. Then, if the post is not null, an XML record is constructed with the post as the parent and comments as the children.

The implementation of the nestElements follows. We chose to use an XML library to build the final record, but please feel free to use whatever means you deem necessary.

```
    public static class PostCommentHierarchyReducer extends
            Reducer<Text, Text, Text, NullWritable> {

        private ArrayList<String> comments = new ArrayList<String>();
        private DocumentBuilderFactory dbf = DocumentBuilderFactory.newInstance();
        private String post = null;

        public void reduce(Text key, Iterable<Text> values, Context context)
                throws IOException, InterruptedException {
            // Reset variables
            post = null;
            comments.clear();

            // For each input value
            for (Text t : values) {
                // If this is the post record, store it, minus the flag
                if (t.charAt(0) == 'P') {
                    post = t.toString().substring(1, t.toString().length())
                            .trim();
                } else {
                    // Else, it is a comment record. Add it to the list, minus
                    // the flag
                    comments.add(t.toString()
                            .substring(1, t.toString().length()).trim());
                }
```

```
        }
        // If there are no comments, the comments list will simply be empty.

        // If post is not null, combine post with its comments.
        if (post != null) {
            // nest the comments underneath the post element
            String postWithCommentChildren = nestElements(post, comments);

            // write out the XML
            context.write(new Text(postWithCommentChildren),
                    NullWritable.get());
        }
    }
}
...
```

The `nestElements` method takes the post and the list of comments to create a new string of XML to output. It uses a `DocumentBuilder` and some additional helper methods to copy the `Element` objects into new ones, in addition to their attributes. This copying occurs to rename the element tags from `row` to either `post` or `comment`. The final `Document` is then transformed into an XML string.

```
private String nestElements(String post, List<String> comments) {
    // Create the new document to build the XML
    DocumentBuilder bldr = dbf.newDocumentBuilder();
    Document doc = bldr.newDocument();

    // Copy parent node to document
    Element postEl = getXmlElementFromString(post);
    Element toAddPostEl = doc.createElement("post");

    // Copy the attributes of the original post element to the new one
    copyAttributesToElement(postEl.getAttributes(), toAddPostEl);

    // For each comment, copy it to the "post" node
    for (String commentXml : comments) {
        Element commentEl = getXmlElementFromString(commentXml);
        Element toAddCommentEl = doc.createElement("comments");

        // Copy the attributes of the original comment element to
        // the new one
        copyAttributesToElement(commentEl.getAttributes(),
                toAddCommentEl);

        // Add the copied comment to the post element
        toAddPostEl.appendChild(toAddCommentEl);
    }

    // Add the post element to the document
    doc.appendChild(toAddPostEl);

    // Transform the document into a String of XML and return
    return transformDocumentToString(doc);
}

private Element getXmlElementFromString(String xml) {
```

```
    // Create a new document builder
    DocumentBuilder bldr = dbf.newDocumentBuilder();

    return bldr.parse(new InputSource(new StringReader(xml)))
            .getDocumentElement();
}

private void copyAttributesToElement(NamedNodeMap attributes,
        Element element) {

    // For each attribute, copy it to the element
    for (int i = 0; i < attributes.getLength(); ++i) {
        Attr toCopy = (Attr) attributes.item(i);
        element.setAttribute(toCopy.getName(), toCopy.getValue());
    }
}

private String transformDocumentToString(Document doc) {

    TransformerFactory tf = TransformerFactory.newInstance();
    Transformer transformer = tf.newTransformer();
    transformer.setOutputProperty(OutputKeys.OMIT_XML_DECLARATION,
            "yes");
    StringWriter writer = new StringWriter();
    transformer.transform(new DOMSource(doc), new StreamResult(
            writer));
    // Replace all new line characters with an empty string to have
    // one record per line.
    return writer.getBuffer().toString().replaceAll("\n|\r", "");
}
}
```

Question/answer building on StackOverflow

This is a continuation of the previous example and will use the previous analytic's output as the input to this analytic. Now that we have the comments associated with the posts, we are going to associate the post answers with the post questions. This needs to be done because posts consist of both answers and questions and are differentiated only by their PostTypeId. We'll group them together by Id in questions and ParentId in answers.

The main difference between the two applications of this pattern is that in this one we are dealing only with one data set. Effectively, we are using a self-join here to correlate the different records from the same data set.

The following descriptions of each code section explain the solution to the problem.

Problem: Given the output of the previous example, perform a self-join operation to create a question, answer, and comment hierarchy.

Mapper code. The first thing the mapper code does is determine whether the record is a question or an answer, because the behavior for each will be different. For a question, we will extract Id as the key and label it as a question. For an answer, we will extract ParentId as the key and label it as an answer.

```
public class QuestionAnswerBuildingDriver {

    public static class PostCommentMapper extends
            Mapper<Object, Text, Text, Text> {

        private DocumentBuilderFactory dbf = DocumentBuilderFactory
                .newInstance();
        private Text outkey = new Text();
        private Text outvalue = new Text();

        public void map(Object key, Text value, Context context)
                throws IOException, InterruptedException {

            // Parse the post/comment XML hierarchy into an Element
            Element post = getXmlElementFromString(value.toString());

            int postType = Integer.parseInt(post.getAttribute("PostTypeId"));

            // If postType is 1, it is a question
            if (postType == 1) {
                outkey.set(post.getAttribute("Id"));
                outvalue.set("Q" + value.toString());
            } else {
                // Else, it is an answer
                outkey.set(post.getAttribute("ParentId"));
                outvalue.set("A" + value.toString());
            }

            context.write(outkey, outvalue);
        }

        private Element getXmlElementFromString(String xml) {
            // same as previous example, "Mapper code" on page 75
        }
    }
}
```

Reducer code. The reducer code is very similar to the that in the previous example. It iterates through the input values and grabs the question and answer, being sure to remove the flag. It then nests the answers inside the question in the same fashion as the previous example. The difference is that tags are "question" instead of the "post" and "answer" instead of "comment." The helper functions are omitted here for brevity. They can be viewed in the previous example.

```
public static class QuestionAnswerReducer extends
        Reducer<Text, Text, Text, NullWritable> {

    private ArrayList<String> answers = new ArrayList<String>();
    private DocumentBuilderFactory dbf = DocumentBuilderFactory
            .newInstance();
    private String question = null;
```

```java
public void reduce(Text key, Iterable<Text> values, Context context)
        throws IOException, InterruptedException {
    // Reset variables
    question = null;
    answers.clear();

    // For each input value
    for (Text t : values) {
        // If this is the post record, store it, minus the flag
        if (t.charAt(0) == 'Q') {
            question = t.toString().substring(1, t.toString().length())
                    .trim();
        } else {
            // Else, it is a comment record. Add it to the list, minus
            // the flag
            answers.add(t.toString()
                    .substring(1, t.toString().length()).trim());
        }
    }

    // If post is not null
    if (question != null) {
        // nest the comments underneath the post element
        String postWithCommentChildren = nestElements(question, answers);

        // write out the XML
        context.write(new Text(postWithCommentChildren),
                NullWritable.get());
    }
}

... // ommitted helper functions
}
```

Partitioning

Pattern Description

The *partitioning* pattern moves the records into categories (i.e., shards, partitions, or bins) but it doesn't really care about the order of records.

Intent

The intent is to take similar records in a data set and partition them into distinct, smaller data sets.

Motivation

If you want to look at a particular set of data—such as postings made on a particular date—the data items are normally spread out across the entire data set. So looking at just one of these subsets requires an entire scan of all of the data. Partitioning means breaking a large set of data into smaller subsets, which can be chosen by some criterion relevant to your analysis. To improve performance, you can run a job that takes the data set and breaks the partitions out into separate files. Then, when a particular subset for the data is to be analyzed, the job needs only to look at that data.

Partitioning by date is one of the most common schemes. This helps when we want to analyze a certain span of time, because the data is already grouped by that criterion. For instance, suppose you have event data that spans three years in your Hadoop cluster, but for whatever reason the records are not ordered at all by date. If you only care about data from January 27 to February 3 of the current year, you must scan all of the data since those events could be anywhere in the data set. If instead you had the events partitioned into months (i.e., you have a file with January data, a file with February data, etc.), you would only need to run your MapReduce job over the January and February partitions. It would be even better if they were partitioned by day!

Partitioning can also help out when you have several different types of records in the same data set, which is increasingly common in NoSQL. For example, in a HTTP server logs, you'll have GET and POST requests, internal system messages, and error messages. Analysis may care about only one category of this data, so partitioning it into these categories will help narrow down the data the job runs over before it even runs.

In an RDBMS, a typical criterion for partitioning is what you normally filter by in the WHERE clause. So, for example, if you are typically filtering down records by country, perhaps you should partition by country. This applies in MapReduce as well. If you find yourself filtering out a bunch of records in the mapper due to the same criteria over and over, you should consider partitioning your data set.

There is no downside to partitioning other than having to build the partitions. A MapReduce job can still run over all the partitions at once if necessary.

Applicability

The one major requirement to apply this pattern is knowing how many partitions you are going to have ahead of time. For example, if you know you are going to partition by day of the week, you know that you will have seven partitions.

You can get around this requirement by running an analytic that determines the number of partitions. For example, if you have a bunch of timestamped data, but you don't know how far back it spans, run a job that figures out the date range for you.

Structure

This pattern is interesting in that it exploits the fact that the partitioner partitions data (imagine that!). There is no actual partitioning logic; all you have to do is define the function that determines what partition a record is going to go to in a custom partitioner. Figure 4-2 shows the structure of this pattern.

- In most cases, the identity mapper can be used.

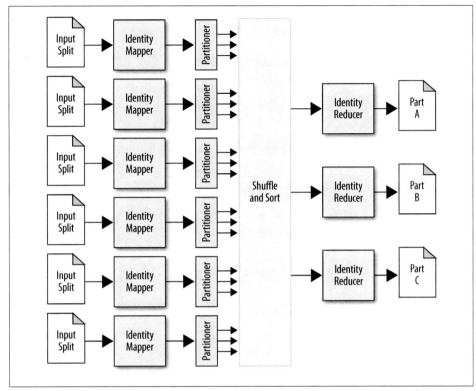

Figure 4-2. The structure of the partitioning pattern

- The custom partitioner is the meat of this pattern. The custom partitioner will determine which reducer to send each record to; each reducer corresponds to particular partitions.

- In most cases, the identity reducer can be used. But this pattern can do additional processing in the reducer if needed. Data is still going to get grouped and sorted, so data can be deduplicated, aggregated, or summarized, per partition.

Consequences

The output folder of the job will have one part file for each par tition.

 Since each category will be written out to one large file, this is a great place to store the data in block-compressed SequenceFiles, which are arguably the most efficient and easy-to-use data format in Hadoop.

Known uses

Partition pruning by continuous value

You have some sort of continuous variable, such as a date or numerical value, and at any one time you care about only a certain subset of that data. Partitioning the data into bins will allow your jobs to load only pertinent data.

Partition pruning by category

Instead of having some sort of continuous variable, the records fit into one of several clearly defined categories, such as country, phone area code, or language.

Sharding

A system in your architecture has divisions of data—such as different disks—and you need to partition the data into these existing shards.

Resemblances

SQL

Some SQL databases allow for automatically partitioned tables. This allows "partition pruning" which allows the database to exclude large portions of irrelevant data before running the SQL.

Other patterns

This pattern is similar to the binning pattern in this chapter. In most cases, binning can perform the same partitioning behavior as this pattern.

Performance analysis

The main performance concern with this pattern is that the resulting partitions will likely not have similar number of records. Perhaps one partition turns out to hold 50% of the data of a very large data set. If implemented naively, all of this data will get sent to one reducer and will slow down processing significantly.

It's pretty easy to get around this, though. Split very large partitions into several smaller partitions, even if just randomly. Assign multiple reducers to one partition and then randomly assign records into each to spread it out a bit better.

For example, consider the "last access date" field for a user in StackOverflow. If we partitioned on this property equally over months, the most recent month will very likely be much larger than any other month. To prevent skew, it may make sense to partition the most recent month into days, or perhaps just randomly.

This method doesn't affect processing over partitions, since you know that these set of files represent one larger partition. Just include all of them as input.

Partitioning Examples

Partitioning users by last access date

In the StackOverflow data set, users are stored in the order in which they registered. Instead, we want to organize the data into partitions based on the year of the last access date. This is done by creating a custom partitioner to assign record to a particular partition based on that date.

The following descriptions of each code section explain the solution to the problem.

Problem: Given a set of user information, partition the records based on the year of last access date, one partition per year.

Driver code. This driver is a little different than the norm. The job needs to be configured to use the custom built partitioner, and this partitioner needs to be configured. The minimum last access year needs to be configured, which is 2008. The reason for this is explained in the partitioner code section. Also, the number of reducers is important to make sure the full range of partitions is accounted for. Given that the authors are running this example in 2012, the maximum last access year was in 2011, spanning 4 years from 2008 to 2011. Users can fall into these dates as well as those in between, meaning the job is configured to have exactly 4 reducers.

```
...
// Set custom partitioner and min last access date
job.setPartitionerClass(LastAccessDatePartitioner.class);
LastAccessDatePartitioner.setMinLastAccessDate(job, 2008);

// Last access dates span between 2008-2011, or 4 years
job.setNumReduceTasks(4);
...
```

Mapper code. The mapper pulls the last access date out of each input record. This date is output as the key, and the full input record is output as the value. This is so the partitioner can do the work of putting each record into its appropriate partition. This key is later ignored during output from the reduce phase.

```
public static class LastAccessDateMapper extends
        Mapper<Object, Text, IntWritable, Text> {

    // This object will format the creation date string into a Date object
    private final static SimpleDateFormat frmt = new SimpleDateFormat(
            "yyyy-MM-dd'T'HH:mm:ss.SSS");

    private IntWritable outkey = new IntWritable();

    protected void map(Object key, Text value, Context context)
            throws IOException, InterruptedException {

        Map<String, String> parsed = MRDPUtils.transformXmlToMap(value
```

```
            .toString());

        // Grab the last access date
        String strDate = parsed.get("LastAccessDate");

        // Parse the string into a Calendar object
        Calendar cal = Calendar.getInstance();
        cal.setTime(frmt.parse(strDate));
        outkey.set(cal.get(Calendar.YEAR));

        // Write out the year with the input value
        context.write(outkey, value);
    }
}
```

Partitioner code. The partitioner examines each key/value pair output by the mapper to determine which partition the key/value pair will be written. Each numbered partition will be copied by its associated reduce task during the reduce phase. The partitioner implements the Configurable interface. The setConf method is called during task construction to configure the partitioner. Here, the minimum value of the last access date is pulled from the configuration. The driver is responsible for calling LastAccessDate Partitioner.setMinLastAccessDate during job configuration. This date is used to subtract from each key (last access date) to determine what partition it goes to. The minimum last access date is 2008, so all users who last logged into StackOverflow in 2008 will be assigned to partition zero.

```
public static class LastAccessDatePartitioner extends
        Partitioner<IntWritable, Text> implements Configurable {

    private static final String MIN_LAST_ACCESS_DATE_YEAR =
            "min.last.access.date.year";

    private Configuration conf = null;
    private int minLastAccessDateYear = 0;

    public int getPartition(IntWritable key, Text value, int numPartitions) {
        return key.get() - minLastAccessDateYear;
    }

    public Configuration getConf() {
        return conf;
    }

    public void setConf(Configuration conf) {
        this.conf = conf;
        minLastAccessDateYear = conf.getInt(MIN_LAST_ACCESS_DATE_YEAR, 0);
    }

    public static void setMinLastAccessDate(Job job,
            int minLastAccessDateYear) {
        job.getConfiguration().setInt(MIN_LAST_ACCESS_DATE_YEAR,
                minLastAccessDateYear);
```

```
        }
    }
```

Reducer code. The reducer code is very simple since we simply want to output the values. The work of paritioning has been done at this point.

```
    public static class ValueReducer extends
            Reducer<IntWritable, Text, Text, NullWritable> {

        protected void reduce(IntWritable key, Iterable<Text> values,
                Context context) throws IOException, InterruptedException {
            for (Text t : values) {
                context.write(t, NullWritable.get());
            }
        }
    }
```

Binning

Pattern Description

The *binning* pattern, much like the previous pattern, moves the records into categories irrespective of the order of records.

Intent

For each record in the data set, file each one into one or more categories.

Motivation

Binning is very similar to partitioning and often can be used to solve the same problem. The major difference is in how the bins or partitions are built using the MapReduce framework. In some situations, one solution works better than the other.

Binning splits data up in the map phase instead of in the partitioner. This has the major advantage of eliminating the need for a reduce phase, usually leading to more efficient resource allocation. The downside is that each mapper will now have one file per possible output bin. This means that, if you have a thousand bins and a thousand mappers, you are going to output a total of one million files. This is bad for NameNode scalability and follow-on analytics. The partitioning pattern will have one output file per category and does not have this problem.

Structure

- This pattern's driver is unique in using the `MultipleOutputs` class, which sets up the job's output to write multiple distinct files.
- The mapper looks at each line, then iterates through a list of criteria for each bin. If the record meets the criteria, it is sent to that bin. See Figure 4-3.

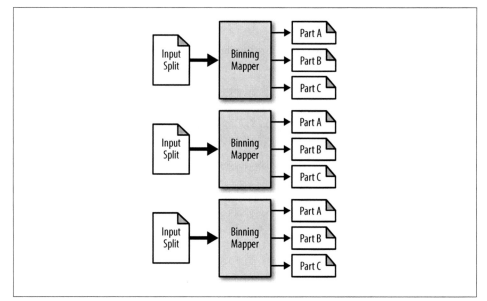

Figure 4-3. The structure of the binning pattern

- No combiner, partitioner, or reducer is used in this pattern.

Consequences

Each mapper outputs one small file per bin.

 Data should not be left as a bunch of tiny files. At some point, you should run some postprocessing that collects the outputs into larger files.

Resemblances

Pig

> The SPLIT operation in Pig implements this pattern.

```
SPLIT data INTO
    eights IF col1 == 8,
    bigs IF col1 > 8,
    smalls IF (col1 < 8 AND col1 > 0);
```

Performance analysis

This pattern has the same scalability and performance properties as other map-only jobs. No sort, shuffle, or reduce needs to be performed, and most of the processing is going to be done on data that is local.

Binning Examples

Binning by Hadoop-related tags

We want to filter data by tag into different bins so that we can run follow-on analysis without having to run over all of the data. We care only about the Hadoop-related tags, specifically hadoop, pig, hive, and hbase. Also, if the post mentions Hadoop anywhere in the text or title, we'll put that into its own bin.

The following descriptions of each code section explain the solution to the problem.

Problem: Given a set of StackOverflow posts, bin the posts into four bins based on the tags hadoop, pig, hive, and hbase. Also, create a separate bin for posts mentioning hadoop in the text or title.

Driver code. The driver is pretty much the same boiler plate code, except that we use `MultipleOutputs` for the different bins. `MultipleOutputs` takes in a name, `bins`, that is used in the mapper to write different output. The name is essentially the output directory of the job. Output counters are disabled by default, so be sure to turn those on if you don't expect a large number of named outputs. We also set the number of reduce tasks to zero, as this is a map-only job.

```
...
// Configure the MultipleOutputs by adding an output called "bins"
// With the proper output format and mapper key/value pairs
MultipleOutputs.addNamedOutput(job, "bins", TextOutputFormat.class,
        Text.class, NullWritable.class);

// Enable the counters for the job
// If there are a significant number of different named outputs, this
// should be disabled
MultipleOutputs.setCountersEnabled(job, true);

// Map-only job
job.setNumReduceTasks(0);
...
```

Mapper code. The setup phase creates an instance of `MultipleOutputs` using the context. The mapper consists of several if-else statements to check each of the tags of a post. Each tag is checked against one of our tags of interest. If the post contains the tag, it is written to the bin. Posts with multiple interesting tags will essentially be duplicated as they are written to the appropriate bins. Finally, we check whether the body of the post contains the word "hadoop". If it does, we output it to a separate bin.

Be sure to close the `MultipleOutputs` during cleanup! Otherwise, you may not have much output at all.

The typical file names, part-*mnnnnn*, will be in the final output directory. These files will be empty unless the Context object is used to write key/value pairs. Instead, files will be named *bin_name-mnnnnn*. In the following example, *bin_name* will be, hadoop-tag, pig-tag, hive-tag, hbase-tag, or hadoop-post.

Note that setting the output format of the job to a NullOutputFormat will remove these empty output files when using the mapred package. In the newer API, the output files are not committed from their _temporary directory into the configured output directory in HDFS. This may be fixed in a newer version of Hadoop.

```
public static class BinningMapper extends
    Mapper<Object, Text, Text, NullWritable> {

    private MultipleOutputs<Text, NullWritable> mos = null;

    protected void setup(Context context) {
        // Create a new MultipleOutputs using the context object
        mos = new MultipleOutputs(context);
    }

    protected void map(Object key, Text value, Context context)
            throws IOException, InterruptedException {

        Map<String, String> parsed = MRDPUtils.transformXmlToMap(value
                .toString());

        String rawtags = parsed.get("Tags");

        // Tags are delimited by ><. i.e. <tag1><tag2><tag3>
        String[] tagTokens = StringEscapeUtils.unescapeHtml(rawtags).split(
                "><");

        // For each tag
        for (String tag : tagTokens) {
            // Remove any > or < from the token
            String groomed = tag.replaceAll(">|<", "").toLowerCase();

            // If this tag is one of the following, write to the named bin
            if (groomed.equalsIgnoreCase("hadoop")) {
                mos.write("bins", value, NullWritable.get(), "hadoop-tag");
            }
            if (groomed.equalsIgnoreCase("pig")) {
                mos.write("bins", value, NullWritable.get(), "pig-tag");
            }
            if (groomed.equalsIgnoreCase("hive")) {
                mos.write("bins", value, NullWritable.get(), "hive-tag");
            }
            if (groomed.equalsIgnoreCase("hbase")) {
                mos.write("bins", value, NullWritable.get(), "hbase-tag");
            }
        }
    }
```

```
            // Get the body of the post
            String post = parsed.get("Body");

            // If the post contains the word "hadoop", write it to its own bin
            if (post.toLowerCase().contains("hadoop")) {
                mos.write("bins", value, NullWritable.get(), "hadoop-post");
            }
        }
    }

    protected void cleanup(Context context) throws IOException,
            InterruptedException {
        // Close multiple outputs!
        mos.close();
    }
}
```

Total Order Sorting

Pattern Description

The *total order sorting* pattern is concerned with the order of the data from record to record.

Intent

You want to sort your data in parallel on a sort key.

Motivation

Sorting is easy in sequential programming. Sorting in MapReduce, or more generally in parallel, is not easy. This is because the typical "divide and conquer" approach is a bit harder to apply here.

Each individual reducer will sort its data by key, but unfortunately, this sorting is not global across all data. What we want to do here is a total order sorting where, if you concatenate the output files, the records are sorted. If we just concatenate the output of a simple MapReduce job, segments of the data will be sorted, but the whole set will not be.

Sorted data has a number of useful properties. Sorted by time, it can provide a timeline view on the data. Finding things in a sorted data set can be done with binary search instead of linear search. In the case of MapReduce, we know the upper and lower boundaries of each file by looking at the last and first records, respectively. This can be useful for finding records, as well, and is one of the primary characteristics of HBase. Some databases can bulk load data faster if the data is sorted on the primary key or index column.

There are countless more reasons to have sorted data from an application standpoint or follow-on system standpoint. However, having data sorted for use in MapReduce serves little purpose, so hopefully this expensive operation only has to be done sparingly.

Applicability

The main requirement here is pretty obvious: your sort key has to implement the `Comparable` interface.

Structure

Total order sorting may be one of the more complicated patterns you'll see. The reason this is that you first have to determine a set of partitions divided by ranges of values that will produce equal-sized subsets of data. These ranges will determine which reducer will sort which range of data. Then something similar to the partitioning pattern is run: a custom partitioner is used to partition data by the sort key. The lowest range of data goes to the first reducer, the next range goes to the second reducer, so on and so forth.

This pattern has two phases: an analyze phase that determines the ranges, and the order phase that actually sorts the data. The analyze phase is optional in some ways. You need to run it only once if the distribution of your data does not change quickly over time, because the value ranges it produces will continue to perform well. Also, in some cases, you may be able to guess the partitions yourself, especially if the data is evenly distributed. For example, if you are sorting comments by user ID, and you have a million users, you can assume that with a thousand reducers, each range is going to have a range of a thousand users. This is because comments by user ID should be spread out evenly and since you know the number of total users, you can divide that number by the number of reducers you want to use.

The analyze phase is a random sampling of the data. The partitions are then based on that random sample. The principle is that partitions that evely split the random sample should evenly split the larger data set well. The structure of the analyze step is as follows:

- The mapper does a simple random sampling. When dividing records, it outputs the sort key as its output key so that the data will show up sorted at the reducer. We don't care at all about the actual record, so we'll just use a null value to save on space.

- Ahead of time, determine the number of records in the total data set and figure out what percentage of records you'll need to analyze to make a reasonable sample. For example, if you plan on running the order with a thousand reducers, sampling about a hundred thousand records should give nice, even partitions. Assuming you have a billion records, divide 100,000 by 1,000,000,000. This gives 0.0001, meaning .01% of the records should be run through the analyze phase.

- Only one reducer will be used here. This will collect the sort keys together into a sorted list (they come in sorted, so that will be easy). Then, when all of them have been collected, the list of keys will be sliced into the data range boundaries.

The order phase is a relatively straightforward application of MapReduce that uses a custom partitioner. The structure of the order step is as follows:

- The mapper extracts the sort key in the same way as the analyze step. However, this time the record itself is stored as the value instead of being ignored.

- A custom partitioner is used that loads up the partition file. In Hadoop, you can use the `TotalOrderPartitioner`, which is built specifically for this purpose. It takes the data ranges from the partition file produced in the previous step and decides which reducer to send the data to.

- The reducer's job here is simple. The shuffle and sort take care of the heavy lifting. The reduce function simply takes the values that have come in and outputs them. The number of reducers needs to be equal to the number of partitions for the `TotalOrderPartitioner` to work properly.

 Note that the number of ranges in the intermediate partition needs to be equal to the number of reducers in the order step. If you decide to change the number of reducers and you've been reusing the same file, you'll need to rebuild it.

 If you want to have a primary sort key and a secondary sort key, concatenate the keys, delimited by something. For example, if you want to sort by last name first, and city second, use a key that looks like `Smith^Baltimore`.

Using Text for nearly everything in Hadoop is very natural since that's the format in which data is coming in. Be careful when sorting on numerical data, though! The string `"10000"` is less than than `"9"` if they are compared as strings, which is not what we want. Either pad the numbers with zeros or use a numerical data type.

Consequences

The output files will contain sorted data, and the output file names will be sorted such that the data is in a total sorting. In Hadoop, you'll be able to issue `hadoop fs -cat output/part-r-*` and retrieve the data in a sorted manner.

Resemblances

SQL

Ordering in SQL is pretty easy!

```
SELECT * FROM data ORDER BY col1;
```

Pig

Ordering in Pig is syntactically pretty easy, but it's a very expensive operation. Behind the scenes, it will run a multi-stage MapReduce job to first find the partitions, and then perform the actual sort.

```
c = ORDER b BY col1;
```

Performance analysis

This operation is expensive because you effectively have to load and parse the data twice: first to build the partition ranges, and then to actually sort the data.

The job that builds the partitions is straightforward and efficient since it has only one reducer and sends a minimal amount of data over the network. The output file is small, so writing it out is trivial. Also, you may only have to run this now and then, which will amortize the cost of building it over time.

The order step of the job has performance characteristics similar o the other data organization patterns, because it has to move all of the data over the network and write all of the data back out. Therefore, you should use a relatively large number of reducers.

Total Order Sorting Examples

Sort users by last visit

The user data in our StackOverflow data set is in the order of the account's creation. Instead, we'd like to have the data ordered by the last time they have visited the site.

For this example, we have a special driver that runs both the analyze and order steps. Also, there are two sets of MapReduce jobs, one for analyze and one for order.

Driver code. Let's break the driver down into two sections: building the partition list via sampling, then perform the sort.

The first section parses the input command line arguments and creates input and output variables from them. It creates path files to the partition list and the staging directory. The partition list is used by the `TotalOrderPartitioner` to make sure the key/value pairs are sorted properly. The staging directory is used to store intermediate output between the two jobs. There is nothing too special with the first job configuration. The main thing to note is that the first job is a map-only only job that uses a `SequenceFileOutput Format`.

```
public static void main(String[] args) throws Exception {
    Configuration conf = new Configuration();
    Path inputPath = new Path(args[0]);
    Path partitionFile = new Path(args[1] + "_partitions.lst");
    Path outputStage = new Path(args[1] + "_staging");
    Path outputOrder = new Path(args[1]);

    // Configure job to prepare for sampling
```

```
Job sampleJob = new Job(conf, "TotalOrderSortingStage");
sampleJob.setJarByClass(TotalOrderSorting.class);

// Use the mapper implementation with zero reduce tasks
sampleJob.setMapperClass(LastAccessDateMapper.class);
sampleJob.setNumReduceTasks(0);

sampleJob.setOutputKeyClass(Text.class);
sampleJob.setOutputValueClass(Text.class);

TextInputFormat.setInputPaths(sampleJob, inputPath);

// Set the output format to a sequence file
sampleJob.setOutputFormatClass(SequenceFileOutputFormat.class);
SequenceFileOutputFormat.setOutputPath(sampleJob, outputStage);

// Submit the job and get completion code.
int code = sampleJob.waitForCompletion(true) ? 0 : 1;

...
```

The second job uses the identity mapper and our reducer implementation. The input is the output from the first job, so we'll use the identity mapper to output the key/value pairs as they are stored from the output. The job is configured to 10 reducers, but any reasonable number can be used. Next, the partition file is configured, even though we have not created it yet.

The next important line uses the InputSampler utility. This sampler writes the partition file by reading through the configured input directory of the job. Using the RandomSampler, it takes a configurable number of samples of the previous job's output. This can be an expensive operation, as the entire output is read using this constructor. Another constructor of RandomSampler allows you to set the number of input splits that will be sampled. This will increase execution time, but you might not get as good a distribution.

After the partition file is written, the job is executed. The partition file and staging directory are then deleted, as they are no longer needed for this example.

 If your data distribution is unlikely to change, it would be worthwhile to keep this partition file around. It can then be used over and over again for this job in the future as new data arrives on the system.

```
...

if (code == 0) {
    Job orderJob = new Job(conf, "TotalOrderSortingStage");
    orderJob.setJarByClass(TotalOrderSorting.class);

    // Here, use the identity mapper to output the key/value pairs in
    // the SequenceFile
    orderJob.setMapperClass(Mapper.class);
```

```
orderJob.setReducerClass(ValueReducer.class);

// Set the number of reduce tasks to an appropriate number for the
// amount of data being sorted
orderJob.setNumReduceTasks(10);

// Use Hadoop's TotalOrderPartitioner class
orderJob.setPartitionerClass(TotalOrderPartitioner.class);

// Set the partition file
TotalOrderPartitioner.setPartitionFile(orderJob.getConfiguration(),
        partitionFile);

orderJob.setOutputKeyClass(Text.class);
orderJob.setOutputValueClass(Text.class);

// Set the input to the previous job's output
orderJob.setInputFormatClass(SequenceFileInputFormat.class);
SequenceFileInputFormat.setInputPaths(orderJob, outputStage);

// Set the output path to the command line parameter
TextOutputFormat.setOutputPath(orderJob, outputOrder);

// Set the separator to an empty string
orderJob.getConfiguration().set(
        "mapred.textoutputformat.separator", "");

// Use the InputSampler to go through the output of the previous
// job, sample it, and create the partition file
InputSampler.writePartitionFile(orderJob,
        new InputSampler.RandomSampler(.001, 10000));

// Submit the job
code = orderJob.waitForCompletion(true) ? 0 : 2;
    }

    // Clean up the partition file and the staging directory
    FileSystem.get(new Configuration()).delete(partitionFile, false);
    FileSystem.get(new Configuration()).delete(outputStage, true);

    System.exit(code);
}
```

Analyze mapper code. This mapper simply pulls the last access date for each user and sets it as the sort key for the record. The input value is output along with it. These key/value pairs, per our job configuration, are written to a SequenceFile that is used to create the partition list for the TotalOrderPartitioner. There is no reducer for this job.

```
public static class LastAccessDateMapper extends
        Mapper<Object, Text, Text, Text> {

    private Text outkey = new Text();

    public void map(Object key, Text value, Context context)
            throws IOException, InterruptedException {
```

```
        Map<String, String> parsed = MRDPUtils.transformXmlToMap(value
                .toString());

        outkey.set(parsed.get("LastAccessDate"));
        context.write(outkey, value);
    }
}
```

Order mapper code. This job simply uses the identity mapper to take each input key/value pair and output them. No special configuration or implementation is needed.

Order reducer code. Because the `TotalOrderPartitioner` took care of all the sorting, all the reducer needs to do is output the values with a `NullWritable` object. This will produce a part file for this reducer that is sorted by last access date. The partitioner ensures that the concatenation of all these part files (in order) produces a totally ordered data set.

```
public static class ValueReducer extends
        Reducer<Text, Text, Text, NullWritable> {

    public void reduce(Text key, Iterable<Text> values, Context context)
            throws IOException, InterruptedException {
        for (Text t : values) {
            context.write(t, NullWritable.get());
        }
    }
}
```

Shuffling

Pattern Description

The total order sorting and *shuffling* patterns are opposites in terms of effect, but the latter is also concerned with the order of data in records.

Intent

You have a set of records that you want to completely randomize.

Motivation

This whole chapter has been about applying some sort of order to your data set except for this pattern which is instead about completely destroying the order.

The use cases for doing such a thing are definitely few and far between, but two stand out. One is shuffling the data for the purposes of anonymizing it. Another is randomizing the data set for repeatable random sampling.

Anonymizing data has recently become important for organizations that want to maintain their users' privacy, but still run analytics. The order of the data can provide some information that might lead to the identity of a user. By shuffling the entire data set, the organization is taking an extra step to anonymize the data.

Another reason for shuffling data is to be able to perform some sort of repeatable random sampling. For example, the first hundred records will be a simple random sampling. Every time we pull the first hundred records, we'll get the same sample. This allows analytics that run over a random sample to have a repeatable result. Also, a separate job won't have to be run to produce a simple random sampling every time you need a new sample.

Structure

- All the mapper does is output the record as the value along with a random key.
- The reducer sorts the random keys, further randomizing the data.

In other words, each record is sent to a random reducer. Then, each reducer sorts on the random keys in the records, producing a random order in that reducer.

 The mapper in the shuffle pattern is barely doing anything. This would be a good time to anonymize the data further by transforming the records into an anonymized form.

Consequences

Each reducer outputs a file containing random records.

Resemblances

SQL

The SQL equivalent to this is to order the data set by a random value, instead of some column in the table. This makes it so each record is compared on the basis of two random numbers, which will produce a random ordering. We don't have to go all the way and do a total ordering in MapReduce, as in the previous pattern. This is because sending data to a random reducer is sufficient.

```
SELECT * FROM data ORDER BY RAND()
```

Pig

Shuffling in Pig can be done as we did it in SQL: performing an ORDER BY on a random column. In this case, doing a total ordering is unnecessary. Instead, we can GROUP BY a random key, and then FLATTEN the grouping. This effectively implements the shuffle pattern we proposed behind the scenes.

```
c = GROUP b BY RANDOM();
d = FOREACH c GENERATE FLATTEN(b);
```

Performance analysis

The shuffle has some very nice performance properties. Since the reducer each record goes to is completely random, the data distribution across reducers will be completely balanced. With more reducers, the data will be more spread out. The size of the files will also be very predictable: each is the size of the data set divided by the number of reducers. This makes it easy to get a specific desired file size as output.

Other than that, the typical performance properties for the other patterns in this chapter apply. The pattern shuffles all of the data over the network and writes all of the data back to HDFS, so a relatively high number of reducers should be used.

Shuffle Examples

Anonymizing StackOverflow comments

To anonymize the StackOverflow comments, this example strips out the user ID and row ID, and truncates the date and time to just the date. Then the data is shuffled.

The following descriptions of each code section explain the solution to the problem.

Problem: Given a large data set of StackOverflow comments, anonymize each comment by removing IDs, removing the time from the record, and then randomly shuffling the records within the data set.

Mapper code. The mapper transforms the data using our utility function that parses the data. Each XML attribute is looked at, and an action is taken based on the attribute to create a new line of XML. If it is a user ID or row ID, it is ignored. If it is a creation date, the characters following the 'T' are removed to ignore the time. Otherwise, just write out the XML attribute and value. A random key is generated and output along with the newly constructed record.

```
public static class AnonymizeMapper extends
        Mapper<Object, Text, IntWritable, Text> {

    private IntWritable outkey = new IntWritable();
    private Random rndm = new Random();
    private Text outvalue = new Text();

    public void map(Object key, Text value, Context context)
            throws IOException, InterruptedException {

        Map<String, String> parsed = MRDPUtils.transformXmlToMap(value
                .toString());

        if (parsed.size() > 0) {
            StringBuilder bldr = new StringBuilder();
            // Create the start of the record
            bldr.append("<row ");

            // For each XML attribute
```

```
            for (Entry<String, String> entry : parsed.entrySet()) {

                // If it is a user ID or row ID, ignore it
                if (entry.getKey().equals("UserId")
                        || entry.getKey().equals("Id")) {
                } else if (entry.getKey().equals("CreationDate")) {

                    // If it is a CreationDate, remove the time from the date
                    // i.e., anything after the 'T' in the value
                    bldr.append(entry.getKey()
                            + "=\""
                            + entry.getValue().substring(0,
                                entry.getValue().indexOf('T')) + "\" ");
                } else {
                    // Otherwise, output the attribute and value as is
                    bldr.append(entry.getKey() + "=\"" + entry.getValue()
                            + "\" ");
                }

            }
            // Add the /> to finish the record
            bldr.append("/>");

            // Set the sort key to a random value and output
            outkey.set(rndm.nextInt());
            outvalue.set(bldr.toString());
            context.write(outkey, outvalue);
        }
    }
}
```

Reducer code. This reducer class just outputs the values in order to strip out the random key.

```
public static class ValueReducer extends
        Reducer<IntWritable, Text, Text, NullWritable> {

    protected void reduce(IntWritable key, Iterable<Text> values,
        Context context) throws IOException, InterruptedException {

    for (Text t : values) {
        context.write(t, NullWritable.get());
    }
    }
}
```

CHAPTER 5

Join Patterns

Having all your data in one giant data set is a rarity. For example, presume you have user information stored in a SQL database because it is updated frequently. Meanwhile, web logs arrive in a constant stream and are dumped directly into HDFS. Also, daily analytics that make sense of these logs are stored somewhere in HDFS and financial records are stored in an encrypted repository. The list goes on.

Data is all over the place, and while it's very valuable on its own, we can discover interesting relationships when we start analyzing these sets together. This is where join patterns come into play. Joins can be used to enrich data with a smaller reference set or they can be used to filter out or select records that are in some type of special list. The use cases go on and on as well.

In SQL, joins are accomplished using simple commands, and the database engine handles all of the grunt work. Sadly for us, joins in MapReduce are not nearly this simple. MapReduce operates on a single key/value pair at a time, typically from the same input. We are now working with at least two data sets that are probably of different structures, so we need to know what data set a record came from in order to process it correctly. Typically, no filtering is done prior to the join operation, so some join operations will require every single byte of input to be sent to the reduce phase, which is very taxing on your network. For example, joining a terabyte of data onto another terabyte data set could require at least two terabytes of network bandwith—and that's before any actual join logic can be done.

On top of all of the complexity so far, one has to determine the best way out of a number of different ways to accomplish the same task. Because the framework is broken down into simple map and reduce tasks, there is a lot of hands-on work to do and a lot of things to keep in mind. After you learn the possibilities, the question to ask is when to use what pattern. As with any MapReduce operation, network bandwith is a very important resource and joins have a tendency to use a lot of it. Anything we can do to make the network transfer more efficient is worthwhile, and network optimizations are what differentiates these patterns.

Each of the upcoming patterns can be used to perform an inner join or at least one type of outer join. As far as what pattern to choose, it depends largely on how large the data sets are, how your data is formatted, and what type of join you want. On the other hand, the Cartesian product is completely different, but we can cross that bridge when we get there.

The first pattern discussed in this chapter, the *reduce side join*, is the most basic, along with a modified version that uses a Bloom filter. After that, we discuss two patterns that perform a join operation on the map-side using either the distributed cache or a merging feature in the Hadoop MapReduce API. Finally, we take a look at how to execute the crafty operation that is the Cartesian product.

Choosing the right type of join for your situation can be challenging. Make sure to pay careful attention to the criteria in the "Applicability" section of each of the pattern descriptions.

A Refresher on Joins

If you come from a strong SQL background, you can probably skip this section, but for those of us that started with Hadoop, joins may be a bit of a foreign concept.

Joins are possibly one of the most complex operations one can execute in MapReduce. By design, MapReduce is very good at processing large data sets by looking at every record or group in isolation, so joining two very large data sets together does not fit into the paradigm gracefully. Before we dive into the patterns themselves, let's go over what we mean when we say *join* and the different types of joins that exist.

A *join* is an operation that combines records from two or more data sets based on a field or set of fields, known as the *foreign key*. The foreign key is the field in a relational table that matches the column of another table, and is used as a means to cross-reference between tables. Examples are the simplest way to go about explaining joins, so let's dive right in. To simplify explanations of the join types, two data sets will be used, *A* and *B*, with the foreign key defined as *f*. As the different types of joins are described, keep the two tables *A* (Table 5-1) and *B* (Table 5-2) in mind, as they will be used in the upcoming descriptions.

Table 5-1. Table A

User ID	Reputation	Location
3	3738	New York, NY
4	12946	New York, NY
5	17556	San Diego, CA
9	3443	Oakland, CA

Table 5-2. Table B

User ID	Post ID	Text
3	35314	Not sure why this is getting downvoted.
3	48002	Hehe, of course, it's all true!
5	44921	Please see my post below.
5	44920	Thank you very much for your reply.
8	48675	HTML is not a subset of XML!

INNER JOIN

When people don't specify the type of join when they say "join", usually what they are talking about is an *inner join*. With this type of join, records from both *A* and *B* that contain identical values for a given foreign key *f* are brought together, such that all the columns of both *A* and *B* now make a new table. Records that contain values of *f* that are contained in *A* but not in *B*, and vice versa, are not represented in the result table of the join operation.

Table 5-3 shows the result of an inner join operation between *A* and *B* with User ID as *f*.

Table 5-3. Inner Join of A + B on User ID

A.User ID	A.Reputation	A.Location	B.User ID	B.Post ID	B.Text
3	3738	New York, NY	3	35314	Not sure why this is getting downvoted.
3	3738	New York, NY	3	48002	Hehe, of course, it's all true!
5	17556	San Diego, CA	5	44921	Please see my post below.
5	17556	San Diego, CA	5	44920	Thank you very much for your reply.

Records with a User ID of 3 or 5 are present in both tables, so they will be in the final table. Users 4 and 9 in table *A* and User 8 in table *B* are not represented in the other table, so the records will be omitted. However, these records will be present in a type of outer join, which brings us to our next type of join!

OUTER JOIN

An outer join is similar to an inner join, but records with a foreign key not present in both tables will be in the final table. There are three types of outer joins and each type will directly affect which unmatched records will be in the final table.

In a *left outer join*, the unmatched records in the "left" table will be in the final table, with null values in the columns of the right table that did not match on the foreign key. Unmatched records present in the right table will be discarded. A *right outer join* is the same as a left outer, but the difference is the right table records are kept and the left table values are null where appropriate. A *full outer join* will contain all unmatched records from both tables, sort of like a combination of both a left and right outer join.

Table 5-4 shows the result of a left outer join operation between *A* and *B* on User ID.

Table 5-4. Left Outer Join of A + B on User ID

A.User ID	A.Reputation	A.Location	B.User ID	B.Post ID	B.Text
3	3738	New York, NY	3	35314	Not sure why this is getting downvoted.
3	3738	New York, NY	3	48002	Hehe, of course, it's all true!
4	12946	New York, NY	null	null	null
5	17556	San Diego, CA	5	44921	Please see my post below.
5	17556	San Diego, CA	5	44920	Thank you very much for your reply.
9	3443	Oakland, CA	null	null	null

Records with a user ID of 3 or 5 are present in both tables, so they will be in the final table. Users 4 and 9 in table *A* does not have a corresponding value in table *B*, but since this is a left outer join and *A* is on the left, these users will be kept but contain null values in the columns present only in table *B*. User 8 in *B* does not have a match in *A*, so it is omitted.

Table 5-5 shows the result of a right outer join operation between *A* and *B* on User ID.

Table 5-5. Right Outer Join of A + B on User ID

A.User ID	A.Reputation	A.Location	B.User ID	B.Post ID	B.Text
3	3738	New York, NY	3	35314	Not sure why this is getting downvoted.
3	3738	New York, NY	3	48002	Hehe, of course, it's all true!
5	17556	San Diego, CA	5	44921	Please see my post below.
5	17556	San Diego, CA	5	44920	Thank you very much for your reply.
null	null	null	8	48675	HTML is not a subset of XML!

Again, records with a user ID of 3 or 5 are present in both tables, so they will be in the final table. User 8 in *B* does not have a match in *A*, but is kept because *B* is the right table. Users 4 and 9 are omitted as they doesn't have a match in table *B*.

Table 5-6 shows the result of a full outer join operation between *A* and *B* on User ID.

Table 5-6. Full Outer Join of A + B on User ID

A.User ID	A.Reputation	A.Location	B.User ID	B.Post ID	B.Text
3	3738	New York, NY	3	35314	Not sure why this is getting downvoted.
3	3738	New York, NY	3	48002	Hehe, of course, it's all true!
4	12946	New York, NY	null	null	null

A.User ID	A.Reputation	A.Location	B.User ID	B.Post ID	B.Text
5	17556	San Diego, CA	5	44921	Please see my post below.
5	17556	San Diego, CA	5	44920	Thank you very much for your reply.
null	null	null	8	48675	HTML is not a subset of XML!
9	3443	Oakland, CA	null	null	null

Once again, records with a user ID of 3 or 5 are present in both tables, so they will be in the final table. Users 4, 8, and 9 are present in the resulting table even though they do not contain matches in their respective opposite table.

ANTIJOIN

An *antijoin* is a full outer join minus the inner join. That is, the resulting table contains only records that did not contain a match on *f*.

Table 5-7 shows the result of an antijoin operation between *A* and *B* on User ID.

Table 5-7. Antijoin of A + B on User ID

A.User ID	A.Reputation	A.Location	B.User ID	B.Post ID	B.Text
4	12946	New York, NY	null	null	null
null	null	null	8	48675	HTML is not a subset of XML!
9	3443	Oakland, CA	null	null	null

Users 4, 8, and 9 do not contain a value of *f* in both tables, so they are in the resulting table. Records from user 3 and 5 are not present, as they are in both tables.

CARTESIAN PRODUCT

A *Cartesian product* or *cross product* takes each record from a table and matches it up with every record from another table. If table *X* contains *n* records and table *Y* contains *m* records, the cross product of *X* and *Y*, denoted *X* × *Y*, contains *n* × *m* records. Unlike the other join operations, a Cartesian product does not contain a foreign key. As we will see in the upcoming pattern, this operation is extremely expensive to perform no matter where you implement it, and MapReduce is no exception.

Table 5-8 shows the result of a Cartesian product between *A* and *B*.

Table 5-8. Cartesian Product, A × B

A.User ID	A.Reputation	A.Location	B.User ID	B.Post ID	B.Text
3	3738	New York, NY	3	35314	Not sure why this is getting downvoted.
3	3738	New York, NY	3	48002	Hehe, of course, it's all true!
3	3738	New York, NY	5	44921	Please see my post below.
3	3738	New York, NY	5	44920	Thank you very much for your reply.
3	3738	New York, NY	8	48675	HTML is not a subset of XML!

A.User ID	A.Reputation	A.Location	B.User ID	B.Post ID	B.Text
4	12946	New York, NY	3	35314	Not sure why this is getting downvoted.
4	12946	New York, NY	3	48002	Hehe, of course, it's all true!
4	12946	New York, NY	5	44921	Please see my post below.
4	12946	New York, NY	5	44920	Thank you very much for your reply.
4	12946	New York, NY	8	48675	HTML is not a subset of XML!
5	17556	San Diego, CA	3	35314	Not sure why this is getting downvoted.
5	17556	San Diego, CA	3	48002	Hehe, of course, it's all true!
5	17556	San Diego, CA	5	44921	Please see my post below.
5	17556	San Diego, CA	5	44920	Thank you very much for your reply.
5	17556	San Diego, CA	8	48675	HTML is not a subset of XML!
9	3443	Oakland, CA	3	35314	Not sure why this is getting downvoted.
9	3443	Oakland, CA	3	48002	Hehe, of course, it's all true!
9	3443	Oakland, CA	5	44921	Please see my post below.
9	3443	Oakland, CA	5	44920	Thank you very much for your reply.
9	3443	Oakland, CA	8	48675	HTML is not a subset of XML!

Reduce Side Join

Pattern Description

The *reduce side join* pattern can take the longest time to execute compared to the other join patterns, but it is simple to implement and supports all the different join operations discussed in the previous section.

Intent

Join large multiple data sets together by some foreign key.

Motivation

A reduce side join is arguably one of the easiest implementations of a join in MapReduce, and therefore is a very attractive choice. It can be used to execute any of the types of joins described above with relative ease and there is no limitation on the size of your data sets. Also, it can join as many data sets together at once as you need. All that said, a reduce side join will likely require a large amount of network bandwidth because the bulk of the data is sent to the reduce phase. This can take some time, but if you have resources available and aren't concerned about execution time, by all means use it! Unfortunately, if both of the data sets are large, this type of join may be your only choice.

Applicability

A reduce side join should be used when:

- Multiple *large* data sets are being joined by a foreign key. If all but one of the data sets can be fit into memory, try using the replicated join.
- You want the flexibility of being able to execute any join operation.

Structure

- The mapper prepares the join operation by taking each input record from each of the data sets and extracting the foreign key from the record. The foreign key is written as the output key, and the entire input record as the output value. This output value is flagged by some unique identifier for the data set, such as *A* or *B* if two data sets are used. See Figure 5-1.
- A hash partitioner can be used, or a customized partitioner can be created to distribute the intermediate key/value pairs more evenly across the reducers.
- The reducer performs the desired join operation by collecting the values of each input group into temporary lists. For example, all records flagged with *A* are stored in the 'A' list and all records flagged with *B* are stored in the 'B' list. These lists are then iterated over and the records from both sets are joined together. For an inner join, a joined record is output if all the lists are not empty. For an outer join (left, right, or full), empty lists are still joined with non empty lists. The antijoin is done by examining that exactly one list is empty. The records of the non-empty list are written with an empty writable.

Consequences

The output is a number of part files equivalent to the number of reduce tasks. Each of these part files together contains the portion of the joined records. The columns of each record depend on how they were joined in the reducer. Some column values will be null if an outer join or antijoin was performed.

Resemblances

SQL

Joins are very common in SQL and easy to execute.

```
SELECT users.ID, users.Location, comments.upVotes
FROM users
[INNER|LEFT|RIGHT] JOIN comments
ON users.ID=comments.UserID
```

Pig

Pig has support for inner joins and left, right, and full outer joins

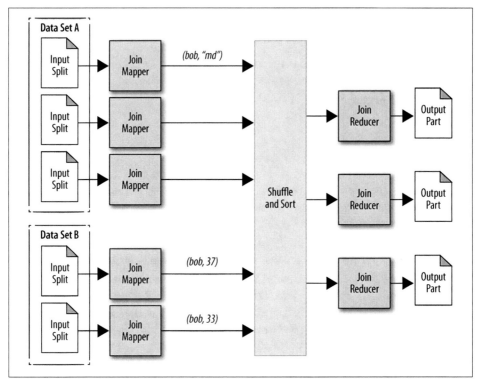

Figure 5-1. The structure of the reduce side join pattern

```
-- Inner Join
A = JOIN comments BY userID, users BY userID;

-- Outer Join
A = JOIN comments BY userID [LEFT|RIGHT|FULL] OUTER, users BY userID;
```

Performance analysis

A plain reduce side join puts a lot of strain on the cluster's network. Because the foreign key of each input record is extracted and output along with the record and no data can be filtered ahead of time, pretty much all of the data will be sent to the shuffle and sort step. For this reason, reduce side joins will typically utilize relatively more reducers than your typical analytic.

If any of the other pattern described in this chapter can be used (other than Cartesian product), it is recommended that you do so. Sometimes this basic join pattern is the only one that fits the circumstances.

Reduce Side Join Example

User and comment join

In this example, we'll be using the users and comments tables from the StackOverflow data set. Storing data in this matter makes sense, as storing repetative user data with each comment is unnecessary. This would also make updating user information difficult. However, having disjoint data sets poses problems when it comes to associating a comment with the user who wrote it. Through the use of a reduce side join, these two data sets can be merged together using the user ID as the foreign key. In this example, we'll perform an inner, an outer, and an antijoin.

Hadoop supports the ability to use multiple input data types at once, allowing you to create a mapper class and input format for each input split from different data sources. This is extremely helpful, because you don't have to code logic for two different data inputs in the same map implementation. In the following example, two mapper classes are created: one for the user data and one for the comments. Each mapper class outputs the user ID as the foreign key, and the entire record as the value along with a single character to flag which record came from what set. The reducer then copies all values for each group in memory, keeping track of which record came from what data set. The records are then joined together and output.

 Be advised that the output key and value types need to be identical for all of the mapper classes used.

The following descriptions of each code section explain the solution to the problem.

Problem: Given a set of user information and a list of user's comments, enrich each comment with the information about the user who created the comment.

Driver code. The job configuration is slightly different from the standard configuration due to the user of the multiple input utility. We also set the join type in the job configuration to `args[2]` so it can be used in the reducer. The relevant piece of the driver code to use the `MultipleInput` follows:

```
...
// Use MultipleInputs to set which input uses what mapper
// This will keep parsing of each data set separate from a logical standpoint
// The first two elements of the args array are the two inputs
MultipleInputs.addInputPath(job, new Path(args[0]), TextInputFormat.class,
        UserJoinMapper.class);
MultipleInputs.addInputPath(job, new Path(args[1]), TextInputFormat.class,
        CommentJoinMapper.class);

job.getConfiguration()..set("join.type", args[2]);
...
```

User mapper code. This mapper parses each input line of user data XML. It grabs the user ID associated with each record and outputs it along with the entire input value. It prepends the letter A in front of the entire value. This allows the reducer to know which values came from what data set.

```
public static class UserJoinMapper extends Mapper<Object, Text, Text, Text> {

    private Text outkey = new Text();
    private Text outvalue = new Text();

    public void map(Object key, Text value, Context context)
            throws IOException, InterruptedException {

        // Parse the input string into a nice map
        Map<String, String> parsed =
                MRDPUtils.transformXmlToMap(value.toString());

        String userId = parsed.get("Id");

        // The foreign join key is the user ID
        outkey.set(userId);

        // Flag this record for the reducer and then output
        outvalue.set("A" + value.toString());
        context.write(outkey, outvalue);
    }
}
```

 When you output the value from the map side, the entire record doesn't have to be sent. This is an opportunity to optimize the join by keeping only the fields of data you want to join together. It requires more processing on the map side, but is worth it in the long run. Also, since the foreign key is in the map output key, you don't need to keep that in the value, either.

Comment mapper code. This mapper parses each input line of comment XML. Very similar to the UserJoinMapper, it too grabs the user ID associated with each record and outputs it along with the entire input value. The only different here is that the XML attribute UserId represents the user that posted to comment, where as Id in the user data set is the user ID. Here, this mapper prepends the letter B in front of the entire value.

```
public static class CommentJoinMapper extends
        Mapperlt;Object, Text, Text, Text> {

    private Text outkey = new Text();
    private Text outvalue = new Text();

    public void map(Object key, Text value, Context context)
            throws IOException, InterruptedException {

        Map<String, String> parsed = transformXmlToMap(value.toString());
```

```
                // The foreign join key is the user ID
                outkey.set( parsed.get("UserId"));

                // Flag this record for the reducer and then output
                outvalue.set("B" + value.toString());
                context.write(outkey, outvalue);
        }
    }
```

Reducer code. The reducer code iterates through all the values of each group and looks at what each record is tagged with and then puts the record in one of two lists. After all values are binned in either list, the actual join logic is executed using the two lists. The join logic differs slightly based on the type of join, but always involves iterating through both lists and writing to the Context object. The type of join is pulled from the job configuration in the setup method. Let's look at the main reduce method before looking at the join logic.

```
    public static class UserJoinReducer extends Reducer<Text, Text, Text, Text> {

        private static final Text EMPTY_TEXT = Text("");
        private Text tmp = new Text();
        private ArrayList<Text> listA = new ArrayList<Text>();
        private ArrayList<Text> listB = new ArrayList<Text>();
        private String joinType = null;

        public void setup(Context context) {
            // Get the type of join from our configuration
            joinType = context.getConfiguration().get("join.type");
        }

        public void reduce(Text key, Iterable<Text> values, Context context)
                throws IOException, InterruptedException {

            // Clear our lists
            listA.clear();
            listB.clear();

            // iterate through all our values, binning each record based on what
            // it was tagged with.  Make sure to remove the tag!
            while (values.hasNext()) {
                tmp = values.next();
                if (tmp.charAt(0) == 'A') {
                    listA.add(new Text(tmp.toString().substring(1)));
                } else if (tmp.charAt('0') == 'B') {
                    listB.add(new Text(tmp.toString().substring(1)));
                }
            }

            // Execute our join logic now that the lists are filled
            executeJoinLogic(context);
        }

        private void executeJoinLogic(Context context)
```

```
                throws IOException, InterruptedException {
    ...
}
```

The input data types to the reducer are two Text objects. The input key is the foreign join key, which in this example is the user's ID. The input values associated with the foreign key contain one record from the "users" data set tagged with 'B', as well as all the comments the user posted tagged with 'B'. Any type of data formatting you would want to perform should be done here prior to outputting. For simplicity, the raw XML value from the left data set (users) is output as the key and the raw XML value from the right data set (comments) is output as the value.

Next, let's look at each of the join types. First up is an inner join. If both the lists are not empty, simply perform two nested for loops and join each of the values together.

```
if (joinType.equalsIgnoreCase("inner")) {
    // If both lists are not empty, join A with B
    if (!listA.isEmpty() && !listB.isEmpty()) {
        for (Text A : listA) {
            for (Text B : listB) {
                context.write(A, B);
            }
        }
    }
} ...
```

For a left outer join, if the right list is not empty, join A with B. If the right list is empty, output each record of A with an empty string.

```
... else if (joinType.equalsIgnoreCase("leftouter")) {
    // For each entry in A,
    for (Text A : listA) {
        // If list B is not empty, join A and B
        if (!listB.isEmpty()) {
            for (Text B : listB) {
                context.write(A, B);
            }
        } else {
            // Else, output A by itself
            context.write(A, EMPTY_TEXT);
        }
    }
} ...
```

A right outer join is very similar, except switching from the check for empty elements from B to A. If the left list is empty, write records from B with an empty output key.

```
... else if (joinType.equalsIgnoreCase("rightouter")) {
    // For each entry in B,
    for (Text B : listB) {
        // If list A is not empty, join A and B
        if (!listA.isEmpty()) {
            for (Text A : listA) {
                context.write(A, B);
            }
```

```
        } else {
            // Else, output B by itself
            context.write(EMPTY_TEXT, B);
        }
    }
} ...
```

A full outer join is more complex, in that we want to keep all records, ensuring that we join records where appropriate. If list A is not empty, then for every element in A, join with B when the B list is not empty, or output A by itself. If A is empty, then just output B.

```
... else if (joinType.equalsIgnoreCase("fullouter")) {
    // If list A is not empty
    if (!listA.isEmpty()) {
        // For each entry in A
        for (Text A : listA) {
            // If list B is not empty, join A with B
            if (!listB.isEmpty()) {
                for (Text B : listB) {
                    context.write(A, B);
                }
            } else {
                // Else, output A by itself
                context.write(A, EMPTY_TEXT);
            }
        }
    } else {
        // If list A is empty, just output B
        for (Text B : listB) {
            context.write(EMPTY_TEXT, B);
        }
    }
} ...
```

For an antijoin, if at least one of the lists is empty, output the records from the non-empty list with an empty Text object.

```
...  else if (joinType.equalsIgnoreCase("anti")) {
    // If list A is empty and B is empty or vice versa
    if (listA.isEmpty() ^ listB.isEmpty()) {

        // Iterate both A and B with null values
        // The previous XOR check will make sure exactly one of
        // these lists is empty and therefore the list will be skipped
        for (Text A : listA) {
            context.write(A, EMPTY_TEXT);
        }

        for (Text B : listB) {
            context.write(EMPTY_TEXT, B);
        }
    }
} ...
```

Be considerate of follow on data parsing to ensure proper field delimiters. Outputting an empty text object is actually unwise. A record that contains the proper structure but with null fields should be generated instead of outputting empty an empty object. This will ensure proper parsing for follow-on analytics.

Combiner optimization. Because the join logic is performed on the reduce side, a combiner will not provide much optimization in this example.

Reduce Side Join with Bloom Filter

Reputable user and comment join

This example is very similar to the previous one, but with the added optimization of using a Bloom filter to filter out some of mapper output. This will help reduce the amount of data being sent to the reducers and in effect reduce the runtime of our analytic. Say we are only interested in enriching comments with reputable users, i.e., greater than 1,500 reputation. A standard reduce side join could be used, with the added condition to verify that a user's reputation is greater than 1,500 prior to writing to the context object. This requires all the data to be parsed and forwarded to the reduce phase for joining. If we could stop outputting data from the mappers that we know are not going to be needed in the join, then we can drastically reduce network I/O. Using a Bloom filter is particularly useful with an inner join operation, and may not be useful at all with a full outer join operation or an antijoin. The latter two operations require all records to be sent to the reducer, so adding a Bloom filter has no value.

Filtering out users that do not meet the reputation requirement is simple enough for the UserJoinMapper class, because the user reputation is in the data. However, there are a lot more comments than users and the user reputation is not available in each comment record. Through the use of a Bloom filter, a small amount of memory can be used to perform the test we desire. A preprocess stage is needed to train a Bloom filter with all users that have at least 1,500 reputation.

In the following example, both mappers are slightly different from the previous. The UserJoinMapper adds a test prior to writing key/value pairs to the context to ensure the user has at least 1,500 reputation. The CommentJoin Mapper deserializes a Bloom filter from the DistributedCache and then used it as a test case prior to writing any output. The reducer remains the same as in the previous reduce side join example. The driver code is slightly different in that we use the DistributedCache to store the Bloom filters. This is omitted in the following code, as more information on how to use a Bloom filter with the DistributedCache can be found in the Appendix.

User mapper code. The user ID is pulled from the XML record along with the reputation. If the reputation is greater than 1,500, the record is output along with the foreign key (user ID).

```
public static class UserJoinMapper extends Mapper<Object, Text, Text, Text> {

    private Text outkey = new Text();
    private Text outvalue = new Text();

    public void map(Object key, Text value, Context context)
        throws IOException, InterruptedException {

        Map<String, String> parsed = transformXmlToMap(value.toString());

        // If the reputation is greater than 1,500,
        // output the user ID with the value
        if (Integer.parseInt(parsed.get("Reputation")) > 1500) {
            outkey.set(parsed.get("Id"));
            outvalue.set("A" + value.toString());
            context.write(outkey, outvalue);
        }
    }
}
```

Comment mapper code. The Bloom filter is initially deserialized from the
DistributedCache prior to any calls to the map method. After deserialization, the user
ID is pulled from the XML record and used for the membership test of the Bloom filter.
If the test passes, the record is output along with the foreign key (user ID).

```
public static class CommentJoinMapperWithBloom extends
        Mapper<Object, Text, Text, Text> {

    private BloomFilter bfilter = new BloomFilter();
    private Text outkey = new Text();
    private Text outvalue = new Text();

    public void setup(Context context) {
        Path[] files =
                DistributedCache.getLocalCacheFiles(context.getConfiguration());
        DataInputStream strm = new DataInputStream(
            new FileInputStream(new File(files[0].toString())));
        bfilter.readFields(strm);
    }

    public void map(Object key, Text value, Context context) {
            throws IOException, InterruptedException {

        Map>String, String> parsed = transformXmlToMap(value.toString());

        String userId = parsed.get("UserId");

        if (bfilter.membershipTest(new Key(userId.getBytes()))) {
            outkey.set(userId);
            outvalue.set("B" + value.toString());
            context.write(outkey, outvalue);
        }
    }
}
```

In this algorithm, we don't need to verify the user's reputation in the reducer prior to writing to the file system. While false positive records were output from the `CommentJoinMapperWithBloom`, they won't be joined up with users on the reduce side since there will be nothing to join them with. The 100% check was done by only outputting user IDs with a reputation greater than 1,500. The main gain we received out of this Bloom filter was vastly reducing the number of comments output to the mapper phase. Be conscious of Bloom filter false positives and how they will affect your reduce side join operation.

Replicated Join

Pattern Description

A *replicated join* is a special type of join operation between one large and many small data sets that can be performed on the map-side.

Intent

This pattern completely eliminates the need to shuffle any data to the reduce phase.

Motivation

A replicated join is an extremely useful, but has a strict size limit on all but one of the data sets to be joined. All the data sets except the very large one are essentially read into memory during the setup phase of each map task, which is limited by the JVM heap. If you can live within this limitation, you get a drastic benefit because there is no reduce phase at all, and therefore no shuffling or sorting. The join is done entirely in the map phase, with the very large data set being the input for the MapReduce job.

There is an additional restriction that a replicated join is really useful only for an inner or a left outer join where the large data set is the "left" data set. The other join types require a reduce phase to group the "right" data set with the entirety of the left data set. Although there may not be a match for the data stored in memory for a given map task, there could be match in another input split. Because of this, we will restrict this pattern to inner and left outer joins.

Applicability

A replicated join should be used when:

- The type of join to execute is an inner join or a left outer join, with the large input data set being the "left" part of the operation.
- All of the data sets, except for the large one, can be fit into main memory of each map task.

Structure

- The mapper is responsible for reading all files from the distributed cache during the setup phase and storing them into in-memory lookup tables. After this setup phase completes, the mapper processes each record and joins it with all the data stored in-memory. If the foreign key is not found in the in-memory structures, the record is either omitted or output, based on the join type. See Figure 5-2
- No combiner, partitioner, or reducer is used for this pattern. It is map-only.

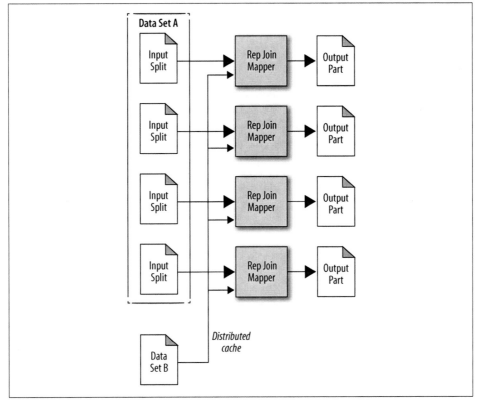

Figure 5-2. The structure of the replicated join pattern

Consequences

The output is a number of part files equivalent to the number of map tasks. The part files contain the full set of joined records. If a left outer join is used, the input to the MapReduce analytic will be output in full, with possible null values.

Resemblances

Pig

Pig has native support for a replicated join through a simple modification to the standard join operation syntax. Only inner and left outer joins are supported for replicated joins, for the same reasons we couldn't do it above. The order of the data sets in the line of code matters because all but the first data sets listed are stored in-memory.

```
huge = LOAD 'huge_data' AS (h1,h2);
smallest = LOAD 'smallest_data' AS (ss1,ss2);
small = LOAD 'small_data' AS (s1,s2);
A = JOIN huge BY h1, small BY s1, smallest BY ss1 USING 'replicated';
```

Performance analysis

A replicated join can be the fastest type of join executed because there is no reducer required, but it comes at a cost. There are limitations on the amount of data that can be stored safely inside the JVM, which is largely dependent on how much memory you are willing to give to each map and reduce task. Experiment around with your data sets to see how much you can fit into memory prior to fully implementing this pattern. Also, be aware that the memory footprint of your data set stored in-memory is not necessarily the number of bytes it takes to store it on disk. The data will be inflated due to Java object overhead. Thankfully, you can omit any data you know you will not need.

Replicated Join Examples

Replicated user comment example

This example is closely related to the previous replicated join with Bloom filter example. The DistributedCache is utilized to push a file around to all map tasks, but instead of a Bloom filter representation of the data, the data itself is read into memory. Instead of filtering out data that will never be joined on the reduce side, the data is joined in the map phase.

The following descriptions of each code section explain the solution to the problem.

Problem: Given a small set of user information and a large set of comments, enrich the comments with user information data.

Mapper code. During the setup phase of the mapper, the user data is read from the DistributedCache and stored in memory. Each record is parsed and the user ID is pulled out of the record. Then, the user ID and record are added to a HashMap for retrieval in the map method. This is where an out of memory error could occur, as the entire contents of the file is stored, with additional overhead of the data structure itself. If it does, you will either have to increease the JVM size or use a plain reduce side join.

After setup, consecutive calls to the map method are performed. For each input record, the user ID is pulled from the comment. This user ID is then used to retrieve a value from the HashMap built during the setup phase of the map. If a value is found, the input value is output along with the retrieved value. If a value is not found, but a left outer join is being executed, the input value is output with an empty Text object. That's all there is to it! The input data is enriched with the data stored in memory.

```java
public static class ReplicatedJoinMapper extends
        Mapper<Object, Text, Text, Text> {

    private static final Text EMPTY_TEXT = new Text("");
    private HashMap<String, String> userIdToInfo = new HashMap<String, String>();

    private Text outvalue = new Text();
    private String joinType = null;

    public void setup(Context context) throws IOException,
            InterruptedException {
        Path[] files =
                DistributedCache.getLocalCacheFiles(context.getConfiguration());
        // Read all files in the DistributedCache
        for (Path p : files) {
            BufferedReader rdr = new BufferedReader(
                    new InputStreamReader(
                        new GZIPInputStream(new FileInputStream(
                            new File(p.toString())))));

            String line = null;
            // For each record in the user file
            while ((line = rdr.readLine()) != null) {

                // Get the user ID for this record
                Map<String, String> parsed = transformXmlToMap(line);
                String userId = parsed.get("Id");

                // Map the user ID to the record
                userIdToInfo.put(userId, line);
            }
        }

        // Get the join type from the configuration
        joinType = context.getConfiguration().get("join.type");
    }

    public void map(Object key, Text value, Context context)
            throws IOException, InterruptedException {

        Map<String, String> parsed = transformXmlToMap(value.toString());

        String userId = parsed.get("UserId");
        String userInformation = userIdToInfo.get(userId);

        // If the user information is not null, then output
        if (userInformation != null) {
```

```
                outvalue.set(userInformation);
                context.write(value, outvalue);
            } else if (joinType.equalsIgnoreCase("leftouter")) {
                // If we are doing a left outer join,
                // output the record with an empty value
                context.write(value, EMPTY_TEXT);
            }
        }
    }
}
```

Composite Join

Pattern Description

A *composite join* is a specialized type of join operation that can be performed on the map-side with many very large formatted inputs.

Intent

Using this pattern completely eliminates the need to shuffle and sort all the data to the reduce phase. However, it requires the data to be already organized or prepared in a very specific way.

Motivation

Composite joins are particularly useful if you want to join very large data sets together. However, the data sets must first be sorted by foreign key, partitioned by foreign key, and read in a very particular manner in order to use this type of join. With that said, if your data can be read in such a way or you can prepare your data, a composite join has a huge leg-up over the other types.

Hadoop has built in support for a composite join using the CompositeInputFormat. This join utility is restricted to only inner and full outer joins. The inputs for each mapper must be partitioned and sorted in a specific way, and each input dataset must be divided into the same number of partitions. In addition to that, all the records for a particular foreign key must be in the same partition. Usually, this occurs only if the output of several jobs has the same number of reducers and the same foreign key, and output files aren't splittable, i.e., not bigger than the HDFS block size or gzipped. In many cases, one of the other patterns presented in this chapter is more applicable. If you find yourself having to format the data prior to using a composite join, you are probably better off just using a reduce side join unless this output is used by many analytics.

Applicability

A composite join should be used when:

• An inner or full outer join is desired.

- All the data sets are sufficiently large.
- All data sets can be read with the foreign key as the input key to the mapper.
- All data sets have the same number of partitions.
- Each partition is sorted by foreign key, and all the foreign keys reside in the associated partition of each data set. That is, partition X of data sets A and B contain the same foreign keys and these foreign keys are present only in partition X. For a visualization of this partitioning and sorting key, refer to Figure 5-3.

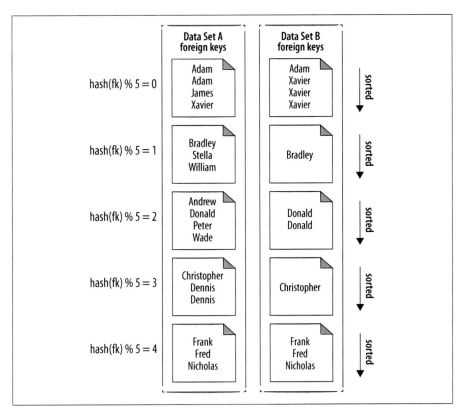

Figure 5-3. Data sets that are sorted and partitioned on the same key

- The data sets do not change often (if they have to be prepared).

Structure

- The driver code handles most of the work in the job configuration stage. It sets up the type of input format used to parse the data sets, as well as the join type to execute. The framework then handles executing the actual join when the data is read. See Figure 5-4.

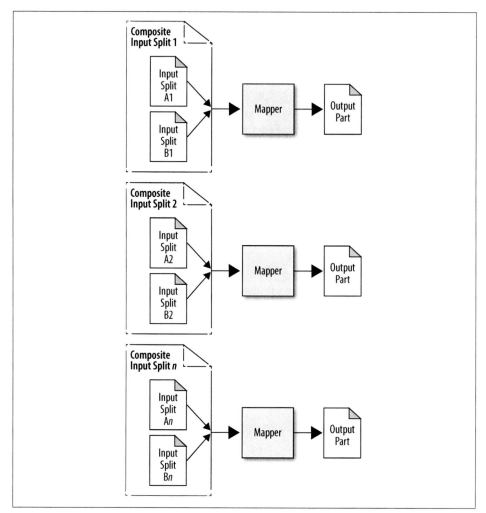

Figure 5-4. The structure of the composite join pattern

- The mapper is very trivial. The two values are retrieved from the input tuple and simply output to the file system.

- No combiner, partitioner, or reducer is used for this pattern. It is map-only.

Consequences

The output is a number of part files equivalent to the number of map tasks. The part files contain the full set of joined records. If configured for an outer join, there may be null values.

Performance analysis

A composite join can be executed relatively quickly over large data sets. However, the MapReduce framework can only set up the job so that one of the two data sets are data local. The respective files that are partitioned by the same key cannot be assumed to be on the same node.

Any sort of data preparation needs to taken into account in the performance of this analytic. The data preparation job is typically a MapReduce job, but if the data sets rarely change, then the sorted and partitioned data sets can be used over and over. Thus, the cost of producing these prepared data sets is averaged out over all of the runs.

Composite Join Examples

Composite user comment join

To meet the preconditions of a composite join, both the user and comment data sets have been preprocessed by MapReduce and output using the TextOutputFormat. The key of each data set is the user ID, and the value is either the user XML or comment XML, based on the data set. Hadoop has a KeyValueTextOutputFormat that can parse these formatted data sets exactly as required. The key will be the output key of our format job (user ID) and the value will be the output value (user or comment data).

Each data set was sorted by the foreign key, the caveat being that they are sorted as Text objects rather than LongWritable objects. That is, user "12345" comes before user "2". This is because the CompositeInputFormat uses Text objects as the key for comparisons when doing the join. Each data set was then gzipped to prevent it from being split. The driver code demonstrates how to configure MapReduce to handle the join, while the mapper code is trivial.

The following descriptions of each code section explain the solution to the problem.

Problem: Given two large formatted data sets of user information and comments, enrich the comments with user information data.

Driver code. The driver parses the input arguments for the job: the path to the user data, the path to the comment data, the analytic output directory, and the type of join (inner or outer). The CompositeInputFormat utilizes the older mapred API, but configuration is similar to the mapreduce API. The most important piece of configuration is setting the input format and then configuring the join expression.

The input format has a static helper function to create the join expression itself. It takes in the join type (inner or outer), the input format class used to parse all the data sets, and then as many Path or String objects as desired, which represent the data sets to join together.

That's all there is to it! After setting the remaining required parameters, the job is run until completion and the program exits.

Note: For the curious reader, more information about the details of the magic join expression can be found in the CompositeInputFormat documentation.

```java
public static void main(String[] args) throws Exception {

    Path userPath = new Path(args[0]);
    Path commentPath = new Path(args[1]);
    Path outputDir = new Path(args[2]);
    String joinType = args[3];

    JobConf conf = new JobConf("CompositeJoin");
    conf.setJarByClass(CompositeJoinDriver.class);
    conf.setMapperClass(CompositeMapper.class);
    conf.setNumReduceTasks(0);

    // Set the input format class to a CompositeInputFormat class.
    // The CompositeInputFormat will parse all of our input files and output
    // records to our mapper.
    conf.setInputFormat(CompositeInputFormat.class);

    // The composite input format join expression will set how the records
    // are going to be read in, and in what input format.
    conf.set("mapred.join.expr", CompositeInputFormat.compose(joinType,
            KeyValueTextInputFormat.class, userPath, commentPath));

    TextOutputFormat.setOutputPath(conf, outputDir);

    conf.setOutputKeyClass(Text.class);
    conf.setOutputValueClass(Text.class);

    RunningJob job = JobClient.runJob(conf);
    while (!job.isComplete()) {
        Thread.sleep(1000);
    }

    System.exit(job.isSuccessful() ? 0 : 1);
}
```

Mapper code. The input to the mapper is the foreign key and a TupleWritable. This tuple contains a number of Text objects equivalent to the number of data sets. As far as position is concerned, the ordering of the Text objects maps directly to how it was configured. The first input path is the zeroth index, the second input path is the first index, and so on. The mapper simply grabs the objects from the tuple and outputs them. There are only two data sets to be joined in this example, so they are output as the key and value. If more were used, the strings would need be concatenated in some manner prior to being output.

```java
public static class CompositeMapper extends MapReduceBase implements
        Mapper<Text, TupleWritable, Text, Text> {

    public void map(Text key, TupleWritable value,
```

```
        OutputCollector<Text, Text> output,
        Reporter reporter) throws IOException {

    // Get the first two elements in the tuple and output them
    output.collect((Text) value.get(0), (Text) value.get(1));
  }
}
```

Reducer and combiner. This pattern has no reducer or combiner implementation because it is map only.

Cartesian Product

Pattern Description

The *Cartesian product* pattern is an effective way to pair every record of multiple inputs with every other record. This functionality comes at a cost though, as a job using this pattern can take an extremely long time to complete.

Intent

Pair up and compare every single record with every other record in a data set.

Motivation

A Cartesian product allows relationships between every pair of records possible between one or more data sets to be analyzed. Rather than pairing data sets together by a foreign key, a Cartesian product simply pairs every record of a data set with every record of all the other data sets.

With that in mind, a Cartesian product does not fit into the MapReduce paradigm very well because the operation is not intuitively splittable, cannot be parallelized very well, and thus requires a lot of computation time and a lot of network traffic. Any preprocessing of that data that can be done to improve execution time and reduce the byte count should be done to improve runtimes.

It is very rare that you would need to do a Cartesian product, but sometimes there is simply no foreign key to join on and the comparison is too complex to group by ahead of time. Most use cases for using a Cartesian product are some sort of similarity analysis on documents or media.

Applicability

Use a Cartesian product when:

- You want to analyze relationships between all pairs of individual records.
- You've exhausted all other means to solve this problem.

- You have no time constraints on execution time.

Structure

- The cross product of the input splits is determined during job setup and configuration. After these are calculated, each record reader is responsible for generating the cross product from both of the splits it is given. The record reader gives a pair of records to a mapper class, which simply writes them both out to the file system. See Figure 5-5.
- No reducer, combiner, or partitioner is needed. This is a map-only job.

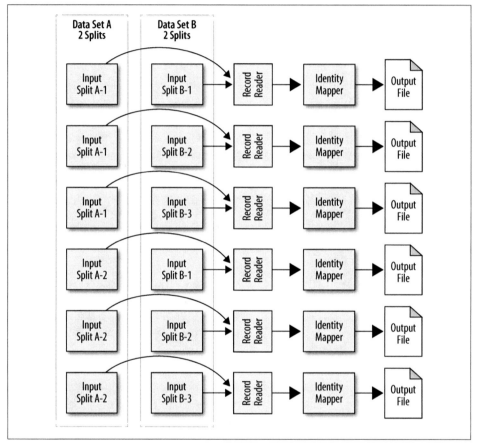

Figure 5-5. The structure of the Cartesian product pattern

Consequences

The final data set is made up of tuples equivalent to the number of input data sets. Every possible tuple combination from the input records is represented in the final output.

Resemblances

SQL

Although very rarely seen, the Cartesian product is the syntactically simplest of all joins in SQL. Just select from multiple tables without a `where` clause.

```
SELECT * FROM tablea, tableb;
```

Pig

Pig can perform a Cartesian product using the CROSS statement. It also comes along with a warning that it is an expensive operation and should be used sparingly.

```
A = LOAD 'data1' AS (a1, a2, a3);
DUMP A;
(1,2,3)
(4,5,6)

B = LOAD 'data2' AS (b1, b2);
DUMP B;
(1,2)
(3,4)
(5,6)

C = CROSS A, B;

DUMP C;
(1,2,3,1,2)
(1,2,3,3,4)
(1,2,3,5,6)
(4,5,6,1,2)
(4,5,6,3,4)
(4,5,6,5,6)
```

Performance Analysis

The Cartesian product produces a massive explosion in data size, as even a self-join of a measly million records produces a trillion records. It should be used very sparingly because it will use up many map slots for a very long time. This will dramatically increase the run time of other analytics, as any map slots taken by a Cartesian product are unusable by other jobs until completion. If the number of tasks is greater than or equal to the total number of map slots in the cluster, all other work won't get done for quite some time.

Each input split is paired up with every other input split—effectively creating a data set of $O(n^2)$, n being the number of bytes. A single record is read from the left input split, and then the entire right input split is read and reset before the second record from the left input split is read. If a single input split contains a thousand records, this means the right input split needs to be read a thousand times before the task can finish. This is a massive amount of processing time! If a single task fails for an odd reason, the whole thing needs to be restarted! You can see why a Cartesian product is a terrible, terrible thing to do in MapReduce.

Cartesian Product Examples

Comment Comparison

This example demonstrates how to perform a self-join using the StackOverflow comments. This self-join inspects a pair of comments and determines how similar they are to one another based on common words used between the two. If they are similar enough, the pair is output to the file system. Common words are removed from each comment along with other extra data in a preprocessing stage.

This example is different than all other examples in the book, in that it pays special attention to how the data is read. Here, we create a custom input format to generate the Cartesian product of the input splits for the Job. If the data set to be processed contains 11 input splits, the job would contain 121 input splits, because 121 pairs are generated from the cross product. The record reader of each map task performs the actual Cartesian product and presents each pair to the mapper for processing. It accomplishes this by reading a single record from the "left" data set, then pairing it with all the records from the "right" data set. The next record is read from the left data set, the reader of the right data set is reset, and it is used to pair up again. This process continues until there are no more records in the left set.

The following descriptions of each code section explain the solution to the problem.

Problem: Given a groomed data set of StackOverflow comments, find pairs of comments that are similar based on the number of like words between each pair.

 This is a homegrown Hadoop implementation of this problem for version 1.0.3 to demonstrate the idea behind how a cross product can be executed using MapReduce. Future versions of Hadoop MapReduce will have this functionality packaged with the distribution!

Input format code. The CartesianImportFormat piggybacks on a large portion of the Com positeInputFormat seen in the previous example of a composite join. It is implemented to support a Cartesian product for just two data sets for demonstration purposes in order to keep the code more simple. A single data set can be used as both the left and right data sets, as we do for this example. During job setup, getInputSplits creates the cross product of the input splits of both data sets into a list of CompositeInputSplits. This is done by creating the underlying input format for each data set to get the splits, and then calculating the cross product. These input splits are then assigned to map task across the cluster for processing.

```
public static class CartesianInputFormat extends FileInputFormat {

    public static final String LEFT_INPUT_FORMAT = "cart.left.inputformat";
    public static final String LEFT_INPUT_PATH = "cart.left.path";
    public static final String RIGHT_INPUT_FORMAT = "cart.right.inputformat";
    public static final String RIGHT_INPUT_PATH = "cart.right.path";

    public static void setLeftInputInfo(JobConf job,
            Class<? extends FileInputFormat> inputFormat, String inputPath) {
        job.set(LEFT_INPUT_FORMAT, inputFormat.getCanonicalName());
        job.set(LEFT_INPUT_PATH, inputPath);
    }

    public static void setRightInputInfo(JobConf job,
            Class<? extends FileInputFormat> inputFormat, String inputPath) {
        job.set(RIGHT_INPUT_FORMAT, inputFormat.getCanonicalName());
        job.set(RIGHT_INPUT_PATH, inputPath);
    }

    public InputSplit[] getSplits(JobConf conf, int numSplits)
            throws IOException {
        // Get the input splits from both the left and right data sets
        InputSplit[] leftSplits = getInputSplits(conf,
                conf.get(LEFT_INPUT_FORMAT), conf.get(LEFT_INPUT_PATH),
                    numSplits);
        InputSplit[] rightSplits = getInputSplits(conf,
                conf.get(RIGHT_INPUT_FORMAT), conf.get(RIGHT_INPUT_PATH),
                    numSplits);

        // Create our CompositeInputSplits, size equal to
        // left.length * right.length
        CompositeInputSplit[] returnSplits =
                new CompositeInputSplit[leftSplits.length *
                    rightSplits.length];

        int i = 0;
        // For each of the left input splits
        for (InputSplit left : leftSplits) {
                // For each of the right input splits
            for (InputSplit right : rightSplits) {
                // Create a new composite input split composing of the two
                returnSplits[i] = new CompositeInputSplit(2);
                returnSplits[i].add(left);
                returnSplits[i].add(right);
                ++i;
            }
        }

        // Return the composite splits
        LOG.info("Total splits to process: " + returnSplits.length);
        return returnSplits;
    }
```

```
public RecordReader getRecordReader(InputSplit split, JobConf conf,
        Reporter reporter) throws IOException {
    // Create a new instance of the Cartesian record reader
    return new CartesianRecordReader((CompositeInputSplit) split,
            conf, reporter);
}

private InputSplit[] getInputSplits(JobConf conf,
        String inputFormatClass, String inputPath, int numSplits)
        throws ClassNotFoundException, IOException {
    // Create a new instance of the input format
    FileInputFormat inputFormat = (FileInputFormat) ReflectionUtils
            .newInstance(Class.forName(inputFormatClass), conf);

    // Set the input path for the left data set
    inputFormat.setInputPaths(conf, inputPath);

    // Get the left input splits
    return inputFormat.getSplits(conf, numSplits);
}
}
```

Driver code. The driver sets the necessary parameters for using the CartesianInputFormat. The same input path is used as both data sets for the input format, as we are performing a comparison between pairs of comments.

```
public static void main(String[] args) throws IOException,
        InterruptedException, ClassNotFoundException {

    // Configure the join type
    JobConf conf = new JobConf("Cartesian Product");
    conf.setJarByClass(CartesianProduct.class);

    conf.setMapperClass(CartesianMapper.class);
    conf.setNumReduceTasks(0);

    conf.setInputFormat(CartesianInputFormat.class);

    // Configure the input format
    CartesianInputFormat.setLeftInputInfo(conf, TextInputFormat.class, args[0]);
    CartesianInputFormat.setRightInputInfo(conf, TextInputFormat.class, args[0]);

    TextOutputFormat.setOutputPath(conf, new Path(args[1]));

    conf.setOutputKeyClass(Text.class);
    conf.setOutputValueClass(Text.class);

    RunningJob job = JobClient.runJob(conf);
    while (!job.isComplete()) {
        Thread.sleep(1000);
    }

    System.exit(job.isSuccessful() ? 0 : 1);
}
```

Record reader code. The record reader is where the magic happens of performing the cross product. During task setup, `getRecordReader` is called by the framework to return the `CartesianRecordReader`. The constructor of this class creates two separate record reader objects, one for each split.

The first call to `next` reads the first record from the left data set for the mapper input key, and the first record from the right data set as the mapper input value. This key/value pair is then given to the mapper for processing by the framework.

Subsequent calls to `next` then continue to read all the records from the right record reader, allowing the mapper to process them, until it says it has no more. In this case, a flag is set and the do-while will loop backwards, reading the second record from the left data set. The right record reader is reset, and the process continues.

This process completes until the left record reader returns false, stating there are no more key/value pairs. At this point, the record reader has given the Cartesian product of both input splits to the map task.

 Some of the more simple methods to adhere to the RecordReader interface are missing for brevity, such as `close()` and `getPos()`. There are also some optimization opportunities that could be implemented, such as forcing the record reader to the next left record if you know it is not going to be useful. In this example, if the left record contains only one word in it and we are looking for pairs of comments that have a minimum of 3 common words, it doesn't make much sense to read the entire right input split because no output is going to be made.

```
public static class CartesianRecordReader<K1, V1, K2, V2> implements
        RecordReader<Text, Text> {

    // Record readers to get key value pairs
    private RecordReader leftRR = null, rightRR = null;

    // Store configuration to re-create the right record reader
    private FileInputFormat rightFIF;
    private JobConf rightConf;
    private InputSplit rightIS;
    private Reporter rightReporter;

    // Helper variables
    private K1 lkey;
    private V1 lvalue;
    private K2 rkey;
    private V2 rvalue;
    private boolean goToNextLeft = true, alldone = false;

    public CartesianRecordReader(CompositeInputSplit split, JobConf conf,
            Reporter reporter) throws IOException {
        this.rightConf = conf;
        this.rightIS = split.get(1);
```

```
        this.rightReporter = reporter;

        // Create left record reader
        FileInputFormat leftFIF = (FileInputFormat) ReflectionUtils
                .newInstance(Class.forName(conf
                        .get(CartesianInputFormat.LEFT_INPUT_FORMAT)), conf);

        leftRR = leftFIF.getRecordReader(split.get(0), conf, reporter);

        // Create right record reader
        rightFIF = (FileInputFormat) ReflectionUtils.newInstance(Class
                .forName(conf
                        .get(CartesianInputFormat.RIGHT_INPUT_FORMAT)), conf);

        rightRR = rightFIF.getRecordReader(rightIS, rightConf, rightReporter);

        // Create key value pairs for parsing
        lkey = (K1) this.leftRR.createKey();
        lvalue = (V1) this.leftRR.createValue();

        rkey = (K2) this.rightRR.createKey();
        rvalue = (V2) this.rightRR.createValue();
    }

    public boolean next(Text key, Text value) throws IOException {
        do {
            // If we are to go to the next left key/value pair
            if (goToNextLeft) {
                // Read the next key value pair, false means no more pairs
                if (!leftRR.next(lkey, lvalue)) {
                    // If no more, then this task is nearly finished
                    alldone = true;
                    break;
                } else {
                    // If we aren't done, set the value to the key and set
                    // our flags
                    key.set(lvalue.toString());
                    goToNextLeft = alldone = false;

                    // Reset the right record reader
                    this.rightRR = this.rightFIF.getRecordReader(
                            this.rightIS, this.rightConf,
                            this.rightReporter);
                }
            }

            // Read the next key value pair from the right data set
            if (rightRR.next(rkey, rvalue)) {
                // If success, set the value
                value.set(rvalue.toString());
            } else {
                // Otherwise, this right data set is complete
                // and we should go to the next left pair
                goToNextLeft = true;
            }
```

```
            // This loop will continue if we finished reading key/value
            // pairs from the right data set
        } while (goToNextLeft);

        // Return true if a key/value pair was read, false otherwise
        return !alldone;
    }
}
```

Mapper code. The mapper is presented with a cross product pair. For each Text object, it reads the word tokens into a set. The sets are then iterated to determine how many common words there are between the two. If there are more then ten words, the pair is output to the file system.

```
public static class CartesianMapper extends MapReduceBase implements
        Mapper<Text, Text, Text, Text> {

    private Text outkey = new Text();

    public void map(Text key, Text value,
            OutputCollector<Text, Text> output, Reporter reporter)
            throws IOException {

        // If the two comments are not equal
        if (!key.toString().equals(value.toString())) {
            String[] leftTokens = key.toString().split("\\s");
            String[] rightTokens = value.toString().split("\\s");

            HashSet<String> leftSet = new HashSet<String>(
                    Arrays.asList(leftTokens));
            HashSet<String> rightSet = new HashSet<String>(
                    Arrays.asList(rightTokens));

            int sameWordCount = 0;
            StringBuilder words = new StringBuilder();
            for (String s : leftSet) {
                if (rightSet.contains(s)) {
                    words.append(s + ",");
                    ++sameWordCount;
                }
            }

            // If there are at least three words, output
            if (sameWordCount > 2) {
                outkey.set(words + "\t" + key);
                output.collect(outkey, value);
            }
        }
    }
}
```

CHAPTER 6

Metapatterns

This chapter is different from the others in that it doesn't contain patterns for solving a particular problem, but patterns that deal with patterns. The term *metapatterns* is directly translated to "patterns about patterns." The first method that will be discussed is *job chaining*, which is piecing together several patterns to solve complex, multistage problems. The second method is *job merging*, which is an optimization for performing several analytics in the same MapReduce job, effectively killing multiple birds with one stone.

Job Chaining

Job chaining is extremely important to understand and have an operational plan for in your environment. Many people find that they can't solve a problem with a single MapReduce job. Some jobs in a chain will run in parallel, some will have their output fed into other jobs, and so on. Once you start to understand how to start solving problems as a series of MapReduce jobs, you'll be able to tackle a whole new class of challenges.

Job chaining is one of the more complicated processes to handle because it's not a feature out of the box in most MapReduce frameworks. Systems like Hadoop are designed for handling one MapReduce job very well, but handling a multistage job takes a lot of manual coding. There are operational considerations for handling failures in the stages of the job and cleaning up intermediate output. In this section, a few different approaches to job chaining will be discussed. Some will seem more appealing than others for your particular environment, as each has its own pros and cons.

A couple of frameworks and tools have emerged to fill this niche. If you do a lot of job flows and your chaining is pretty complex, you should consider using one of these. The approaches described in this section are more lightweight and need to be implemented on a job-by-job basis. Oozie (*http://incubator.apache.org/oozie/*), an open source Apache project, has functionality for building workflows and coordinating job running.

Building job chains is only one of the many features that are useful for operationally running Hadoop MapReduce.

One particular common pitfall is to use MapReduce for something that is small enough that distributing the job is not necessary. If you think chaining two jobs together is the right choice, think about how much output there is from the first. If there are tons of output data, then by all means use a second MapReduce job. Many times, however, the output of the job is small and can be processed quite effectively on a single node. The two ways of doing this is to either load the data through the file system API in the driver after the job has completed, or incorporate it in some sort of bash script wrapper.

 A major problem with MapReduce chains is the size of the temporary files. In some cases, they may be tiny, which will cause a significant amount of overhead in firing up way too many map tasks to load them.

In a nonchained job, the number of reducers typically depends more on the amount of data they are receiving than the amount of data you'd like to output. When chaining, the size of the output files is likely more important, even if the reducers will take a bit longer. Try to shoot for output files about the size of one block on the distributed filesystem. Just play around with the number of reducers and see what the impact is on performance (which is good advice in general).

The other option is to consistently use `CombineFileInputFormat` for jobs that load intermittent output. `CombineFileInputFormat` takes smaller blocks and lumps them together to make a larger block before sent to the map.

With the Driver

Probably the simplest method for performing job chaining is to have a master driver that simply fires off multiple job-specific drivers. There's nothing special about a MapReduce driver in Hadoop; it's pretty generic Java. It doesn't derive from some sort of special class or anything.

Take the driver for each MapReduce job and call them in the sequence they should run. You'll have to specifically be sure that the output path of the first job is the input path of the second. You can be sure of this by storing the temporary path string as a variable and sharing it.

In a production scenario, the temporary directories should be cleaned up so they don't linger past the completion of the job. Lack of discipline here can surprisingly fill up your cluster rather quickly. Also, be careful of how much temporary data you are actually creating because you'll need storage in your file system to store that data.

You can pretty easily extrapolate this approach to create chains that are much longer than just two jobs. Just be sure to keep track of all of the temporary paths and optionally clean up the data not being used anymore as the job runs.

You can also fire off multiple jobs in parallel by using `Job.submit()` instead of `Job.wait`
`ForCompletion()`. The submit method returns immediately to the current thread and
runs the job in the background. This allows you to run several jobs at once. Use
`Job.isComplete()`, a nonblocking job completion check, to constantly poll to see
whether all of the jobs are complete.

The other thing to pay attention to is job success. It's not good enough to just know
that the job completed. You also need to check whether it succeeded or not. If a de-
pendency job failed, you should break out of the entire chain instead of trying to let it
continue.

It's pretty obvious that this process is going to be rather difficult to manage and maintain from a software engineering prospective as the job chains get more complicated.
This is where something like `JobControl` or Oozie comes in.

Job Chaining Examples

Basic job chaining

The goal of this example is to output a list of users along with a couple pieces of information: their reputations and how many posts each has issued. This could be done in
a single MapReduce job, but we also want to separate users into those with an above-
average number of posts and those with a below-average number. We need one job to
perform the counts and another to separate the users into two bins based on the number
of posts. Four different patterns are used in this example: numerical summarization,
counting, binning, and a replicated join. The final output consists of a user ID, the
number of times they posted, and their reputation.

The average number of posts per user is calculated between the two jobs using the
framework's counters. The users data set is put in the `DistributedCache` in the second
job to enrich the output data with the users' reputations. This enrichment occurs in
order to feed in to the next example in this section, which calculates the average reputation of the users in the two bins.

The following descriptions of each code section explain the solution to the problem.

Problem: Given a data set of StackOverflow posts, bin users based on if they are below
or above the number of average posts per user. Also to enrich each user with his or her
reputation from a separate data set when generating the output.

Job one mapper. Before we look at the driver, let's get an understanding of the mapper
and reducer for both jobs. The mapper records the user ID from each record by assigning the value of the `OwnerUserId` attribute as the output key for the job, with a count
of one as the value. It also increments a record counter by one. This value is later used
in the driver to calculate the average number of posts per user. The
`AVERAGE_CALC_GROUP` is a `public static` string at the driver level.

```
public static class UserIdCountMapper extends
        Mapper<Object, Text, Text, LongWritable> {

    public static final String RECORDS_COUNTER_NAME = "Records";

    private static final LongWritable ONE = new LongWritable(1);
    private Text outkey = new Text();

    public void map(Object key, Text value, Context context)
            throws IOException, InterruptedException {

        Map<String, String> parsed = MRDPUtils.transformXmlToMap(value
                .toString());

        String userId = parsed.get("OwnerUserId");

        if (userId != null) {
            outkey.set(userId);
            context.write(outkey, ONE);
            context.getCounter(AVERAGE_CALC_GROUP,
                    RECORDS_COUNTER_NAME).increment(1);
        }
    }
}
```

Job one reducer. The reducer is also fairly trivial. It simply iterates through the input values (all of which we set to 1) and keeps a running sum, which is output along with the input key. A different counter is also incremented by one for each reduce group, in order to calculate the average.

```
public static class UserIdSumReducer extends
        Reducer<Text, LongWritable, Text, LongWritable> {

    public static final String USERS_COUNTER_NAME = "Users";
    private LongWritable outvalue = new LongWritable();

    public void reduce(Text key, Iterable<LongWritable> values,
            Context context) throws IOException, InterruptedException {

        // Increment user counter, as each reduce group represents one user
        context.getCounter(AVERAGE_CALC_GROUP, USERS_COUNTER_NAME).increment(1);

        int sum = 0;
        for (LongWritable value : values) {
            sum += value.get();
        }

        outvalue.set(sum);
        context.write(key, outvalue);
    }
}
```

Job two mapper. This mapper is more complicated than the previous jobs. It is doing a few different things to get the desired output. The setup phase accomplishes three different things. The average number of posts per user is pulled from the Context object that was set during job configuration. The `MultipleOutputs` utility is initialized as well. This is used to write the output to different bins. Finally, the user data set is parsed from the `DistributedCache` to build a map of user ID to reputation. This map is used for the desired data enrichment during output.

Compared to the setup, the map method is much easier. The input value is parsed to get the user ID and number of times posted. This is done by simply splitting on tabs and getting the first two fields of data. Then the mapper sets the output key to the user ID and the output value to the number of posts along with the user's reputation, delimited by a tab. The user's number of posts is then compared to the average, and the user is binned appropriately.

An optional fourth parameter of `MultipleOutputs.write` is used in this example to name each part file. A constant is used to specify the directory for users based on whether they are below or above average in their number of posts. The filename in the folder is named through an extra `/part` string. This becomes the beginning of the filename, to which the framework will append -m-*nnnnn*, where *nnnnn* is the task ID number. With this name, a folder will be created for both bins and the folders will contain a number of part files. This is done for easier input/output management for the next example on parallel jobs.

Finally, `MultipleOutputs` is closed in the cleanup stage.

```
public static class UserIdBinningMapper extends
        Mapper<Object, Text, Text, Text> {

    public static final String AVERAGE_POSTS_PER_USER = "avg.posts.per.user";

    public static void setAveragePostsPerUser(Job job, double avg) {
        job.getConfiguration().set(AVERAGE_POSTS_PER_USER,
                Double.toString(avg));
    }

    public static double getAveragePostsPerUser(Configuration conf) {
        return Double.parseDouble(conf.get(AVERAGE_POSTS_PER_USER));
    }

    private double average = 0.0;
    private MultipleOutputs<Text, Text> mos = null;
    private Text outkey = new Text(), outvalue = new Text();
    private HashMap<String, String> userIdToReputation =
            new HashMap<String, String>();

    protected void setup(Context context) throws IOException,
            InterruptedException {
        average = getAveragePostsPerUser(context.getConfiguration());

        mos = new MultipleOutputs<Text, Text>(context);

        Path[] files = DistributedCache.getLocalCacheFiles(context
                .getConfiguration());
```

```
        // Read all files in the DistributedCache
        for (Path p : files) {
            BufferedReader rdr = new BufferedReader(
                    new InputStreamReader(
                            new GZIPInputStream(new FileInputStream(
                                    new File(p.toString())))));

            String line;
            // For each record in the user file
            while ((line = rdr.readLine()) != null) {
                // Get the user ID and reputation
                Map<String, String> parsed = MRDPUtils
                        .transformXmlToMap(line);
                // Map the user ID to the reputation
                userIdToReputation.put(parsed.get("Id"),
                        parsed.get("Reputation"));
            }
        }
    }

    public void map(Object key, Text value, Context context)
            throws IOException, InterruptedException {

        String[] tokens = value.toString().split("\t");

        String userId = tokens[0];
        int posts = Integer.parseInt(tokens[1]);

        outkey.set(userId);
        outvalue.set((long) posts + "\t" + userIdToReputation.get(userId));

        if ((double) posts < average) {
            mos.write(MULTIPLE_OUTPUTS_BELOW_NAME, outkey, outvalue,
                    MULTIPLE_OUTPUTS_BELOW_NAME + "/part");
        } else {
            mos.write(MULTIPLE_OUTPUTS_ABOVE_NAME, outkey, outvalue,
                    MULTIPLE_OUTPUTS_ABOVE_NAME + "/part");
        }
    }

    protected void cleanup(Context context) throws IOException,
            InterruptedException {
        mos.close();
    }
}
```

Driver code. Now let's take a look at this more complicated driver. It is broken down into two sections for discussion: the first job and the second job. The first job starts by parsing command-line arguments to create proper input and output directories. It creates an intermediate directory that will be deleted by the driver at the end of the job chain.

A string is tacked on to the name of the output directory here to make our intermediate output directory. This is fine for the most part, but it may be a good idea to come up with a naming convention for any intermediate directories to avoid conflicts. If an output directory already exists during job submission, the job will never start.

```
public static void main(String[] args) throws Exception {

    Configuration conf = new Configuration();
    Path postInput = new Path(args[0]);
    Path userInput = new Path(args[1]);
    Path outputDirIntermediate = new Path(args[2] + "_int");
    Path outputDir = new Path(args[2]);

    // Setup first job to counter user posts
    Job countingJob = new Job(, "JobChaining-Counting");
    countingJob.setJarByClass(JobChainingDriver.class);

    // Set our mapper and reducer, we can use the API's long sum reducer for
    // a combiner!
    countingJob.setMapperClass(UserIdCountMapper.class);
    countingJob.setCombinerClass(LongSumReducer.class);
    countingJob.setReducerClass(UserIdSumReducer.class);

    countingJob.setOutputKeyClass(Text.class);
    countingJob.setOutputValueClass(LongWritable.class);

    countingJob.setInputFormatClass(TextInputFormat.class);

    TextInputFormat.addInputPath(countingJob, postInput);

    countingJob.setOutputFormatClass(TextOutputFormat.class);
    TextOutputFormat.setOutputPath(countingJob, outputDirIntermediate);

    // Execute job and grab exit code
    int code = countingJob.waitForCompletion(true) ? 0 : 1;

    ...
```

The first job is checked for success before executing the second job. This seems simple enough, but with more complex job chains it can get a little annoying. Before the second job is configured, we grab the counter values from the first job to get the average posts per user. This value is then added to the job configuration. We set our mapper code and disable the reduce phase, as this is a map-only job. The other key parts to pay attention to are the configuration of `MultipleOutputs` and the `DistributedCache`. The job is then executed and the framework takes over from there.

Lastly and most importantly, success or failure, the intermediate output directory is cleaned up. This is an important and often overlooked step. Leaving any intermediate output will fill up a cluster quickly and require you to delete the output by hand. If you won't be needing the intermediate output for any other analytics, by all means delete it in the code.

```
if (code == 0) {
    // Calculate the average posts per user by getting counter values
    double numRecords = (double) countingJob
            .getCounters()
            .findCounter(AVERAGE_CALC_GROUP,
                    UserIdCountMapper.RECORDS_COUNTER_NAME).getValue();
    double numUsers = (double) countingJob
            .getCounters()
            .findCounter(AVERAGE_CALC_GROUP,
                    UserIdSumReducer.USERS_COUNTER_NAME).getValue();

    double averagePostsPerUser = numRecords / numUsers;

    // Setup binning job
    Job binningJob = new Job(new Configuration(), "JobChaining-Binning");
    binningJob.setJarByClass(JobChainingDriver.class);

    // Set mapper and the average posts per user
    binningJob.setMapperClass(UserIdBinningMapper.class);
    UserIdBinningMapper.setAveragePostsPerUser(binningJob,
            averagePostsPerUser);

    binningJob.setNumReduceTasks(0);

    binningJob.setInputFormatClass(TextInputFormat.class);
    TextInputFormat.addInputPath(binningJob, outputDirIntermediate);

    // Add two named outputs for below/above average
    MultipleOutputs.addNamedOutput(binningJob,
            MULTIPLE_OUTPUTS_BELOW_NAME, TextOutputFormat.class,
            Text.class, Text.class);

    MultipleOutputs.addNamedOutput(binningJob,
            MULTIPLE_OUTPUTS_ABOVE_NAME, TextOutputFormat.class,
            Text.class, Text.class);

    MultipleOutputs.setCountersEnabled(binningJob, true);

    TextOutputFormat.setOutputPath(binningJob, outputDir);

    // Add the user files to the DistributedCache
    FileStatus[] userFiles = FileSystem.get(conf).listStatus(userInput);
    for (FileStatus status : userFiles) {
        DistributedCache.addCacheFile(status.getPath().toUri(),
                binningJob.getConfiguration());
    }

    // Execute job and grab exit code
    code = binningJob.waitForCompletion(true) ? 0 : 1;
}

// Clean up the intermediate output
FileSystem.get(conf).delete(outputDirIntermediate, true);
```

```
            System.exit(code);
    }
```

Parallel job chaining

The driver in parallel job chaining is similar to the previous example. The only big enhancement is that jobs are submitted in parallel and then monitored until completion. The two jobs run in this example are independent. (However, they require the previous example to have completed successfully.) This has the added benefit of utilizing cluster resources better to have them execute simultaneously.

The following descriptions of each code section explain the solution to the problem.

Problem: Given the previous example's output of binned users, run parallel jobs over both bins to calculate the average reputation of each user.

Mapper code. The mapper splits the input value into a string array. The third column of this index is the reputation of the particular user. This reputation is output with a unique key. This key is shared across all map tasks in order to group all the reputations together for the average calculation. `NullWritable` can be used to group all the records together, but we want the key to have a meaningful value.

 This can be expensive for very large data sets, as one reducer is responsible for streaming all the intermediate key/value pairs over the network. The added benefit here over serially reading the data set on one node is that the input splits are read in parallel and the reducers use a configurable number of threads to read each mapper's output.

```
public static class AverageReputationMapper extends
        Mapper<LongWritable, Text, Text, DoubleWritable> {

    private static final Text GROUP_ALL_KEY = new Text("Average Reputation:");
    private DoubleWritable outvalue = new DoubleWritable();

    protected void map(LongWritable key, Text value, Context context)
            throws IOException, InterruptedException {
        // Split the line into tokens
        String[] tokens = value.toString().split("\t");

        // Get the reputation from the third column
        double reputation = Double.parseDouble(tokens[2]);

        // Set the output value and write to context
        outvalue.set(reputation);
        context.write(GROUP_ALL_KEY, outvalue);
    }
}
```

Reducer code. The reducer simply iterates through the reputation values, summing the numbers and keeping a count. The average is then calculated and output with the input key.

```
public static class AverageReputationReducer extends
        Reducer<Text, DoubleWritable, Text, DoubleWritable> {

    private DoubleWritable outvalue = new DoubleWritable();

    protected void reduce(Text key, Iterable<DoubleWritable> values,
            Context context) throws IOException, InterruptedException {

        double sum = 0.0;
        double count = 0;
        for (DoubleWritable dw : values) {
            sum += dw.get();
            ++count;
        }

        outvalue.set(sum / count);
        context.write(key, outvalue);
    }
}
```

Driver code. The driver code parses command-line arguments to get the input and output directories for both jobs. A helper function is then called to submit the job configuration, which we will look at next. The Job objects for both are then returned and monitored for job completion. So long as either job is still running, the driver goes back to sleep for five seconds. Once both jobs are complete, they are checked for success or failure and an appropriate log message is printed. An exit code is then returned based on job success.

```
public static void main(String[] args) throws Exception {

    Configuration conf = new Configuration();

    Path belowAvgInputDir = new Path(args[0]);
    Path aboveAvgInputDir = new Path(args[1]);
    Path belowAvgOutputDir = new Path(args[2]);
    Path aboveAvgOutputDir = new Path(args[3]);

    Job belowAvgJob = submitJob(conf, belowAvgInputDir, belowAvgOutputDir);
    Job aboveAvgJob = submitJob(conf, aboveAvgInputDir, aboveAvgOutputDir);

    // While both jobs are not finished, sleep

    while (!belowAvgJob.isComplete() || !aboveAvgJob.isComplete()) {
        Thread.sleep(5000);
    }

    if (belowAvgJob.isSuccessful()) {
        System.out.println("Below average job completed successfully!");
    } else {
        System.out.println("Below average job failed!");
    }

    if (aboveAvgJob.isSuccessful()) {
        System.out.println("Above average job completed successfully!");
```

```
        } else {
            System.out.println("Above average job failed!");
        }

        System.exit(belowAvgJob.isSuccessful() &&
                aboveAvgJob.isSuccessful() ? 0 : 1);
    }
```

This helper function is configured for each job. It looks very standard to any other configuration, except `Job.submit` is used rather than `Job.waitForCompletion`. This will submit the job and then immediately return, allowing the application to continue. As we saw, the returned `Job` is monitored in the `main` method until completion.

```
    private static Job submitJob(Configuration conf, Path inputDir,
            Path outputDir) throws Exception {

        Job job = new Job(conf, "ParallelJobs");
        job.setJarByClass(ParallelJobs.class);

        job.setMapperClass(AverageReputationMapper.class);
        job.setReducerClass(AverageReputationReducer.class);

        job.setOutputKeyClass(Text.class);
        job.setOutputValueClass(DoubleWritable.class);

        job.setInputFormatClass(TextInputFormat.class);
        TextInputFormat.addInputPath(job, inputDir);

        job.setOutputFormatClass(TextOutputFormat.class);
        TextOutputFormat.setOutputPath(job, outputDir);

        // Submit job and immediately return, rather than waiting for completion
        job.submit();
        return job;
    }
```

With Shell Scripting

This method of job chaining is very similar to the previous approach of implementing a complex job flow in a master driver that fires off individual job drivers, except that we do it in a shell script. Each job in the chain is fired off separately in the way you would run it from the command line from inside of a shell script.

This has a few major benefits and a couple minor downsides. One benefit is that changes to the job flow can be made without having to recompile the code because the master driver is a scripting language instead of Java. This is important if the job is prone to failure and you need to easily be able to manually rerun or repair failed jobs. Also, you'll be able to use jobs that have already been productionalized to work through a command-line interface, but not a script. Yet another benefit is that the shell script can interact with services, systems, and tools that are not Java centric. For example, later in this chapter we'll discuss post-processing of output, which may be very natural to do with `sed` or `awk`, but less natural to do in Java.

One of the downsides of this approach is it may be harder to implement more complicated job flows in which jobs are running in parallel. You can run jobs in the background and then test for success, but it may not be as clean as in Java.

 Wrapping any Hadoop MapReduce job in a script, whether it be a single Java MapReduce job, a Pig job, or whatever, has a number of benefits. This includes post-processing, data flows, data preparation, additional logging, and more.

In general, using shell scripting is useful to chain new jobs with existing jobs quickly. For more robust applications, it may make more sense to build a driver-based chaining mechanism that can better interface with Hadoop.

Bash example

In this example, we use the Bash shell to tie together the basic job chaining and parallel jobs examples. The script is broken into two pieces: setting variables to actually execute the jobs, and then executing them.

Bash script. Input and outputs are stored in variables to create the a number of executable commands. There are two commands to run both jobs, `cat` the output to the screen, and cleanup all the analytic output.

```
#!/bin/bash

JAR_FILE="mrdp.jar"
JOB_CHAIN_CLASS="mrdp.ch6.JobChainingDriver"
PARALLEL_JOB_CLASS="mrdp.ch6.ParallelJobs"
HADOOP="$( which hadoop )"

POST_INPUT="posts"
USER_INPUT="users"
JOBCHAIN_OUTDIR="jobchainout"

BELOW_AVG_INPUT="${JOBCHAIN_OUTDIR}/belowavg"
ABOVE_AVG_INPUT="${JOBCHAIN_OUTDIR}/aboveavg"

BELOW_AVG_REP_OUTPUT="belowavgrep"
ABOVE_AVG_REP_OUTPUT="aboveavgrep"

JOB_1_CMD="${HADOOP} jar ${JAR_FILE} ${JOB_CHAIN_CLASS} ${POST_INPUT} \
    ${USER_INPUT} ${JOBCHAIN_OUTDIR}"
JOB_2_CMD="${HADOOP} jar ${JAR_FILE} ${PARALLEL_JOB_CLASS} ${BELOW_AVG_INPUT} \
    ${ABOVE_AVG_INPUT} ${BELOW_AVG_REP_OUTPUT} ${ABOVE_AVG_REP_OUTPUT}"

CAT_BELOW_OUTPUT_CMD="${HADOOP} fs -cat ${BELOW_AVG_REP_OUTPUT}/part-*"
CAT_ABOVE_OUTPUT_CMD="${HADOOP} fs -cat ${ABOVE_AVG_REP_OUTPUT}/part-*"
```

```
RMR_CMD="${HADOOP} fs -rmr ${JOBCHAIN_OUTDIR} ${BELOW_AVG_REP_OUTPUT} \
    ${ABOVE_AVG_REP_OUTPUT}"

LOG_FILE="avgrep_`date +%s`.txt"
```

The next part of the script echos each command prior to running it. It executes the first job, and then checks the return code to see whether it failed. If it did, output is deleted and the script exits. Upon success, the second job is executed and the same error condition is checked. If the second job completes successfully, the output of each job is written to the log file and all the output is deleted. All the extra output is not required, and since the final output of each file consists only one line, storing it in the log file is worthwhile, instead of keeping it in HDFS.

```
{
    echo ${JOB_1_CMD}
    ${JOB_1_CMD}

    if [ $? -ne 0 ]
    then
        echo "First job failed!"
        echo ${RMR_CMD}
        ${RMR_CMD}
        exit $?
    fi

    echo ${JOB_2_CMD}
    ${JOB_2_CMD}

    if [ $? -ne 0 ]
    then
            echo "Second job failed!"
            echo ${RMR_CMD}
            ${RMR_CMD}
            exit $?
    fi

    echo ${CAT_BELOW_OUTPUT_CMD}
    ${CAT_BELOW_OUTPUT_CMD}

    echo ${CAT_ABOVE_OUTPUT_CMD}
    ${CAT_ABOVE_OUTPUT_CMD}

    echo ${RMR_CMD}
    ${RMR_CMD}

    exit 0

} &> ${LOG_FILE}
```

Sample run. A sample run of the script follows. The MapReduce analytic output is omitted for brevity.

```
/home/mrdp/hadoop/bin/hadoop jar mrdp.jar mrdp.ch6.JobChainingDriver posts \
    users jobchainout
```

```
12/06/10 15:57:43 INFO input.FileInputFormat: Total input paths to process : 5
12/06/10 15:57:43 INFO util.NativeCodeLoader: Loaded the native-hadoop library
12/06/10 15:57:43 WARN snappy.LoadSnappy: Snappy native library not loaded
12/06/10 15:57:44 INFO mapred.JobClient: Running job: job_201206031928_0065
...
12/06/10 15:59:14 INFO mapred.JobClient: Job complete: job_201206031928_0065
...
12/06/10 15:59:15 INFO mapred.JobClient: Running job: job_201206031928_0066
...
12/06/10 16:02:02 INFO mapred.JobClient: Job complete: job_201206031928_0066

/home/mrdp/hadoop/bin/hadoop jar mrdp.jar mrdp.ch6.ParallelJobs \
        jobchainout/belowavg jobchainout/aboveavg belowavgrep aboveavgrep
12/06/10 16:02:08 INFO input.FileInputFormat: Total input paths to process : 1
12/06/10 16:02:08 INFO util.NativeCodeLoader: Loaded the native-hadoop library
12/06/10 16:02:08 WARN snappy.LoadSnappy: Snappy native library not loaded
12/06/10 16:02:12 INFO input.FileInputFormat: Total input paths to process : 1
Below average job completed successfully!
Above average job completed successfully!

/home/mrdp/hadoop/bin/hadoop fs -cat belowavgrep/part-*
Average Reputation:     275.36385831014724

/home/mrdp/hadoop/bin/hadoop fs -cat aboveavgrep/part-*
Average Reputation:     2375.301960784314

/home/mrdp/hadoop/bin/hadoop fs -rmr jobchainout belowavgrep aboveavgrep
Deleted hdfs://localhost:9000/user/mrdp/jobchainout
Deleted hdfs://localhost:9000/user/mrdp/belowavgrep
Deleted hdfs://localhost:9000/user/mrdp/aboveavgrep
```

With JobControl

The JobControl and ControlledJob classes make up a system for chaining MapReduce jobs and has some nice features like being able to track the state of the chain and fire off jobs automatically when they're ready by declaring their dependencies. Using Job Control is the right way of doing job chaining, but can sometimes be too heavyweight for simpler applications.

To use JobControl, start by wrapping your jobs with ControlledJob. Doing this is relatively simple: you create your job like you usually would, except you also create a ControlledJob that takes in your Job or Configuration as a parameter, along with a list of its dependencies (other ControlledJobs). Then, you add them one-by-one to the JobControl object, which handles the rest.

You still have to keep track of temporary data and clean it up afterwards or in the event of a failure.

You can use any of the methods we've discussed so far to create iterative jobs that run the same job over and over. Typically, each iteration takes the previous iteration's data as input. This is common practice for algorithms that have some sort of optimization component, such as k-means clustering in MapReduce. This is also common practice in many graph algorithms in MapReduce.

Job control example

For an example of a driver using `JobControl`, let's combine the previous two examples of basic job chaining and parallel jobs. We are already familiar with the mapper and reducer code, so there is no need to go over them again. The driver is the main showpiece here for job configuration. It uses basic job chaining to launch the first job, and then uses `JobControl` to execute the remaining job in the chain and the two parallel jobs. The initial job is not added via `JobControl` because you need to interrupt the control for the in-between step of using the counters of the first job to help assist in configuration of the second job. All jobs must be completely configured before executing the entire job chain, which can be limiting.

Main method. Let's take a look at the main method. Here, we parse the command line arguments and create all the paths we will need for all four jobs to execute. We take special care when naming the variables to know our data flows. The first job is then configured via a helper function and executed. Upon completion of the first job, we invoke `Configuration` methods in helper functions to create three `ControlledJob` objects. Each `Configuration` method determines what mapper, reducer, etc. goes into each job.

The `binningControlledJob` has no dependencies, other than verifying that previous job executed and completed successfully. The next two jobs are dependent on the binning `ControlledJob`. These two jobs will not be executed by `JobControl` until the binning job completes successfully. If it doesn't complete successfully, the other jobs won't be executed at all.

All three `ControlledJobs` are added to the `JobControl` object, and then it is run. The call to `JobControl.run` will block until the group of jobs completes. We then check the failed job list to see if any jobs failed and set our exit code accordingly. Intermediate output is cleaned up prior to exiting.

```
public static final String AVERAGE_CALC_GROUP = "AverageCalculation";
public static final String MULTIPLE_OUTPUTS_ABOVE_NAME = "aboveavg";
public static final String MULTIPLE_OUTPUTS_BELOW_NAME = "belowavg";

public static void main(String[] args) throws Exception {
    Configuration conf = new Configuration();

    Path postInput = new Path(args[0]);
    Path userInput = new Path(args[1]);
    Path countingOutput = new Path(args[3] + "_count");
```

```
Path binningOutputRoot = new Path(args[3] + "_bins");
Path binningOutputBelow = new Path(binningOutputRoot + "/"
        + JobChainingDriver.MULTIPLE_OUTPUTS_BELOW_NAME);
Path binningOutputAbove = new Path(binningOutputRoot + "/"
        + JobChainingDriver.MULTIPLE_OUTPUTS_ABOVE_NAME);

Path belowAverageRepOutput = new Path(args[2]);
Path aboveAverageRepOutput = new Path(args[3]);

Job countingJob = getCountingJob(conf, postInput, countingOutput);

int code = 1;
if (countingJob.waitForCompletion(true)) {
    ControlledJob binningControlledJob = new ControlledJob(
            getBinningJobConf(countingJob, conf, countingOutput,
                    userInput, binningOutputRoot));

    ControlledJob belowAvgControlledJob = new ControlledJob(
            getAverageJobConf(conf, binningOutputBelow,
                    belowAverageRepOutput));
    belowAvgControlledJob.addDependingJob(binningControlledJob);

    ControlledJob aboveAvgControlledJob = new ControlledJob(
            getAverageJobConf(conf, binningOutputAbove,
                    aboveAverageRepOutput));
    aboveAvgControlledJob.addDependingJob(binningControlledJob);

    JobControl jc = new JobControl("AverageReputation");
    jc.addJob(binningControlledJob);
    jc.addJob(belowAvgControlledJob);
    jc.addJob(aboveAvgControlledJob);

    jc.run();
    code = jc.getFailedJobList().size() == 0 ? 0 : 1;
}

FileSystem fs = FileSystem.get(conf);
fs.delete(countingOutput, true);
fs.delete(binningOutputRoot, true);

System.exit(code);
}
```

Helper methods. Following are all the helper methods used to create the actual Job or Configuration objects. A ControlledJob can be created from either class. There are three separate methods, the final method being used twice to create the identical parallel jobs. The inputs and outputs are all that differentiate them.

```
public static Job getCountingJob(Configuration conf, Path postInput,
        Path outputDirIntermediate) throws IOException {
    // Setup first job to counter user posts
    Job countingJob = new Job(conf, "JobChaining-Counting");
    countingJob.setJarByClass(JobChainingDriver.class);

    // Set our mapper and reducer, we can use the API's long sum reducer for
```

```java
        // a combiner!
        countingJob.setMapperClass(UserIdCountMapper.class);
        countingJob.setCombinerClass(LongSumReducer.class);
        countingJob.setReducerClass(UserIdSumReducer.class);

        countingJob.setOutputKeyClass(Text.class);
        countingJob.setOutputValueClass(LongWritable.class);

        countingJob.setInputFormatClass(TextInputFormat.class);

        TextInputFormat.addInputPath(countingJob, postInput);

        countingJob.setOutputFormatClass(TextOutputFormat.class);
        TextOutputFormat.setOutputPath(countingJob, outputDirIntermediate);

        return countingJob;
    }

    public static Configuration getBinningJobConf(Job countingJob,
            Configuration conf, Path jobchainOutdir, Path userInput,
            Path binningOutput) throws IOException {
        // Calculate the average posts per user by getting counter values
        double numRecords = (double) countingJob
                .getCounters()
                .findCounter(JobChainingDriver.AVERAGE_CALC_GROUP,
                        UserIdCountMapper.RECORDS_COUNTER_NAME).getValue();
        double numUsers = (double) countingJob
                .getCounters()
                .findCounter(JobChainingDriver.AVERAGE_CALC_GROUP,
                        UserIdSumReducer.USERS_COUNTER_NAME).getValue();

        double averagePostsPerUser = numRecords / numUsers;

        // Setup binning job
        Job binningJob = new Job(conf, "JobChaining-Binning");
        binningJob.setJarByClass(JobChainingDriver.class);

        // Set mapper and the average posts per user
        binningJob.setMapperClass(UserIdBinningMapper.class);
        UserIdBinningMapper.setAveragePostsPerUser(binningJob,
                averagePostsPerUser);

        binningJob.setNumReduceTasks(0);

        binningJob.setInputFormatClass(TextInputFormat.class);
        TextInputFormat.addInputPath(binningJob, jobchainOutdir);

        // Add two named outputs for below/above average
        MultipleOutputs.addNamedOutput(binningJob,
                JobChainingDriver.MULTIPLE_OUTPUTS_BELOW_NAME,
                TextOutputFormat.class, Text.class, Text.class);

        MultipleOutputs.addNamedOutput(binningJob,
                JobChainingDriver.MULTIPLE_OUTPUTS_ABOVE_NAME,
                TextOutputFormat.class, Text.class, Text.class);
```

```
        MultipleOutputs.setCountersEnabled(binningJob, true);

        // Configure multiple outputs
        conf.setOutputFormat(NullOutputFormat.class);
        FileOutputFormat.setOutputPath(conf, outputDir);
        MultipleOutputs.addNamedOutput(conf, MULTIPLE_OUTPUTS_ABOVE_5000,
                TextOutputFormat.class, Text.class, LongWritable.class);
        MultipleOutputs.addNamedOutput(conf, MULTIPLE_OUTPUTS_BELOW_5000,
                TextOutputFormat.class, Text.class, LongWritable.class);

        // Add the user files to the DistributedCache
        FileStatus[] userFiles = FileSystem.get(conf).listStatus(userInput);
        for (FileStatus status : userFiles) {
            DistributedCache.addCacheFile(status.getPath().toUri(),
                    binningJob.getConfiguration());
        }

        // Execute job and grab exit code
        return binningJob.getConfiguration();
    }

    public static Configuration getAverageJobConf(Configuration conf,
            Path averageOutputDir, Path outputDir) throws IOException {

        Job averageJob = new Job(conf, "ParallelJobs");
        averageJob.setJarByClass(ParallelJobs.class);

        averageJob.setMapperClass(AverageReputationMapper.class);
        averageJob.setReducerClass(AverageReputationReducer.class);

        averageJob.setOutputKeyClass(Text.class);
        averageJob.setOutputValueClass(DoubleWritable.class);

        averageJob.setInputFormatClass(TextInputFormat.class);

        TextInputFormat.addInputPath(averageJob, averageOutputDir);

        averageJob.setOutputFormatClass(TextOutputFormat.class);
        TextOutputFormat.setOutputPath(averageJob, outputDir);

        // Execute job and grab exit code
        return averageJob.getConfiguration();
    }
```

Chain Folding

Chain folding is an optimization that is applied to MapReduce job chains. Basically, it is a rule of thumb that says each record can be submitted to multiple mappers, or to a reducer and then a mapper. Such combined processing would save a lot of time reading files and transmitting data. The structure of the jobs often make these feasible because a map phase is completely shared-nothing: it looks at each record alone, so it doesn't really matter what the organization of the data is or if it is grouped or not. When building large MapReduce chains, folding the chain to combine map phases will have some drastic performance benefits.

The main benefit of chain folding is reducing the amount of data movement in the MapReduce pipeline, whether it be the I/O of loading and storing to disk, or shuffling data over the network. In chained MapReduce jobs, temporary data is stored in HDFS, so if we can reduce the number of times we hit the disks, we're reducing the total I/O in the chain.

There are a number of patterns in chains to look for to determine what to fold.

1. Take a look at the map phases in the chain. If multiple map phases are adjacent, merge them into one phase. This would be the case if you had a map-only job (such as a replicated join), followed by a numerical aggregation. In this step, we are reducing the amount of times we're hitting the disks. Consider a two-job chain in which the first job is a map-only job, which is then followed by a traditional Map-Reduce job with a map phase and a reduce phase. Without this optimization, the first map-only job will write its output out to the distributed file system, and then that data will be loaded by the second job.

   Instead, if we merge the map phase of the map-only job and the traditional job, that temporary data never gets written, reducing the I/O significantly. Also, fewer tasks are started, reducing overhead of task management. Chaining many map tasks together is an even more drastic optimization. In this case, there really isn't any downside to do this other than having to possibly alter already existing code.

2. If the job ends with a map phase (combined or otherwise), push that phase into the reducer right before it. This is a special case with the same performance benefits as the previous step. It removes the I/O of writing temporary data out and then running a map-only job on it. It also reduces the task start-up overhead.

3. Note that the the first map phase of the chain cannot benefit from this next optimization. As much as possible, split up each map phase (combined or otherwise) between operations that *decrease* the amount of data (e.g., filtering) and operations that *increase* the amount of data (e.g., enrichment). In some cases, this is not possible because you may need some enrichment data in order to do the filtering. In these cases, look at dependent phases as one larger phase that cumulatively increases or decreases the amount of data. Push the processes that decrease the amount of data into the previous reducer, while keeping the processes that increase the amount of data where they are.

   This step is a bit more complex and the difference is more subtle. The gain here is that if you push minimizing map-phase processing into the previous reducer, you will reduce the amount of data written to temporary storage, as well as the amount of data loaded off disk into the next part of the chain. This can be pretty significant if a drastic amount of filtering is done.

Be careful when merging phases that require lots of memory. For example, merging five replicated joins together might not be a good idea because it will exceed the total memory available to the task. In these cases, it might be better to just leave them separate.

 Regardless of whether a job is a chain or not, try to filter as much data as early as possible. The most expensive parts of a MapReduce job are typically pushing data through the pipeline: loading the data, the shuffle/sort, and storing the data. For example, if you care only about data from item 2012, filter that out in the map phase, not after the reducer has grouped the data together.

Let's run through a couple of examples to help explain the idea and why it is so useful.

To exemplify step one, consider the chain in Figure 6-1. The original chain (on top) is optimized so that the replicated join is folded into the mapper of the second MapReduce job (bottom).

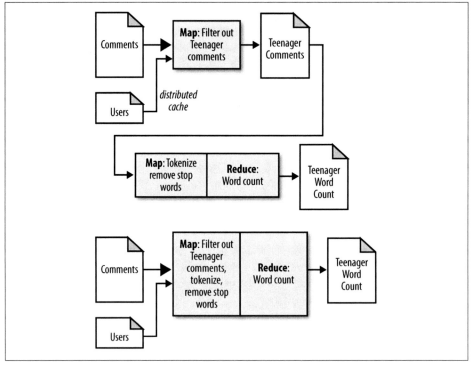

Figure 6-1. Original chain and optimizing mappers

This job performs a word count on comments from teenagers. We do this to find out what topics are interesting to our youngest users. The age of the user isn't with the comment, which is why we need to do a join. In this case, the map-only replicated join can be merged into the preprocessing of the second job.

To exemplify step two, consider the following chain in Figure 6-2. The original chain (top) is optimized so that the replicated join is folded into the reducer of the second MapReduce job (bottom).

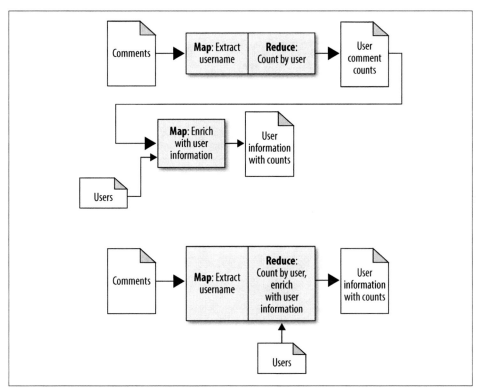

Figure 6-2. Original chain and optimizing a reducer with a mapper

This job enriches each user's information with the number of comments that user has posted. It uses a generic counting MapReduce job, then uses a replicated join to add in the user information to the count. In this case, the map-only replicated join can be merged into the reducer.

To exemplify step three, consider the following chain in Figure 6-3. The original chain (top) is optimized so that the replicated join is folded into the reducer of the second MapReduce job (bottom). This job is a bit more complicated than the others, as is evident from the long chain used to solve it. The intent is to find the most popular tags per age group, which is is done by finding a count of each user, enriching their user information onto it, filtering out counts less than 5, then finally grouping by the age group and summing up the original counts. When we look at the map tasks (enrichment

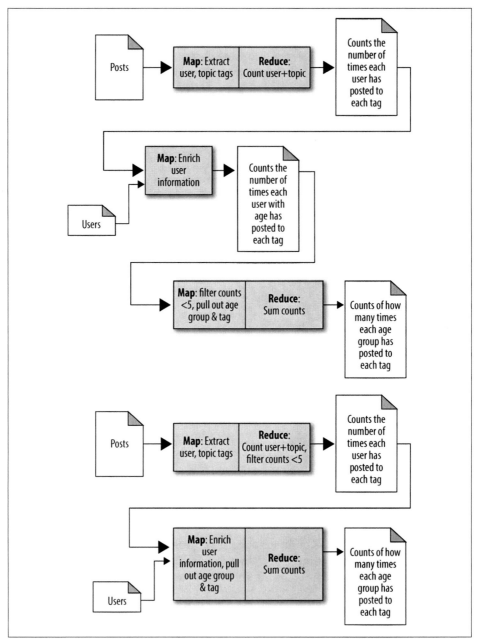

Figure 6-3. Original chain and optimizing a mapper with a reducer

and filtering), the replicated join is adding data, while the filter is removing data. Following step three, we are going to move the filtering to the first MapReduce job, and then move the replicated join into the map phase of the second MapReduce job. This gives us the new chain that can be seen at the bottom of Figure 6-3. Now the first MapReduce job will write out significantly less data than before and then it follows that the second MapReduce job is loading less data.

There are two primary methods for implementing chain folding: manually cutting and pasting code together, and a more elegant approach that uses special classes called `ChainMapper` and `ChainReducer`. If this is a one-time job and logically has multiple map phases, just implement it in one shot with the manual approach. If several of the map phases are reused (in a software reuse sense), then you should use the `ChainMapper` and `ChainReducer` approach to follow good software engineering practice.

The ChainMapper and ChainReducer Approach

`ChainMapper` and `ChainReducer` are special mapper and reducer classes that allow you to run multiple map phases in the mapper and multiple map phases after the reducer. You are effectively expanding the traditional map and reduce paradigm into several map phases, followed by a reduce phase, followed by several map phases. However, only one map phase and one reduce phase is ever invoked.

Each chained map phase feeds into the next in the pipeline. The output of the first is then processed by the second, which is then processed by the third, and so on. The map phases on the backend of the reducer take the output of the reducer and do additional computation. This is useful for post-processing operations or additional filtering.

 Be sure that the input types and output types between each chain match up. If the first phase outputs a `<LongWritable, Text>`, be sure the second phase takes its input as `<LongWritable, Text>`.

Chain Folding Example

Bin users by reputation

This example is a slight modification of the job chaining example. Here, we use two mapper implementations for the initial map phase. The first formats each input XML record and writes out the user ID with a count of one. The second mapper then enriches the user ID with his or her reputation, which is read during the setup phase via the `DistributedCache`.

These two individual mapper classes are then chained together to feed a single reducer. This reducer is a basic `LongSumReducer` that simply iterates through all the values and sums the numbers. This sum is then output along with the input key.

Finally, a third mapper is called that will bin the records based on whether their reputation is below or above 5,000. This entire flow is executed in one MapReduce job using `ChainMapper` and `ChainReducer`.

This example uses the deprecated `mapred` API, because `ChainMapper` and `ChainReducer` were not available in the `mapreduce` package when this example was written.

The following descriptions of each code section explain the solution to the problem.

Problem: Given a set of user posts and user information, bin users based on whether their reputation is below or above 5,000.

Parsing mapper code. This mapper implementation gets the user ID from the input post record and outputs it with a count of 1.

```
public static class UserIdCountMapper extends MapReduceBase implements
        Mapper<Object, Text, Text, LongWritable> {

    public static final String RECORDS_COUNTER_NAME = "Records";
    private static final LongWritable ONE = new LongWritable(1);
    private Text outkey = new Text();

    public void map(Object key, Text value,
            OutputCollector<Text, LongWritable> output, Reporter reporter)
            throws IOException {

        Map<String, String> parsed = MRDPUtils.transformXmlToMap(value
                .toString());

        // Get the value for the OwnerUserId attribute
        outkey.set(parsed.get("OwnerUserId"));
        output.collect(outkey, ONE);
    }
}
```

Replicated join mapper code. This mapper implementation is fed the output from the previous mapper. It reads the users data set during the setup phase to create a map of user ID to reputation. This map is used in the calls to map to enrich the output value with the user's reputation. This new key is then output along with the input value.

```
public static class UserIdReputationEnrichmentMapper extends MapReduceBase
        implements Mapper<Text, LongWritable, Text, LongWritable> {

    private Text outkey = new Text();
    private HashMap<String, String> userIdToReputation =
            new HashMap<String, String>();

    public void configure(JobConf job) {

        Path[] files = DistributedCache.getLocalCacheFiles(job);

        // Read all files in the DistributedCache
        for (Path p : files) {
            BufferedReader rdr = new BufferedReader(
                    new InputStreamReader(
                            new GZIPInputStream(new FileInputStream(
                                    new File(p.toString())))));
```

```
            String line;
            // For each record in the user file
            while ((line = rdr.readLine()) != null) {
                // Get the user ID and reputation
                Map<String, String> parsed = MRDPUtils
                        .transformXmlToMap(line);

                // Map the user ID to the reputation
                userIdToReputation.put(parsed.get("Id",
                        parsed.get("Reputation")));
            }
        }
    }

    public void map(Text key, LongWritable value,
            OutputCollector<Text, LongWritable> output, Reporter reporter)
            throws IOException {

        String reputation = userIdToReputation.get(key.toString());
        if (reputation != null) {
            outkey.set(value.get() + "\t" + reputation);
            output.collect(outkey, value);
        }
    }
}
```

Reducer code. This reducer implementation sums the values together and outputs this summation with the input key: user ID and reputation.

```
public static class LongSumReducer extends MapReduceBase implements
        Reducer<Text, LongWritable, Text, LongWritable> {

    private LongWritable outvalue = new LongWritable();

    public void reduce(Text key, Iterator<LongWritable> values,
            OutputCollector<Text, LongWritable> output, Reporter reporter)
            throws IOException {

        int sum = 0;
        while (values.hasNext()) {
            sum += values.next().get();
        }
        outvalue.set(sum);
        output.collect(key, outvalue);
    }
}
```

Binning mapper code. This mapper uses `MultipleOutputs` to bin users into two data sets. The input key is parsed to pull out the reputation. This reputation value is then compared to the value 5,000 and the record is binned appropriately.

```
public static class UserIdBinningMapper extends MapReduceBase implements
        Mapper<Text, LongWritable, Text, LongWritable> {
```

```
            private MultipleOutputs mos = null;

            public void configure(JobConf conf) {
                mos = new MultipleOutputs(conf);
            }

            public void map(Text key, LongWritable value,
                    OutputCollector<Text, LongWritable> output, Reporter reporter)
                    throws IOException {

                if (Integer.parseInt(key.toString().split("\t")[1]) < 5000) {
                    mos.getCollector(MULTIPLE_OUTPUTS_BELOW_5000, reporter)
                            .collect(key, value);
                } else {
                    mos.getCollector(MULTIPLE_OUTPUTS_ABOVE_5000, reporter)
                            .collect(key, value);
                }
            }

            public void close() {
                mos.close();
            }
        }
```

Driver code. The driver handles configuration of the ChainMapper and ChainReducer. The most interesting piece here is adding mappers and setting the reducer. The order in which they are added affects the execution of the different mapper implementations. ChainMapper is first used to add the two map implementations that will be called back to back before any sorting and shuffling occurs. Then, the ChainReducer static methods are used to set the reducer implementation, and then finally a mapper on the end. Note that you don't use ChainMapper to add a mapper after a reducer: use ChainReducer.

The signature of each method takes in the JobConf of a mapper/reducer class, the input and output key value pair types, and another JobConf for the mapper/reducer class. This can be used in case the mapper or reducer has overlapping configuration parameters. No special configuration is required, so we simply pass in empty JobConf objects. The seventh parameter in the signature is a flag as to pass values in the chain by reference or by value. This is an added optimization you can use if the collector does not modify the keys or values in either the mapper or the reducer. Here, we make these assumptions, so we pass objects by reference (byValue = false).

In addition to configuring the chain mappers and reducers, we also add the user data set to the DistributedCache so our second mapper can perform the enrichment. We also set configure the MultipleOutputs and use a NullOutputFormat rather than the typical TextOutputFormat. Use of this output format will prevent the framework from creating the default empty part files.

Due to a bug, using NullOutputFormat in the mapreduce will not commit files from their _temporary directory to the configured output directory. This is present in version 1.0.3 of Hadoop, but may be fixed in a newer version.

```
public static void main(String[] args) throws Exception {
    JobConf conf = new JobConf("ChainMapperReducer");
    conf.setJarByClass(ChainMapperDriver.class);

    Path postInput = new Path(args[0]);
    Path userInput = new Path(args[1]);
    Path outputDir = new Path(args[2]);

    ChainMapper.addMapper(conf, UserIdCountMapper.class,
            LongWritable.class, Text.class, Text.class, LongWritable.class,
            false, new JobConf(false));

    ChainMapper.addMapper(conf, UserIdReputationEnrichmentMapper.class,
            Text.class, LongWritable.class, Text.class, LongWritable.class,
            false, new JobConf(false));

    ChainReducer.setReducer(conf, LongSumReducer.class, Text.class,
            LongWritable.class, Text.class, LongWritable.class, false,
            new JobConf(false));

    ChainReducer.addMapper(conf, UserIdBinningMapper.class, Text.class,
            LongWritable.class, Text.class, LongWritable.class, false,
            new JobConf(false));

    conf.setCombinerClass(LongSumReducer.class);

    conf.setInputFormat(TextInputFormat.class);
    TextInputFormat.setInputPaths(conf, postInput);

    // Configure multiple outputs
    conf.setOutputFormat(NullOutputFormat.class);
    FileOutputFormat.setOutputPath(conf, outputDir);
    MultipleOutputs.addNamedOutput(conf, MULTIPLE_OUTPUTS_ABOVE_5000,
            TextOutputFormat.class, Text.class, LongWritable.class);
    MultipleOutputs.addNamedOutput(conf, MULTIPLE_OUTPUTS_BELOW_5000,

    conf.setOutputKeyClass(Text.class);
    conf.setOutputValueClass(LongWritable.class);

    // Add the user files to the DistributedCache
    FileStatus[] userFiles = FileSystem.get(conf).listStatus(userInput);
    for (FileStatus status : userFiles) {
        DistributedCache.addCacheFile(status.getPath().toUri(), conf);
    }

    RunningJob job = JobClient.runJob(conf);

    while (!job.isComplete()) {
        Thread.sleep(5000);
```

```
        }
        System.exit(job.isSuccessful() ? 0 : 1);
    }
```

Job Merging

Like job folding, *job merging* is another optimization aimed to reduce the amount of I/O through the MapReduce pipeline. Job merging is a process that allows two unrelated jobs that are loading the same data to share the MapReduce pipeline. The main benefit of merging is that the data needs to be loaded and parsed only once. For some large-scale jobs, that task might be the most expensive part of the whole operation. One of the downsides of "schema-on-load" and storing the data in its original form is having to parse it over and over again, which can really impact performance if parsing is complicated (e.g., XML).

Assume we have two jobs that need to run over the exact same massive amount of data. These two jobs both load and parse the data, then perform their computations. With job merging, we'll have one MapReduce job that logically performs the two jobs at once without mixing the two applications as seen in Figure 6-4. The original chain (top) is optimized so that the two mappers run on the same data, and the two reducers run on the same data (bottom).

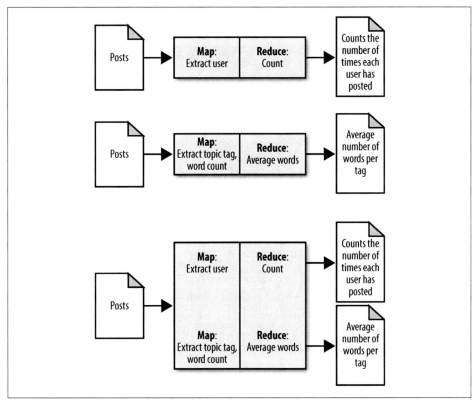

Figure 6-4. Original jobs and merged jobs

Nothing is stopping you from applying job merging to more than two jobs at once. The more the merrier! The more you consolidate a shared burden across jobs, the more compute resources you'll have available in your cluster.

Likely, this process will be relevant only for important and already existing jobs in a production cluster. Development groups that take the time to consolidate their core analytics will see significant reductions in cluster utilization. When the jobs are merged, they'll have to run together and the source code will have to be kept together. This is likely not worth it for jobs that are run in an ad hoc manner or are relatively new to the environment.

Unfortunately, you must satisfy a number of prerequisites before applying this pattern. The most obvious one is that both jobs need to have the same intermediate keys and output formats, because they'll be sharing the pipeline and thus need to use the same data types. Serialization or polymorphism can be used if this is truly a problem, but adds a bit of complexity.

Job merging is a dirty procedure. Some hacks will have to be done to get it to work, but definitely more work can be put into a merging solution to make it a bit cleaner.

From a software engineering perspective, this complicates the code organization, because unrelated jobs now share the same code. At a high level, the same map function will now be performing the original duties of the old map functions, while the reduce function will perform one action or another based on a tag on the key that tells which data set it came from. The steps for merging two jobs are as follows:

1. Bring the code for the two mappers together.

   There are a couple of ways to do this. Copying and pasting the code works, but may complicate which piece of code is doing what. Good in-code comments can help you compensate for this. The other method is to separate the code into two helper map functions that process the input for each algorithm.

2. In the mapper, change the writing of the key and value to "tag" the key with the map source.

   Tagging the key to indicate which map it came from is critical so that the data from the different maps don't get mixed up. There are a few ways to do this depending on the original data type. If it is a string, you can simply make the first character the tag, so for instance you could change "parks" to "Aparks" when it comes from the first map, and "Bparks" when it comes from the second map.

   The general way to tag is to make a custom composite tuple-like key that stores the tag separately from the original data. This is definitely the cleaner way of doing things, but takes a bit more work.

3. In the reducer, parse out the tag and use an if-statement to switch what reducer code actually gets executed.

   As in the mapper, you can either just copy and paste the code into an if-statement or have the if-statement call out to helper functions. The if-statement controls the path of execution based on the tag.

4. Use `MultipleOuputs` to separate the output for the jobs.

   `MultipleOutputs` is a special output format helper class that allows you to write to different folders of output for the same reducer, instead of just a single folder. Make it so the one reducer path always writes to one folder of the `MultipleOutputs`, while the other reducer path writes to the other folder.

Job Merging Examples

Anonymous comments and distinct users

This example combines "Anonymizing StackOverflow comments" on page 95 and "Distinct user IDs" on page 65. Both examples used the comments data set as input. However, their outputs were very different. One created a distinct set of users, while the other created an anonymized version of each record. The comment portion of the StackOverflow data set is the largest we have, so merging these jobs together will definitely cut our processing time down. This way, the data set needs to be read only once.

The following descriptions of each code section explain the solution to the problem.

Problem: Given a set of comments, generate an anonymized version of the data and a distinct set of user IDs.

Tagged text WritableComparable. A custom `WritableComparable` object is created to tag a `Text` with a string. This is a cleaner way of splitting the logic between the two jobs, and saves us some string parsing in the reducer.

This object has two private member variables and getters and setters for each variable. It holds a `String` that the mapper uses to tag each `Text` value that is also held by this object. The reducer then examines the tag to find out which reduce logic to execute. The `compareTo` method is what makes this object also comparable and allowed for use as a key in the MapReduce framework. This method first examines the tag for equality. If they are equal, the text inside the object is then compared and the value immediately returned. If they are not equal, the value of the comparison is then returned. Items are sorted by tag first, and then by the text value. This type of comparison will produce output such as:

```
A:100004122
A:120019879
D:10
D:22
D:23
```

```java
public static class TaggedText implements WritableComparable<TaggedText> {

    private String tag = "";
    private Text text = new Text();

    public TaggedText() { }

    public void setTag(String tag) {
        this.tag = tag;
    }

    public String getTag() {
        return tag;
    }

    public void setText(Text text) {
        this.text.set(text);
    }

    public void setText(String text) {
        this.text.set(text);
    }

    public Text getText() {
        return text;
    }

    public void readFields(DataInput in) throws IOException {
```

```
        tag = in.readUTF();
        text.readFields(in);
    }

    public void write(DataOutput out) throws IOException {
        out.writeUTF(tag);
        text.write(out);
    }

    public int compareTo(TaggedText obj) {
        int compare = tag.compareTo(obj.getTag());
        if (compare == 0) {
            return text.compareTo(obj.getText());
        } else {
            return compare;
        }
    }

    public String toString() {
        return tag.toString() + ":" + text.toString();
    }
}
```

Merged mapper code. The map method simply passes the parameters to two helper functions, each of which processes the map logic individual to write output to context. The map methods were slightly changed from their original respective examples in order to both output Text objects as the key and value. This is a necessary change so we can have the same type of intermediate key/value pairs we had in the separate map logic. The anonymizeMap method generates an anonymous record from the input value, whereas the distinctMap method grabs the user ID from the record and outputs it. Each intermediate key/value pair written out from each helper map method is tagged with either "A" for anonymize or "D" for distinct.

 Each helper math method parses the input record, but this parsing should instead be done inside the actual map method, The resulting Map<String,String> can then be passed to both helper methods. Any little optimizations like this can be very beneficial in the long run and should be implemented!

```
public static class AnonymizeDistinctMergedMapper extends
            Mapper<Object, Text, TaggedText, Text> {

    private static final Text DISTINCT_OUT_VALUE = new Text();

    private Random rndm = new Random();
    private TaggedText anonymizeOutkey = new TaggedText(),
            distinctOutkey = new TaggedText();
    private Text anonymizeOutvalue = new Text();

    public void map(Object key, Text value, Context context)
            throws IOException, InterruptedException {
```

```
                anonymizeMap(key, value, context);
                distinctMap(key, value, context);
        }

        private void anonymizeMap(Object key, Text value, Context context)
                throws IOException, InterruptedException {

            Map<String, String> parsed = MRDPUtils.transformXmlToMap(value
                    .toString());

            if (parsed.size() > 0) {
                StringBuilder bldr = new StringBuilder();
                bldr.append("<row ");
                for (Entry<String, String> entry : parsed.entrySet()) {

                    if (entry.getKey().equals("UserId")
                            || entry.getKey().equals("Id")) {
                        // ignore these fields
                    } else if (entry.getKey().equals("CreationDate")) {
                    // Strip out the time, anything after the 'T' in the value
                        bldr.append(entry.getKey()
                                + "=\""
                                + entry.getValue().substring(0,
                                        entry.getValue().indexOf('T')) + "\" ");
                    } else {
                        // Otherwise, output this.
                        bldr.append(entry.getKey() + "=\"" + entry.getValue()
                                + "\" ");
                    }
                }

                bldr.append(">");
                anonymizeOutkey.setTag("A");
                anonymizeOutkey.setText(Integer.toString(rndm.nextInt()));
                anonymizeOutvalue.set(bldr.toString());
                context.write(anonymizeOutkey, anonymizeOutvalue);
            }
        }

        private void distinctMap(Object key, Text value, Context context)
                throws IOException, InterruptedException {

            Map<String, String> parsed = MRDPUtils.transformXmlToMap(value
                    .toString());

            // Otherwise, set our output key to the user's id, tagged with a "D"
            distinctOutkey.setTag("D");
            distinctOutkey.setText(parsed.get("UserId"));

            // Write the user's id with a null value
            context.write(distinctOutkey, DISTINCT_OUT_VALUE);
        }
    }
```

Merged reducer code. The reducer's calls to setup and cleanup handle the creation and closing of the MultipleOutputs utility. The reduce method checks the tag of each input key and calls a helper reducer method based on the tag. The reduce methods are passed the Text object inside the TaggedText.

For the anonymous call, all the input values are iterated over and written to a named output of anonymize/part. Adding the slash and the "part" creates a folder under the configured output directory that contains a number of part files equivalent to the number of reduce tasks.

For the distinct reduce call, the input key is written to MultipleOutputs with a Null Writable to a named output of distinct/part. Again, this will create a folder called distinct underneath the job's configured output directory.

 In this example, we are outputting the same essential format—a Text object and a NullWritable object— from each of the reduce calls. This won't always be the case! If your jobs have conflicting output key/value types, you can utilize the Text object to normalize the outputs.

```
public static class AnonymizeDistinctMergedReducer extends
        Reducer<TaggedText, Text, Text, NullWritable> {

    private MultipleOutputs<Text, NullWritable> mos = null;

    protected void setup(Context context) throws IOException,
            InterruptedException {
        mos = new MultipleOutputs<Text, NullWritable>(context);
    }

    protected void reduce(TaggedText key, Iterable<Text> values,
            Context context) throws IOException, InterruptedException {

        if (key.getTag().equals("A")) {
            anonymizeReduce(key.getText(), values, context);
        } else {
            distinctReduce(key.getText(), values, context);
        }
    }

    private void anonymizeReduce(Text key, Iterable<Text> values,
            Context context) throws IOException, InterruptedException {

        for (Text value : values) {
            mos.write(MULTIPLE_OUTPUTS_ANONYMIZE, value,
                    NullWritable.get(), MULTIPLE_OUTPUTS_ANONYMIZE + "/part");
        }
    }

    private void distinctReduce(Text key, Iterable<Text> values,
            Context context) throws IOException, InterruptedException {
        mos.write(MULTIPLE_OUTPUTS_DISTINCT, key, NullWritable.get(),
                MULTIPLE_OUTPUTS_DISTINCT + "/part");
```

```
    }
    protected void cleanup(Context context) throws IOException,
            InterruptedException {
        mos.close();
    }
}
```

Driver code. The driver code looks just like any other driver that uses MultipleOutputs.
All the logic of merging jobs is done inside the mapper and reducer implementation.

```
public static void main(String[] args) throws Exception {

    // Configure the merged job
    Job job = new Job(new Configuration(), "MergedJob");
    job.setJarByClass(MergedJobDriver.class);

    job.setMapperClass(AnonymizeDistinctMergedMapper.class);
    job.setReducerClass(AnonymizeDistinctMergedReducer.class);
    job.setNumReduceTasks(10);

    TextInputFormat.setInputPaths(job, new Path(args[0]));
    TextOutputFormat.setOutputPath(job, new Path(args[1]));

    MultipleOutputs.addNamedOutput(job, MULTIPLE_OUTPUTS_ANONYMIZE,
            TextOutputFormat.class, Text.class, NullWritable.class);
    MultipleOutputs.addNamedOutput(job, MULTIPLE_OUTPUTS_DISTINCT,
            TextOutputFormat.class, Text.class, NullWritable.class);

    job.setOutputKeyClass(TaggedText.class);
    job.setOutputValueClass(Text.class);

    System.exit(job.waitForCompletion(true) ? 0 : 1);
}
```

Input and Output Patterns

In this chapter, we'll be focusing on what is probably the most often overlooked way to improve the value of MapReduce: customizing input and output. You will not always want to load or store data the way Hadoop MapReduce does out of the box. Sometimes you can skip the time-consuming step of storing data in HDFS and just accept data from some original source, or feed it directly to some process that uses it after Map-Reduce is finished. Sometimes the basic Hadoop paradigm of file blocks and input splits doesn't do what you need, so this is where a custom `InputFormat` or `OutputFormat` comes into play.

Three patterns in this chapter deal with input: *generating data*, *external source input*, and *partition pruning*. All three input patterns share an interesting property: the map phase is completely unaware that tricky things are going on before it gets its input pairs. Customizing an input format is a great way to abstract away details of the method you use to load data.

On the flip side, Hadoop will not always store data in the way you need it to. There is one pattern in this chapter, *external source output*, that writes data to a system outside of Hadoop and HDFS. Just like the custom input formats, custom output formats keep the map or reduce phase from realizing that tricky things are going on as the data is going out.

Customizing Input and Output in Hadoop

Hadoop allows you to modify the way data is loaded on disk in two major ways: con-figuring how contiguous chunks of input are generated from blocks in HDFS (or maybe more exotic sources), and configuring how records appear in the map phase. The two classes you'll be playing with to do this are `RecordReader` and `InputFormat`. These work with the Hadoop MapReduce framework in a very similar way to how mappers and reducers are plugged in.

Hadoop also allows you to modify the way data is stored in an analogous way: with an `OutputFormat` and a `RecordWriter`.

InputFormat

Hadoop relies on the input format of the job to do three things:

1. Validate the input configuration for the job (i.e., checking that the data is there)
2. Split the input blocks and files into logical chunks of type InputSplit, each of which is assigned to a map task for processing
3. Create the RecordReader implementation to be used to create key/value pairs from the raw InputSplit. These pairs are sent one by one to their mapper

The most common input formats are subclasses of FileInputFormat, with the Hadoop default being TextInputFormat. The input format first validates the input into the job by ensuring that all of the input paths exist. Then it logically splits each input file based on the total size of the file in bytes, using the block size as an upper bound. For example, a 160 megabyte file in HDFS will generate three input splits along the byte ranges 0MB-64MB, 64MB-128MB and 128MB-160MB. Each map task will be assigned exactly one of these input splits, and then RecordReader implementation is responsible for generate key/value pairs out of all the bytes it has been assigned.

Typically, the RecordReader has the additional responsibility of fixing boundaries, because the input split boundary is arbitrary and probably will not fall on a record boundary. For example, the TextInputFormat reads text files uses a LineRecordReader to create key/value pairs for each map task for each line of text (i.e., separated by a newline character). The key is the number of bytes read in the file so far and the value is a string of characters up to a newline character. Because it is very unlikely that the chunk of bytes for each input split will be lined up with a newline character, the LineRecordReader will read past its given "end" in order to make sure a complete line is read. This bit of data comes from a different data block and is therefore not stored on the same node, so it is streamed from a DataNode hosting the block. This streaming is all handled by an instance of the FSDataInputStream class, and we (thankfully) don't have to deal with any knowledge of where these blocks are.

Don't be afraid to go past split boundaries in your own formats, just be sure to test thoroughly so you aren't duplicating or missing any data!

 Custom input formats are not limited to file-based input. As long as you can express the input as InputSplit objects and key/value pairs, custom or otherwise, you can read anything into the map phase of a MapReduce job in parallel. Just be sure to keep in mind what an input split represents and try to take advantage of data locality.

The InputFormat abstract class contains two abstract methods:

getSplits

The implementation of `getSplits` typically uses the given `JobContext` object to retrieve the configured input and return a `List` of `InputSplit` objects. The input splits
have a method to return an array of machines associated with the locations of the
data in the cluster, which gives clues to the framework as to which TaskTracker
should process the map task. This method is also a good place to verify the configuration and throw any necessary exceptions, because the method is used on the
front-end (i.e. before the job is submitted to the JobTracker).

createRecordReader

This method is used on the back-end to generate an implementation of `Record
Reader`, which we'll discuss in more detail shortly. Typically, a new instance is
created and immediately returned, because the record reader has an `initialize`
method that is called by the framework.

RecordReader

The `RecordReader` abstract class creates key/value pairs from a given `InputSplit`. While
the `InputSplit` represents the byte-oriented view of the split, the `RecordReader` makes
sense out of it for processing by a mapper. This is why Hadoop and MapReduce is
considered *schema on read*. It is in the `RecordReader` that the schema is defined, based
solely on the record reader implementation, which changes based on what the expected
input is for the job. Bytes are read from the input source and turned into a `Writable
Comparable` key and a `Writable` value. Custom data types are very common when cre-
ating custom input formats, as they are a nice object-oriented way to present information to a mapper.

A `RecordReader` uses the data within the boundaries created by the input split to generate
key/value pairs. In the context of file-based input, the "start" is the byte position in the
file where the `RecordReader` should start generating key/value pairs. The "end" is where
it should stop reading records. These are not hard boundaries as far as the API is concerned—there is nothing stopping a developer from reading the entire file for each map
task. While reading the entire file is not advised, reading outside of the boundaries it
often necessary to ensure that a complete record is generated.

Consider the case of XML. While using a `TextInputFormat` to grab each line works,
XML elements are typically not on the same line and will be split by a typical MapReduce input. By reading past the "end" input split boundary, you can complete an entire
record. After finding the bottom of the record, you just need to ensure that each record
reader starts at the beginning of an XML element. After seeking to the start of the input
split, continue reading until the beginning of the configured XML tag is read. This will
allow the MapReduce framework to cover the entire contents of an XML file, while not
duplicating any XML records. Any XML that is skipped by seeking forward to the start
of an XML element will be read by the preceding map task.

The `RecordReader` abstract class has a number of methods that must be overridden.

initialize

This method takes as arguments the map task's assigned `InputSplit` and `TaskAt temptContext`, and prepares the record reader. For file-based input formats, this is a good place to seek to the byte position in the file to begin reading.

getCurrentKey and getCurrentValue

These methods are used by the framework to give generated key/value pairs to an implementation of `Mapper`. Be sure to reuse the objects returned by these methods if at all possible!

nextKeyValue

Like the corresponding method of the `InputFormat` class, this reads a single key/ value pair and returns `true` until the data is consumed.

getProgress

Like the corresponding method of the `InputFormat` class, this is an optional method used by the framework for metrics gathering.

close

This method is used by the framework for cleanup after there are no more key/ value pairs to process.

OutputFormat

Similarly to an input format, Hadoop relies on the output format of the job for two main tasks:

1. Validate the output configuration for the job
2. Create the `RecordWriter` implementation that will write the output of the job

On the flip side of the `FileInputFormat`, there is a `FileOutputFormat` to work with file-based output. Because most output from a MapReduce job is written to HDFS, the many file-based output formats that come with the API will solve most of yours needs. The default used by Hadoop is the `TextOutputFormat`, which stores key/value pairs to HDFS at a configured output directory with a tab delimiter. Each reduce task writes an individual part file to the configured output directory. The `TextOutputFormat` also validates that the output directory does not exist prior to starting the MapReduce job.

The `TextOutputFormat` uses a `LineRecordWriter` to write key/value pairs for each map task or reduce task, depending on whether there is a reduce phase or not. This class uses the `toString` method to serialize each each key/value pair to a part file in HDFS, delimited by a tab. This tab delimiter is the default and can be changed via job configuration.

Again, much like an `InputFormat`, you are not restricted to storing data to HDFS. As long as you can write key/value pairs to some other source with Java (e.g., a JDBC database connection), you can use MapReduce to do a parallel bulk write. Just make sure whatever you are writing to can handle the large number of connections from the many tasks.

The `OutputFormat` abstract class contains three abstract methods for implementation:

checkOutputSpecs
> This method is used to validate the output specification for the job, such as making sure the directory does not already exist prior to it being submitted. Otherwise, the output would be overwritten.

getRecordWriter
> This method returns a `RecordWriter` implementation that serializes key/value pairs to an output, typically a `FileSystem` object.

getOutputCommiter
> The output committer of a job sets up each task during initialization, commits the task upon successful completion, and cleans up each task when it finishes — successful or otherwise. For file-based output, a `FileOutputCommitter` can be used to handle all the heavy lifting. It will create temporary output directories for each map task and move the successful output to the configured output directory when necessary.

RecordWriter

The `RecordWriter` abstract class writes key/value pairs to a file system, or another output. Unlike its `RecordReader` counterpart, it does not contain an initialize phase. However, the constructor can always be used to set up the record writer for whatever is needed. Any parameters can be passed in during construction, because the record writer instance is created via `OutputFormat.getRecordWriter`.

The `RecordWriter` abstract class is a much simpler interface, containing only two methods:

write
> This method is called by the framework for each key/value pair that needs to be written. The implementation of this method depends very much on your use case. The examples we'll show will write each key/value pair to an external in-memory key/value store rather than a file system.

close
> This method is used by the framework after there are no more key/value pairs to write out. This can be used to release any file handles, shut down any connections to other services, or any other cleanup tasks needed.

Generating Data

Pattern Description

The *generating data* pattern is interesting because instead of loading data that comes from somewhere outside, it generates that data on the fly and in parallel.

Intent

You want to generate a lot of data from scratch.

Motivation

This pattern is different from all of the others in the book in that it doesn't load data. With this pattern, you generate the data and store it back in the distributed file system.

Generating data isn't common. Typically you'll generate a bunch of the data at once then use it over and over again. However, when you do need to generate data, Map-Reduce is an excellent system for doing it.

The most common use case for this pattern is generating random data. Building some sort of representative data set could be useful for large scale testing for when the real data set is still too small. It can also be useful for building "toy domains" for researching a proof of concept for an analytic at scale.

Generating random data is also used often used as part of a benchmark, such as the commonly used TeraGen/TeraSort and DFSIO.

Unfortunately, the implementation of this pattern isn't straightforward in Hadoop because one of the foundational pieces of the framework is assigning one map task to an input split and assigning one map function call to one record. In this case, there are no input splits and there are no records, so we have to fool the framework to think there are.

Structure

To implement this pattern in Hadoop, implement a custom `InputFormat` and let a `RecordReader` generate the random data. The map function is completely oblivious to the origin of the data, so it can be built on the fly instead of being loaded out of some file in HDFS. For the most part, using the identity mapper is fine here, but you might want to do some post-processing in the map task, or even analyze it right away. See Figure 7-1.

This pattern is map-only.

- The `InputFormat` creates the fake splits from nothing. The number of splits it creates should be configurable.
- The `RecordReader` takes its fake split and generates random records from it.

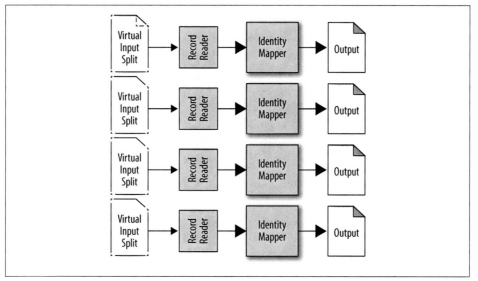

Figure 7-1. The structure of the generating data pattern

In some cases, you can assign some information in the input split to tell the record reader what to generate. For example, to generate random date/time data, have each input split account for an hour.

- In most cases, the `IdentityMapper` is used to just write the data out as it comes in.

 The lazy way of doing implementing this pattern is to seed the job with fake empty files. Then, you can just use a generic `InputFormat` and `RecordReader` and generate the data in the map function. The empty input files are then deleted on application exit.

Consequences

Each mapper outputs a file containing random data.

Resemblances

There are a number of ways to create random data with SQL and Pig, but nothing that is eloquent or terse.

Performance analysis

The major consideration here in terms of performance is how many worker map tasks are needed to generate the data. In general, the more map tasks you have, the faster you can generate data since you are better utilizing the parallelism of the cluster. However, it makes little sense to fire up more map tasks than you have map slots since they are all doing the same thing.

Generating Data Examples

Generating random StackOverflow comments

To generate random StackOverflow data, we'll take a list of 1,000 words and just make random blurbs. We also have to generate a random score, a random row ID (we can ignore that it likely won't be unique), a random user ID, and a random creation date.

The following descriptions of each code section explain the solution to the problem.

Driver code. The driver parses the four command line arguments to configure this job. It sets our custom input format and calls the static methods to configure it further. All the output is written to the given output directory. The identity mapper is used for this job, and the reduce phase is disabled by setting the number of reduce tasks to zero.

```
public static void main(String[] args) throws Exception {
    Configuration conf = new Configuration();

    int numMapTasks = Integer.parseInt(args[0]);
    int numRecordsPerTask = Integer.parseInt(args[1]);
    Path wordList = new Path(args[2]);
    Path outputDir = new Path(args[3]);

    Job job = new Job(conf, "RandomDataGenerationDriver");
    job.setJarByClass(RandomDataGenerationDriver.class);

    job.setNumReduceTasks(0);

    job.setInputFormatClass(RandomStackOverflowInputFormat.class);

    RandomStackOverflowInputFormat.setNumMapTasks(job, numMapTasks);
    RandomStackOverflowInputFormat.setNumRecordPerTask(job,
            numRecordsPerTask);
    RandomStackOverflowInputFormat.setRandomWordList(job, wordList);

    TextOutputFormat.setOutputPath(job, outputDir);

    job.setOutputKeyClass(Text.class);
    job.setOutputValueClass(NullWritable.class);

    System.exit(job.waitForCompletion(true) ? 0 : 2);
}
```

InputSplit code. The FakeInputSplit class simply extends InputSplit and implements Writable. There is no implementation for any of the overridden methods, or for methods requiring return values return basic values. This input split is used to trick the framework into assigning a task to generate the random data.

```
public static class FakeInputSplit extends InputSplit implements
        Writable {

    public void readFields(DataInput arg0) throws IOException {
    }

    public void write(DataOutput arg0) throws IOException {
    }

    public long getLength() throws IOException, InterruptedException {
        return 0;
    }

    public String[] getLocations() throws IOException,
            InterruptedException {
        return new String[0];
    }
}
```

InputFormat code. The input format has two main purposes: returning the list of input
splits for the framework to generate map tasks from, and then creating the RandomStack
OverflowRecordReader for the map task. We override the getSplits method to return a
configured number of FakeInputSplit splits. This number is pulled from the configuration.   When   the   framework   calls   createRecordReader,   a
RandomStackOverflowRecordReader is instantiated, initialized, and returned.

```
public static class RandomStackOverflowInputFormat extends
        InputFormat<Text, NullWritable> {

    public static final String NUM_MAP_TASKS = "random.generator.map.tasks";
    public static final String NUM_RECORDS_PER_TASK =
            "random.generator.num.records.per.map.task";
    public static final String RANDOM_WORD_LIST =
            "random.generator.random.word.file";

    public List<InputSplit> getSplits(JobContext job) throws IOException {

        // Get the number of map tasks configured for
        int numSplits = job.getConfiguration().getInt(NUM_MAP_TASKS, -1);

        // Create a number of input splits equivalent to the number of tasks
        ArrayList<InputSplit> splits = new ArrayList<InputSplit>();
        for (int i = 0; i < numSplits; ++i) {
            splits.add(new FakeInputSplit());
        }

        return splits;
    }

    public RecordReader<Text, NullWritable> createRecordReader(
            InputSplit split, TaskAttemptContext context)
            throws IOException, InterruptedException {
        // Create a new RandomStackOverflowRecordReader and initialize it
        RandomStackOverflowRecordReader rr =
```

```
                new RandomStackOverflowRecordReader();
        rr.initialize(split, context);
        return rr;
    }

    public static void setNumMapTasks(Job job, int i) {
        job.getConfiguration().setInt(NUM_MAP_TASKS, i);
    }

    public static void setNumRecordPerTask(Job job, int i) {
        job.getConfiguration().setInt(NUM_RECORDS_PER_TASK, i);
    }

    public static void setRandomWordList(Job job, Path file) {
        DistributedCache.addCacheFile(file.toUri(), job.getConfiguration());
    }
}
```

RecordReader code. This record reader is where the data is actually generated. It is given during our FakeInputSplit during initialization, but simply ignores it. The number of records to create is pulled from the job configuration, and the list of random words is read from the DistributedCache. For each call to nextKeyValue, a random record is created using a simple random number generator. The body of the comment is generated by a helper function that random selects words from the list, between one and thirty words (also random). The counter is incremented to keep track of how many records have been generated. Once all the records are generated, the record reader returns false, signaling the framework that there is no more input for the mapper.

```
public static class RandomStackOverflowRecordReader extends
        RecordReader<Text, NullWritable> {

    private int numRecordsToCreate = 0;
    private int createdRecords = 0;
    private Text key = new Text();
    private NullWritable value = NullWritable.get();
    private Random rndm = new Random();
    private ArrayList<String> randomWords = new ArrayList<String>();

    // This object will format the creation date string into a Date
    // object
    private SimpleDateFormat frmt = new SimpleDateFormat(
            "yyyy-MM-dd'T'HH:mm:ss.SSS");

    public void initialize(InputSplit split, TaskAttemptContext context)
            throws IOException, InterruptedException {

        // Get the number of records to create from the configuration
        this.numRecordsToCreate = context.getConfiguration().getInt(
                NUM_RECORDS_PER_TASK, -1);

        // Get the list of random words from the DistributedCache
        URI[] files = DistributedCache.getCacheFiles(context
                .getConfiguration());
```

```java
    // Read the list of random words into a list
    BufferedReader rdr = new BufferedReader(new FileReader(
            files[0].toString()));

    String line;
    while ((line = rdr.readLine()) != null) {
        randomWords.add(line);
    }
    rdr.close();
}

public boolean nextKeyValue() throws IOException,
        InterruptedException {
    // If we still have records to create
    if (createdRecords < numRecordsToCreate) {
        // Generate random data
        int score = Math.abs(rndm.nextInt()) % 15000;
        int rowId = Math.abs(rndm.nextInt()) % 1000000000;
        int postId = Math.abs(rndm.nextInt()) % 100000000;
        int userId = Math.abs(rndm.nextInt()) % 1000000;
        String creationDate = frmt
                .format(Math.abs(rndm.nextLong()));

        // Create a string of text from the random words
        String text = getRandomText();

        String randomRecord = "<row Id=\"" + rowId + "\" PostId=\""
                + postId + "\" Score=\"" + score + "\" Text=\""
                + text + "\" CreationDate=\"" + creationDate
                + "\" UserId\"=" + userId + "\" />";

        key.set(randomRecord);
        ++createdRecords;
        return true;
    } else {
        // We are done creating records
        return false;
    }
}

private String getRandomText() {
    StringBuilder bldr = new StringBuilder();
    int numWords = Math.abs(rndm.nextInt()) % 30 + 1;

    for (int i = 0; i < numWords; ++i) {
        bldr.append(randomWords.get(Math.abs(rndm.nextInt())
                % randomWords.size())
                + " ");
    }
    return bldr.toString();
}

public Text getCurrentKey() throws IOException,
        InterruptedException {
    return key;
```

```
    }

    public NullWritable getCurrentValue() throws IOException,
            InterruptedException {
        return value;
    }

    public float getProgress() throws IOException, InterruptedException {
        return (float) createdRecords / (float) numRecordsToCreate;
    }

    public void close() throws IOException {
        // nothing to do here...
    }
}
```

External Source Output

Pattern Description

As stated earlier in this chapter, the *external source output* pattern writes data to a system outside of Hadoop and HDFS.

Intent

You want to write MapReduce output to a nonnative location.

Motivation

With this pattern, we are able to output data from the MapReduce framework directly to an external source. This is extremely useful for direct loading into a system instead of staging the data to be delivered to the external source. The pattern skips storing data in a file system entirely and sends output key/value pairs directly where they belong. MapReduce is rarely ever hosting an applications as-is, so using MapReduce to bulk load into an external source in parallel has its uses.

In a MapReduce approach, the data is written out in parallel. As with using an external source for input, you need to be sure the destination system can handle the parallel ingest it is bound to endure with all the open connections.

Structure

Figure 7-2 shows the external source output structure, explained below.

- The OutputFormat verifies the output specification of the job configuration prior to job submission. This is a great place to ensure that the external source is fully functional, as it won't be good to process all the data only to find out the external

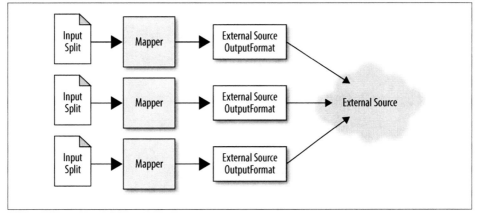

Figure 7-2. The structure of the external source output pattern

source was unable when it was time to commit the data. This method also is responsible for creating and initializing a `RecordWriter` implementation.

- The `RecordWriter` writes all key/value pairs to the external source. Much like a `RecordReader`, the implementation varies depending on the external data source being written to. During construction of the object, establish any needed connections using the external source's API. These connections are then used to write out all the data from each map or reduce task.

Consequences

The output data has been sent to the external source and that external source has loaded it successfully.

 Note that task failures are bound to happen, and when they do, any key/value pairs written in the `write` method can't be reverted. In a typical MapReduce job, temporary output is written to the file system. In the event of a failure, this output is simply discarded. When writing to an external source directly, it will receive the data in a stream. If a task fails, the external source won't automatically know about it and discard all the data it received from a task. If this is unacceptable, consider using a custom `OutputCommitter` to write temporary output to the file system. This temporary output can then be read, delivered to the external source, and deleted upon success, or deleted from the file system outright in the event of a failure.

Performance analysis

From a MapReduce perspective, there isn't much to worry about since the map and reduce are generic. However, you do have to be very careful that the receiver of the data can handle the parallel connections. Having a thousand tasks writing to a single SQL database is not going to work well. To avoid this, you may have to have each reducer handle a bit more data than you typically would to reduce the number of parallel writes to the data sink. This is not necessarily a problem if the destination of the data is parallel in nature and supports parallel ingestation. For example, for writing to a sharded SQL database, you could have each reducer write to a specific database instance.

External Source Output Example

Writing to Redis instances

This example is a basic means for writing to a number of Redis instances in parallel from MapReduce. Redis (*www.redis.io*) is an open-source, in-memory, key-value store. It is often referred to as a data structure server, since keys can contain strings, hashes, lists, sets, and sorted sets. Redis is written in ANSI C and works in most POSIX systems, such as Linux, without any external dependencies.

In order to work with the Hadoop framework, Jedis (*https://github.com/xetorthio/jedis/*) is used to communicate with Redis. Jedis is an open-source "blazingly small and sane Redis java client." A list of clients written for other languages is available on their website.

Unlike other examples in this book, there is no actual analysis in this example (along with the rest of the examples in this chapter). It focuses on how to take a data set stored in HDFS and store it in an external data source using a custom `FileOutputFormat`. In this example, the Stack Overflow users data set is written to a configurable number of Redis instances, specifically the user-to-reputation mappings. These mappings are randomly distributed evenly among a single Redis hash.

A Redis hash is a map between string fields and string values, similar to a Java `Hash Map`. Each hash is given a key to identify the hash. Every hash can store more than four billion field-value pairs.

The sections below with its corresponding code explain the following problem.

Problem: Given a set of user information, randomly distributed user-to-reputation mappings to a configurable number of Redis instances in parallel.

OutputFormat code. The `RedisHashOutputFormat` is responsible for establishing and verifying the job configuration prior to being submitted to the JobTracker. Once the job has been submitted, it also creates the `RecordWriter` to serialize all the output key/value pairs. Typically, this is a file in HDFS. However, we are not bound to using HDFS, as we will see in the `RecordWriter` later on.

The output format contains configuration variables that must be set by the driver to ensure it has all the information required to do its job. Here, we have a couple `public static` methods to take some of the guess work out of what a developer needs to set. This output format takes in a list of Redis instance hosts as a CSV structure and a Redis hash key to write all the output to. In the `checkOutputSpecs` method, we ensure that both of these parameters are set before we even both launching the job, as it will surely fail without them. This is where you'll want to verify your configuration!

The getRecordWriter method is used on the back end to create an instance of a Record Writer for the map or reduce task. Here, we get the configuration variables required by the RedisHashRecordWriter and return a new instance of it. This record writer is a nested class of the RedisHashOutputFormat, which is not required but is more of a convention. The details of this class are in the following section.

The final method of this output format is getOutputCommitter. The output committer is used by the framework to manage any temporary output before committing in case the task fails and needs to be reexecuted. For this implementation, we don't typically care whether the task fails and needs to be re-executed. As long as the job finishes we are okay. An output committer is required by the framework, but the NullOutputFormat contains an output committer implementation that doesn't do anything.

```
public static class RedisHashOutputFormat extends OutputFormat<Text, Text> {

    public static final String REDIS_HOSTS_CONF =
            "mapred.redishashoutputformat.hosts";
    public static final String REDIS_HASH_KEY_CONF =
            "mapred.redishashinputformat.key";

    public static void setRedisHosts(Job job, String hosts) {
        job.getConfiguration().set(REDIS_HOSTS_CONF, hosts);
    }

    public static void setRedisHashKey(Job job, String hashKey) {
        job.getConfiguration().set(REDIS_HASH_KEY_CONF, hashKey);
    }

    public RecordWriter<Text, Text> getRecordWriter(TaskAttemptContext job)
            throws IOException, InterruptedException {
        return new RedisHashRecordWriter(job.getConfiguration().get(
                REDIS_HASH_KEY_CONF), job.getConfiguration().get(
                REDIS_HOSTS_CONF));
    }

    public void checkOutputSpecs(JobContext job) throws IOException {
        String hosts = job.getConfiguration().get(REDIS_HOSTS_CONF);
        if (hosts == null || hosts.isEmpty()) {
            throw new IOException(REDIS_HOSTS_CONF
                    + " is not set in configuration.");
        }

        String hashKey = job.getConfiguration().get(
                REDIS_HASH_KEY_CONF);
        if (hashKey == null || hashKey.isEmpty()) {
            throw new IOException(REDIS_HASH_KEY_CONF
                    + " is not set in configuration.");
        }
    }
}
```

```
        public OutputCommitter getOutputCommitter(TaskAttemptContext context)
                throws IOException, InterruptedException {
            return (new NullOutputFormat<Text, Text>()).getOutputCommitter(context);
        }

        public static class RedisHashRecordWriter extends RecordWriter<Text, Text> {
            // code in next section
        }
    }
```

RecordReader code. The RedisHashRecordWriter handles connecting to Redis via the Jedis
client and writing out the data. Each key/value pair is randomly written to a Redis
instance, providing an even distribution of all data across all Redis instances. The constructor stores the hash key to write to and creates a new Jedis instance.

The code then connects to the Jedis instance and maps it to an integer. This map is
used in the write method to get the assigned Jedis instance. The hash code is the key
is taken modulo the number of configured Redis instances. The key/value pair is then
written to the returned Jedis instance to the configured hash. Finally, all Jedis instances
are disconnected in the close method.

```
    public static class RedisHashRecordWriter extends RecordWriter<Text, Text> {

        private HashMap<Integer, Jedis> jedisMap = new HashMap<Integer, Jedis>();
        private String hashKey = null;

        public RedisHashRecordWriter(String hashKey, String hosts) {
            this.hashKey = hashKey;

            // Create a connection to Redis for each host
            // Map an integer 0-(numRedisInstances - 1) to the instance
            int i = 0;
            for (String host : hosts.split(",")) {
                Jedis jedis = new Jedis(host);
                jedis.connect();
                jedisMap.put(i, jedis);
                ++i;
            }
        }

        public void write(Text key, Text value) throws IOException,
                InterruptedException {
            // Get the Jedis instance that this key/value pair will be
            // written to
            Jedis j = jedisMap.get(Math.abs(key.hashCode()) % jedisMap.size());

            // Write the key/value pair
            j.hset(hashKey, key.toString(), value.toString());
        }

        public void close(TaskAttemptContext context) throws IOException,
                InterruptedException {
            // For each jedis instance, disconnect it
            for (Jedis jedis : jedisMap.values()) {
```

```
                jedis.disconnect();
            }
        }
    }
```

Mapper Code. The Mapper instance is very straightforward and looks like any other mapper. The user ID and reputation are retrieved from the record and then output. The output format does all the heavy lifting for us, allowing it to be reused multiple times to write whatever we want to a Redis hash.

```
public static class RedisOutputMapper extends
        Mapper<Object, Text, Text, Text> {

    private Text outkey = new Text();
    private Text outvalue = new Text();

    public void map(Object key, Text value, Context context)
            throws IOException, InterruptedException {

        Map<String, String> parsed = MRDPUtils.transformXmlToMap(value
                .toString());

        String userId = parsed.get("Id");
        String reputation = parsed.get("Reputation");

        // Set our output key and values
        outkey.set(userId);
        outvalue.set(reputation);

        context.write(outkey, outvalue);
    }
}
```

Driver Code. The driver code parses the command lines and calls our public static methods to set up writing data to Redis. The job is then submitted just like any other.

```
public static void main(String[] args) throws Exception {
    Configuration conf = new Configuration();

    Path inputPath = new Path(args[0]);
    String hosts = args[1];
    String hashName = args[2];

    Job job = new Job(conf, "Redis Output");
    job.setJarByClass(RedisOutputDriver.class);

    job.setMapperClass(RedisOutputMapper.class);
    job.setNumReduceTasks(0);

    job.setInputFormatClass(TextInputFormat.class);
    TextInputFormat.setInputPaths(job, inputPath);

    job.setOutputFormatClass(RedisHashOutputFormat.class);
    RedisHashOutputFormat.setRedisHosts(job, hosts);
    RedisHashOutputFormat.setRedisHashKey(job, hashName);
```

```
        job.setOutputKeyClass(Text.class);
        job.setOutputValueClass(Text.class);

        int code = job.waitForCompletion(true) ? 0 : 2;

        System.exit(code);
    }
```

External Source Input

Pattern Description

The *external source input* pattern doesn't load data from HDFS, but instead from some system outside of Hadoop, such as an SQL database or a web service.

Intent

You want to load data in parallel from a source that is not part of your MapReduce framework.

Motivation

The typical model for using MapReduce to analyze your data is to store it into your storage platform first (i.e., HDFS), then analyze it. With this pattern, you can hook up the MapReduce framework into an external source, such as a database or a web service, and pull the data directly into the mappers.

There are a few reasons why you might want to analyze the data directly from the source instead of staging it first. It may be faster to load the data from outside of Hadoop without having to stage it into files first. For example, dumping a database to the file system is likely to be an expensive operation, and taking it from the database directly ensures that the MapReduce job has the most up-to-date data available. A lot can happen on a busy cluster, and dumping a database prior to running an analytics can also fail, causing a stall in the entire pipeline.

In a MapReduce approach, the data is loaded in parallel rather than in a serial fashion. The caveat to this is that the source needs to have well-defined boundaries on which data is read in parallel in order to scale. For example, in the case of a sharded databases, each map task can be assigned a shard to load from the a table, thus allowing for very quick parallel loads of data without requiring a database scan.

Structure

Figure 7-3 shows the external source input structure.

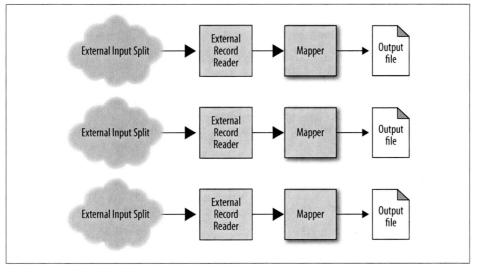

Figure 7-3. The structure of the external source input pattern

- The `InputFormat` creates all the `InputSplit` objects, which may be based on a custom object. An input split is a chunk of logical input, and that largely depends on the format in which it will be reading data. In this pattern, the input is not from a file-based input but an external source. The input could be from a series of SQL tables or a number of distributed services spread through the cluster. As long as the input can be read in parallel, this is a good fit for MapReduce.

- The `InputSplit` contains all the knowledge of where the sources are and how much of each source is going to be read. The framework uses the location information to help determine where to assign the map task. A custom `InputSplit` must also implement the `Writable` interface, because the framework uses the methods of this interface to transmit the input split information to a TaskTracker. The number of map tasks distributed among TaskTrackers is equivalent to the number of input splits generated by the input format. The `InputSplit` is then used to initialize a `RecordReader` for processing.

- The `RecordReader` uses the job configuration provided and `InputSplit` information to read key/value pairs. The implementation of this class depends on the data source being read. It sets up any connections required to read data from the external source, such as using JDBC to load from a database or creating a REST call to access a RESTful service.

Consequences

Data is loaded from the external source into the MapReduce job and the map phase doesn't know or care where that data came from.

Performance analysis

The bottleneck for a MapReduce job implementing this pattern is going to be the source or the network. The source may not scale well with multiple connections (e.g., a single-threaded SQL database isn't going to like 1,000 mappers all grabbing data at once). Another problem may be the network infrastructure. Given that the source is probably not in the MapReduce cluster's network backplane, the connections may be reaching out on a single connection on a slower public network. This should not be a problem if the source is inside the cluster.

External Source Input Example

Reading from Redis Instances

This example demonstrates how to read data we just wrote to Redis. Again, we take in a CSV list of Redis instance hosts in order to connect to and read all the data from the hash. Since we distributed the data across a number of Redis instances, this data can be read in parallel. All we need to do is create a map task for each Redis instance, connect to Redis, and then create key/value pairs out of all the data we retrieve. This example uses the identity mapper to simply output each key/value pair received from Redis.

The sections below with its corresponding code explain the following problem.

Problem: Given a list of Redis instances in CSV format, read all the data stored in a configured hash in parallel.

InputSplit code. The RedisInputSplit represents the data to be processed by an individual Mapper. In this example, we store the Redis instance hostname as the location of the input split, as well as the hash key. The input split implements the Writable interface, so that it is serializable by the framework, and includes a default constructor in order for the framework to create a new instance via reflection. We return the location via the getLocations method, in the hopes that the JobTracker will assign each map task to a TaskTracker that is hosting the data.

```
public static class RedisHashInputSplit extends InputSplit implements Writable {

    private String location = null;
    private String hashKey = null;

    public RedisHashInputSplit() {
        // Default constructor for reflection
    }

    public RedisHashInputSplit(String redisHost, String hash) {
        this.location = redisHost;
        this.hashKey = hash;
    }
```

```
        public String getHashKey() {
            return this.hashKey;
        }

        public void readFields(DataInput in) throws IOException {
            this.location = in.readUTF();
            this.hashKey = in.readUTF();
        }

        public void write(DataOutput out) throws IOException {
            out.writeUTF(location);
            out.writeUTF(hashKey);
        }

        public long getLength() throws IOException, InterruptedException {
            return 0;
        }

        public String[] getLocations() throws IOException, InterruptedException {
            return new String[] { location };
        }
    }
```

InputFormat code. The RedisHashInputFormat mirrors that of the RedisHashOutputFormat in many ways. It contains configuration variables to know which Redis instances to connect to and which hash to read from. In the getSplits method, the configuration is verified and a number of RedisHashInputSplits is created based on the number of Redis hosts. This will create one map task for each configured Redis instance. The Redis hostname and hash key are stored in the input split in order to be retrieved later by the RedisHashRecordReader. The createRecordReader method is called by the framework to get a new instance of a record reader. The record reader's initialize method is called by the framework, so we can just create a new instance and return it. Again by convention, this class contains two nested classes for the record reader and input split implementations.

```
    public static class RedisHashInputFormat extends InputFormat<Text, Text> {

        public static final String REDIS_HOSTS_CONF =
                "mapred.redishashinputformat.hosts";
        public static final String REDIS_HASH_KEY_CONF =
                "mapred.redishashinputformat.key";
        private static final Logger LOG = Logger
                .getLogger(RedisHashInputFormat.class);

        public static void setRedisHosts(Job job, String hosts) {
            job.getConfiguration().set(REDIS_HOSTS_CONF, hosts);
        }

        public static void setRedisHashKey(Job job, String hashKey) {
            job.getConfiguration().set(REDIS_HASH_KEY_CONF, hashKey);
        }

        public List<InputSplit> getSplits(JobContext job) throws IOException {
```

```
    String hosts = job.getConfiguration().get(REDIS_HOSTS_CONF);

    if (hosts == null || hosts.isEmpty()) {
        throw new IOException(REDIS_HOSTS_CONF
                + " is not set in configuration.");
    }

    String hashKey = job.getConfiguration().get(REDIS_HASH_KEY_CONF);
    if (hashKey == null || hashKey.isEmpty()) {
        throw new IOException(REDIS_HASH_KEY_CONF
                + " is not set in configuration.");
    }

    // Create an input split for each host
    List<InputSplit> splits = new ArrayList<InputSplit>();
    for (String host : hosts.split(",")) {
        splits.add(new RedisHashInputSplit(host, hashKey));
    }

    LOG.info("Input splits to process: " + splits.size());
    return splits;
}

public RecordReader<Text, Text> createRecordReader(InputSplit split,
        TaskAttemptContext context) throws IOException,
        InterruptedException {
    return new RedisHashRecordReader();
}

public static class RedisHashRecordReader extends RecordReader<Text, Text> {
    // code in next section
}

public static class RedisHashInputSplit extends InputSplit implements Writable {
    // code in next section
}
}
```

RecordReader code. The RedisHashRecordReader is where the most of the work is done. The initialize method is called by the framework and provided with an input split we created in the input format. Here, we get the Redis instance to connect to and the hash key. We then connect to Redis and get the number of key/value pairs we will be reading from Redis. The hash doesn't have a means to iterate or stream the data one at a time or in bulk, so we simply pull everything over and disconnect from Redis. We store an iterator over the entries and log some helpful statements along the way.

In nextKeyValue, we iterate through the map of entries one at a time and set the record reader's writable objects for the key and value. A return value of true informs the framework that there is a key/value pair to process. Once we have exhausted all the key/value pairs, false is returned so the map task can complete.

The other methods of the record reader are used by the framework to get the current key and value for the mapper to process. It is worthwhile to reuse this object whenever possible. The `getProgress` method is useful for reporting gradual status to the Job-Tracker and should also be reused if possible. Finally, the `close` method is for finalizing the process. Since we pulled all the information and disconnected from Redis in the `initialize` method, there is nothing to do here.

```java
public static class RedisHashRecordReader extends RecordReader<Text, Text> {

    private static final Logger LOG =
            Logger.getLogger(RedisHashRecordReader.class);
    private Iterator<Entry<String, String>> keyValueMapIter = null;
    private Text key = new Text(), value = new Text();
    private float processedKVs = 0, totalKVs = 0;
    private Entry<String, String> currentEntry = null;

    public void initialize(InputSplit split, TaskAttemptContext context)
            throws IOException, InterruptedException {
        // Get the host location from the InputSplit
        String host = split.getLocations()[0];
        String hashKey = ((RedisHashInputSplit) split).getHashKey();

        LOG.info("Connecting to " + host + " and reading from "
                + hashKey);

        Jedis jedis = new Jedis(host);
        jedis.connect();
        jedis.getClient().setTimeoutInfinite();

        // Get all the key/value pairs from the Redis instance and store
        // them in memory
        totalKVs = jedis.hlen(hashKey);
        keyValueMapIter = jedis.hgetAll(hashKey).entrySet().iterator();
        LOG.info("Got " + totalKVs + " from " + hashKey);
        jedis.disconnect();
    }

    public boolean nextKeyValue() throws IOException,
            InterruptedException {

        // If the key/value map still has values
        if (keyValueMapIter.hasNext()) {
            // Get the current entry and set the Text objects to the entry
            currentEntry = keyValueMapIter.next();
            key.set(currentEntry.getKey());
            value.set(currentEntry.getValue());
            return true;
        } else {
            // No more values? return false.
            return false;
        }
    }

    public Text getCurrentKey() throws IOException,
            InterruptedException {
        return key;
    }
```

```
public Text getCurrentValue() throws IOException,
        InterruptedException {
    return value;
}

public float getProgress() throws IOException, InterruptedException {
    return processedKVs / totalKVs;
}

public void close() throws IOException {
    // nothing to do here
}
}
```

Driver code. Much like the previous example's driver, we use the `public static` methods provided by the input format to modify the job configuration. Since we are just using the identity mapper, we don't need to set any special classes. The number of reduce tasks is set to zero to specify that this is a map-only job.

```
public static void main(String[] args) throws Exception {
    Configuration conf = new Configuration();

    String hosts = otherArgs[0];
    String hashKey = otherArgs[1];
    Path outputDir = new Path(otherArgs[2]);

    Job job = new Job(conf, "Redis Input");
    job.setJarByClass(RedisInputDriver.class);

    // Use the identity mapper
    job.setNumReduceTasks(0);

    job.setInputFormatClass(RedisHashInputFormat.class);
    RedisHashInputFormat.setRedisHosts(job, hosts);
    RedisHashInputFormat.setRedisHashKey(job, hashKey);

    job.setOutputFormatClass(TextOutputFormat.class);
    TextOutputFormat.setOutputPath(job, outputDir);

    job.setOutputKeyClass(Text.class);
    job.setOutputValueClass(Text.class);

    System.exit(job.waitForCompletion(true) ? 0 : 3);
}
```

Partition Pruning

Pattern Description

Partition pruning configures the way the framework picks input splits and drops files from being loaded into MapReduce based on the name of the file.

Intent

You have a set of data that is partitioned by a predetermined value.

Motivation

Typically, all the data loaded into a MapReduce job is assigned into map tasks and read in parallel. If entire files are going to be thrown out based on the query, loading all of the files is a large waste of processing time. By partitioning the data by a common value, you can avoid significant amounts of processing time by looking only where the data would exist. For example, if you are commonly analyzing data based on data ranges, partitioning your data by date will make it so you only need to load the data inside of that range.

The added caveat to this pattern is this should be handled transparently, so you can run the same MapReduce job over and over again, but over different data sets. This is done by simply changing the data you are querying for, rather than changing the implementation of the job. A great way to do this would be to strip away how the data is stored on the file system and instead put it inside an input format. The input format knows where to locate and get the data, allowing the number of map tasks generated to change based on the query.

 This is exceptionally useful if the data storage is volatile and likely to change. If you have dozens of analytics using some type of partitioned input format, you can change the input format implementation and simply recompile all analytics using the new input format code. Since all your analytics get input from a query rather than a file, you don't need to re-implement how the data is read into the analytic. This can save a massive amount of development time, making you look really good to your boss!

Structure

Figure 7-4 shows the structure for partition pruning, explained below.

- The InputFormat is where this pattern comes to life. The getSplits method is where we pay special attention, because it determines the input splits that will be created, and thus the number of map tasks. While the configuration is typically a set of files, configuration turns into more of a query than a set of file paths. For instance, if data is stored on a file system by date, the InputFormat can accept a date range as input, then determine which folders to pull into the MapReduce job. If data is sharded in an external service by date, say 12 shards for each month, only one shard needs to be read by the MapReduce job when looking for data in March. The key here is that the input format determines where the data comes from based on a query, rather than passing in a set of files.

- The `RecordReader` implementation depends on how the data is being stored. If it is a file-based input, something like a `LineRecordReader` can be used to read key/value pairs from a file. If it is an external source, you'll have to customize something more to your needs.

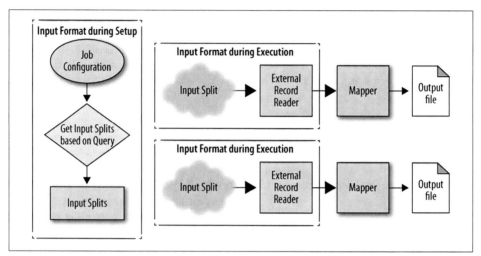

Figure 7-4. The structure of the partition pruning pattern

Consequences

Partition pruning changes only the amount of data that is read by the MapReduce job, not the eventual outcome of the analytic. The main reason for partition pruning is to reduce the overall processing time to read in data. This is done by ignoring input that will not produce any output before it even gets to a map task.

Resemblances

SQL

Many modern relational databases handle partition pruning transparently. When you create the table, you specify how the database should partition the data and the database will handle the rest on inserts. Hive also supports partitioning.

```
CREATE TABLE parted_data
(foo_date    DATE)
PARTITION BY RANGE(foo_date)
(
PARTITION foo_2012 VALUES LESS THAN(TO_DATE('01/01/2013','DD/MM/YYYY')),
PARTITION foo_2011 VALUES LESS THAN(TO_DATE('01/01/2012','DD/MM/YYYY')),
PARTITION foo_2010 VALUES LESS THAN(TO_DATE('01/01/2011','DD/MM/YYYY')),
);
```

Then, when you query with a specific value in the `WHERE` clause, the database will automatically use only the relevant partitions.

```
SELECT * FROM parted_data WHERE foo_date=TO_DATE('01/31/2012');
```

Performance analysis

The data in this pattern is loaded into each map task is as fast as in any other pattern. Only the number of tasks changes based on the query at hand. Utilizing this pattern can provide massive gains by reducing the number of tasks that need to be created that would not have generated output anyways. Outside of the I/O, the performance depends on the other pattern being applied in the map and reduce phases of the job.

Partition Pruning Examples

Partitioning by last access date to Redis instances

This example demonstrates a smarter way to store and read data in Redis. Rather than randomly distributing the user-to-reputation mappings, we can partition this data on particular criteria. The user-to-reputation mappings are partitioned based on last access date and stored in six different Redis instances. Two months of data are stored in separate hashes on each Redis instance. That is, January and February are stored in different hashes on Redis instance 0, March and April on instance 1, and so on

By distributing the data in this manner, we can more intelligently read it based on a user query. Whereas the previous examples took in a list of Redis instances and a hash key via the command line, this pattern hardcodes all the logic of where and how to store the data in the output format, as well as in the input format. This completely strips away knowledge from the mapper and reducer of where the data is coming from, which has its advantages and disadvantages for a developer using our input and output formats.

 It may not be the best idea to actually hardcode information into the Java code itself, but instead have a rarely-changing configuration file that can be found by your formats. This way, things can still be changed if necessary and prevent a recompile. Environment variables work nicely, or it can just be passed in via the command line.

The sections below with its corresponding code explain the following problem.

Problem: Given a set of user data, partition the user-to-reputation mappings by last access date across six Redis instances.

Custom WritableComparable code. To help better store information, a custom `WritableCom parable` is implemented in order to allow the mapper to set information needed by the record writer. This class contains methods to set and get the field name to be stored in Redis, as well as the last access month. The last access month accepts a zero-based integer value for the month, but is later turned into a string representation for easier querying in the next example. Take the time to implement the compareTo, toString, and hashCode methods (like every good Java developer!).

```java
public static class RedisKey implements WritableComparable<RedisKey> {

    private int lastAccessMonth = 0;
    private Text field = new Text();

    public int getLastAccessMonth() {
        return this.lastAccessMonth;
    }

    public void setLastAccessMonth(int lastAccessMonth) {
        this.lastAccessMonth = lastAccessMonth;
    }

    public Text getField() {
        return this.field;
    }

    public void setField(String field) {
        this.field.set(field);
    }

    public void readFields(DataInput in) throws IOException {
        lastAccessMonth = in.readInt();
        this.field.readFields(in);
    }

    public void write(DataOutput out) throws IOException {
        out.writeInt(lastAccessMonth);
        this.field.write(out);
    }

    public int compareTo(RedisKey rhs) {
        if (this.lastAccessMonth == rhs.getLastAccessMonth()) {
            return this.field.compareTo(rhs.getField());
        } else {
            return this.lastAccessMonth < rhs.getLastAccessMonth() ? -1 : 1;
        }
    }

    public String toString() {
        return this.lastAccessMonth + "\t" + this.field.toString();
    }

    public int hashCode() {
        return toString().hashCode();
    }
}
```

OutputFormat code. This output format is extremely basic, as all the grunt work is handled in the record writer. The main thing to focus on is the templated arguments when extending the InputFormat class. This output format accepts our custom class as the output key and a Text object as the output value. Any other classes will cause errors when trying to write any output.

Since our record writer implementation is coded to a specific and known output, there is no need to verify any output specification of the job. An output committer is still required by the framework, so we use NullOutputFormat's output committer.

```
public static class RedisLastAccessOutputFormat
        extends OutputFormat<RedisKey, Text> {

    public RecordWriter<RedisKey, Text> getRecordWriter(
            TaskAttemptContext job) throws IOException, InterruptedException {
        return new RedisLastAccessRecordWriter();
    }

    public void checkOutputSpecs(JobContext context) throws IOException,
            InterruptedException {
    }

    public OutputCommitter getOutputCommitter(TaskAttemptContext context)
            throws IOException, InterruptedException {
        return (new NullOutputFormat<Text, Text>()).getOutputCommitter(context);
    }

    public static class RedisLastAccessRecordWriter
            extends RecordWriter<RedisKey, Text> {
        // Code in next section
    }
}
```

RecordWriter code. The RedisLastAccessRecordWriter is templated to accept the same classes as the output format. The construction of the class connects to all six Redis instances and puts them in a map. This map stores the month-to-Redis-instance mappings and is used in the write method to retrieve the proper instance. The write method then uses a map of month int to a three character month code for serialization. This map is omitted for brevity, but looks stores something like 0→JAN, 1→FEB, ..., 11→DEC. This means all the hashes in Redis are named based on the three-character month code. The close method disconnects all the Redis instances.

```
public static class RedisLastAccessRecordWriter
        extends RecordWriter<RedisKey, Text> {

    private HashMap<Integer, Jedis> jedisMap = new HashMap<Integer, Jedis>();

    public RedisLastAccessRecordWriter() {
        // Create a connection to Redis for each host
        int i = 0;
        for (String host : MRDPUtils.REDIS_INSTANCES) {
            Jedis jedis = new Jedis(host);
            jedis.connect();
            jedisMap.put(i, jedis);
            jedisMap.put(i + 1, jedis);
            i += 2;
```

```
      }
    }

    public void write(RedisKey key, Text value) throws IOException,
        InterruptedException {
      // Get the Jedis instance that this key/value pair will be
      // written to -- (0,1)->0, (2-3)->1, ... , (10-11)->5
      Jedis j = jedisMap.get(key.getLastAccessMonth());

      // Write the key/value pair
      j.hset(MONTH_FROM_INT.get(key.getLastAccessMonth()), key
          .getField().toString(), value.toString());
    }

    public void close(TaskAttemptContext context) throws IOException,
        InterruptedException {
      // For each jedis instance, disconnect it
      for (Jedis jedis : jedisMap.values()) {
        jedis.disconnect();
      }
    }
  }
}
```

Mapper code. The mapper code parses each input record and sets the values for the output RedisKey and the output value. The month of the last access data is parsed via the Calendar and SimpleDateFormat classes.

```
public static class RedisLastAccessOutputMapper extends
    Mapper<Object, Text, RedisKey, Text> {

  // This object will format the creation date string into a Date object
  private final static SimpleDateFormat frmt = new SimpleDateFormat(
      "yyyy-MM-dd'T'HH:mm:ss.SSS");

  private RedisKey outkey = new RedisKey();
  private Text outvalue = new Text();

  public void map(Object key, Text value, Context context)
      throws IOException, InterruptedException {

    Map<String, String> parsed = MRDPUtils.transformXmlToMap(value
        .toString());

    String userId = parsed.get("Id");
    String reputation = parsed.get("Reputation");

    // Grab the last access date
    String strDate = parsed.get("LastAccessDate");

    // Parse the string into a Calendar object
    Calendar cal = Calendar.getInstance();
    cal.setTime(frmt.parse(strDate));

    // Set our output key and values
    outkey.setLastAccessMonth(cal.get(Calendar.MONTH));
```

```
            outkey.setField(userId);
            outvalue.set(reputation);

            context.write(outkey, outvalue);
        }
    }
```

Driver code. The driver looks very similar to a more basic job configuration. All the special configuration is entirely handled by the output format class and record writer. Again, an output directory is set but later deleted after the job completes.

```
    public static void main(String[] args) throws Exception {
        Configuration conf = new Configuration();

        Path inputPath = new Path(args[0]);

        Job job = new Job(conf, "Redis Last Access Output");
        job.setJarByClass(PartitionPruningOutputDriver.class);

        job.setMapperClass(RedisLastAccessOutputMapper.class);
        job.setNumReduceTasks(0);

        job.setInputFormatClass(TextInputFormat.class);
        TextInputFormat.setInputPaths(job, inputPath);

        job.setOutputFormatClass(RedisHashSetOutputFormat.class);

        job.setOutputKeyClass(RedisKey.class);
        job.setOutputValueClass(Text.class);

        int code = job.waitForCompletion(true) ? 0 : 2;

        System.exit(code);
    }
```

Querying for user reputation by last access date

This example demonstrates how to query for the information we just stored in Redis. Unlike most examples, where you provide some path to files in HDFS, we instead just pass in the months of data we want. Figuring out where to get the data is entirely handled intelligently by the input format.

The heart of partition pruning is to avoid reading data that you don't have to read. By storing the user-to-reputation mappings across six different Redis servers, we need to connect only to the instances that are hosting the requested month's data. Even better, we need to read only from the hashes that are holding the specific month. For instance, passing in "JAN,FEB,MAR,NOV" on the command line will create three input splits, one for each Redis instance hosting the data (0, 1, and 5). All the data on Redis instance 0 will be read, but only the first months on Redis instances 1 and 5 will be pulled. This is much better than having to connect to all the desired instances and read all the data, only to throw most of it away!

The sections below with its corresponding code explain the following problem.

Problem: Given a query for user to reputation mappings by months, read only the data required to satisfy the query in parallel.

InputSplit code. The input split shown here is very similar to the input split in "External Source Input Example" on page 186. Instead of storing one hash key, we are going to store multiple hash keys. This is because the data is partitioned based on month, instead of all the data being randomly distributed in one hash.

```
public static class RedisLastAccessInputSplit
        extends InputSplit implements Writable {

    private String location = null;
    private List<String> hashKeys = new ArrayList<String>();

    public RedisLastAccessInputSplit() {
        // Default constructor for reflection
    }

    public RedisLastAccessInputSplit(String redisHost) {
        this.location = redisHost;
    }

    public void addHashKey(String key) {
        hashKeys.add(key);
    }

    public void removeHashKey(String key) {
        hashKeys.remove(key);
    }

    public List<String> getHashKeys() {
        return hashKeys;
    }

    public void readFields(DataInput in) throws IOException {
        location = in.readUTF();
        int numKeys = in.readInt();
        hashKeys.clear();
        for (int i = 0; i < numKeys; ++i) {
            hashKeys.add(in.readUTF());
        }
    }

    public void write(DataOutput out) throws IOException {
        out.writeUTF(location);
        out.writeInt(hashKeys.size());
        for (String key : hashKeys) {
            out.writeUTF(key);
        }
    }

    public long getLength() throws IOException, InterruptedException {
        return 0;
```

```
    }
    public String[] getLocations() throws IOException, InterruptedException {
        return new String[] { location };
    }
}
```

InputFormat code. This input format class intelligently creates RedisLastAccessInputS
plit objects from the selected months of data. Much like the output format we showed
earlier in "OutputFormat code" on page 194 writes RedisKey objects, this input format
reads the same objects and is templated to enforce this on mapper implementations. It
initially creates a hash map of host-to-input splits in order to add the hash keys to the
input split, rather than adding both months of data to the same split. If a split has not
been created for a particular month, a new one is created and the month hash key is
added. Otherwise, the hash key is added to the split that has already been created. A
List is then created out of the values stored in the map. This will create a number of
input splits equivalent to the number of Redis instances required to satisfy the query.

There are a number of helpful hash maps to help convert a month string to an integer,
as well as figure out which Redis instance hosts which month of data. The initialization
of these hash maps are ommitted from the **static** block for brevity.

```
public static class RedisLastAccessInputFormat
        extends InputFormat<RedisKey, Text> {

    public static final String REDIS_SELECTED_MONTHS_CONF =
            "mapred.redilastaccessinputformat.months";
    private static final HashMap<String, Integer> MONTH_FROM_STRING =
            new HashMap<String, Integer>();
    private static final HashMap<String, String> MONTH_TO_INST_MAP =
            new HashMap<String, String>();
    private static final Logger LOG = Logger
            .getLogger(RedisLastAccessInputFormat.class);

    static {
        // Initialize month to Redis instance map
        // Initialize month 3 character code to integer
    }

    public static void setRedisLastAccessMonths(Job job, String months) {
        job.getConfiguration().set(REDIS_SELECTED_MONTHS_CONF, months);
    }

    public List<InputSplit> getSplits(JobContext job) throws IOException {

        String months = job.getConfiguration().get(
                REDIS_SELECTED_MONTHS_CONF);

        if (months == null || months.isEmpty()) {
            throw new IOException(REDIS_SELECTED_MONTHS_CONF
                    + " is null or empty.");
        }
```

```
        // Create input splits from the input months
        HashMap<String, RedisLastAccessInputSplit> instanceToSplitMap =
                new HashMap<String, RedisLastAccessInputSplit>();

        for (String month : months.split(",")) {
            String host = MONTH_TO_INST_MAP.get(month);
            RedisLastAccessInputSplit split = instanceToSplitMap.get(host);
            if (split == null) {
                split = new RedisLastAccessInputSplit(host);
                split.addHashKey(month);
                instanceToSplitMap.put(host, split);
            } else {
                split.addHashKey(month);
            }
        }

        LOG.info("Input splits to process: " +
                instanceToSplitMap.values().size());
        return new ArrayList<InputSplit>(instanceToSplitMap.values());
    }

    public RecordReader<RedisKey, Text> createRecordReader(
            InputSplit split, TaskAttemptContext context)
            throws IOException, InterruptedException {
        return new RedisLastAccessRecordReader();
    }

    public static class RedisLastAccessRecordReader
            extends RecordReader<RedisKey, Text> {
        // Code in next section
    }
}
```

RecordReader code. The RedisLastAccessRecordReader is a bit more complicated than the other record readers we have seen. It needs to read from multiple hashes, rather than just reading everything at once in the initialize method. Here, the configuration is simply read in this method.

In nextKeyValue, a new connection to Redis is created if the iterator through the hash is null, or if we have reached the end of all the hashes to read. If the iterator through the hashes does not have a next value, we immediately return false, as there is no more data for the map task. Otherwise, we connect to Redis and pull all the data from the specific hash. The hash iterator is then used to exhaust all the field value pairs from Redis. A do-while loop is used to ensure that once a hash iterator is complete, it will loop back around to get data from the next hash or inform the task there is no more data to be read.

The implementation of the remaining methods are identical to that of the RedisHashRe cordReader and are omitted.

```
    public static class RedisLastAccessRecordReader
            extends RecordReader<RedisKey, Text> {
```

```
private static final Logger LOG = Logger
        .getLogger(RedisLastAccessRecordReader.class);
private Entry<String, String> currentEntry = null;
private float processedKVs = 0, totalKVs = 0;
private int currentHashMonth = 0;
private Iterator<Entry<String, String>> hashIterator = null;
private Iterator<String> hashKeys = null;
private RedisKey key = new RedisKey();
private String host = null;
private Text value = new Text();

public void initialize(InputSplit split, TaskAttemptContext context)
        throws IOException, InterruptedException {

    // Get the host location from the InputSplit
    host = split.getLocations()[0];

    // Get an iterator of all the hash keys we want to read
    hashKeys = ((RedisLastAccessInputSplit) split)
            .getHashKeys().iterator();

    LOG.info("Connecting to " + host);
}

public boolean nextKeyValue() throws IOException,
        InterruptedException {

    boolean nextHashKey = false;
    do {
        // if this is the first call or the iterator does not have a
        // next
        if (hashIterator == null || !hashIterator.hasNext()) {
            // if we have reached the end of our hash keys, return
            // false
            if (!hashKeys.hasNext()) {
                // ultimate end condition, return false
                return false;
            } else {
                // Otherwise, connect to Redis and get all
                // the name/value pairs for this hash key
                Jedis jedis = new Jedis(host);
                jedis.connect();
                String strKey = hashKeys.next();
                currentHashMonth = MONTH_FROM_STRING.get(strKey);
                hashIterator = jedis.hgetAll(strKey).entrySet()
                        .iterator();
                jedis.disconnect();
            }
        }

        // If the key/value map still has values
        if (hashIterator.hasNext()) {
            // Get the current entry and set
            // the Text objects to the entry
            currentEntry = hashIterator.next();
```

```
                    key.setLastAccessMonth(currentHashMonth);
                    key.setField(currentEntry.getKey());
                    value.set(currentEntry.getValue());
                } else {
                    nextHashKey = true;
                }
            } while (nextHashKey);

            return true;
        }


        ...

    }
```

Driver code. The driver code sets the months most recently accessed passed in via the command line. This configuration parameter is used by the input format to determine which Redis instances to read from, rather than reading from every Redis instance. It also sets the output directory for the job. Again, it uses the identity mapper rather than performing any analysis on the data retrieved.

```
public static void main(String[] args) throws Exception {
    Configuration conf = new Configuration();

    String lastAccessMonths = args[0];
    Path outputDir = new Path(args[1]);

    Job job = new Job(conf, "Redis Input");
    job.setJarByClass(PartitionPruningInputDriver.class);

    // Use the identity mapper
    job.setNumReduceTasks(0);

    job.setInputFormatClass(RedisLastAccessInputFormat.class);
    RedisLastAccessInputFormat.setRedisLastAccessMonths(job,
            lastAccessMonths);

    job.setOutputFormatClass(TextOutputFormat.class);
    TextOutputFormat.setOutputPath(job, outputDir);

    job.setOutputKeyClass(RedisKey.class);
    job.setOutputValueClass(Text.class);

    System.exit(job.waitForCompletion(true) ? 0 : 2);
}
```

CHAPTER 8

Final Thoughts and the Future of Design Patterns

At the time of this book's writing, MapReduce is moving quickly. New features and new systems are popping up every day and new users are out in droves. More importantly for the subject of *MapReduce Design Patterns*, a growing number of users brings along a growing number of experts. These experts are the ones that will drive the community's documentation of design patterns not only by sharing new ones, but also by maturing the already existing ones.

In this chapter, we'll discuss and speculate what the future holds for MapReduce design patterns. Where will they come from? What systems will benefit from design patterns? How will today's design patterns change with the technology? What trends in data will affect the design patterns of today?

Trends in the Nature of Data

MapReduce systems such as Hadoop aren't being used just for text analysis anymore. Increasing number of users are deploying MapReduce jobs that analyze data once thought to be too hard for the paradigm. New design patterns are surely to arise to deal with this to transform a solution from pushing the limits of the system to making it daily practice.

Images, Audio, and Video

One of the most obvious trends in the nature of data is the rise of image, audio, and video analysis. This form of data is a good candidate for a distributed system using MapReduce because these files are typically very large. Retailers want to analyze their security video to detect what stores are busiest. Medical imaging analysis is becoming harder with the astronomical resolutions of the pictures. Unfortunately, as a text processing platform, some artifacts remain in MapReduce that make this type of analysis challenging. Since this is a MapReduce book, we'll acknowledge the fact that analyzing this type of data is really hard, even on a single node with not much data, but we will not go into more detail.

One place we may see a surge in design patterns is dealing with multidimensional data. Videos have colored pixels that change over time, laid out on a two-dimensional grid. To top it off, they also may have an audio track. MapReduce follows a very straight-forward, one-dimensional tape paradigm. The data is in order from front to back and that is how it is analyzed. Therefore, it's challenging to take a look at 10-pixel by 10-pixel by 5-second section of video and audio as a "record." As multidimensional data increases in popularity, we'll see more patterns showing how to logically split the data into records and input splits properly. Or, it is possible that new systems will fill this niche. For example, SciDB, an open-source analytical database, is specifically built to deal with multi-dimensional data.

Streaming Data

MapReduce is traditionally a batch analytics system, but streaming analytics feels like a natural progression. In many production MapReduce systems, data is constantly streaming in and then gets processed in batch on an interval. For example, data from web server logs are streaming in, but the MapReduce job is only executed every hour.

This is inconvenient for a few reasons. First, processing an hour's worth of data at once can strain resources. Because it's coming in gradually, processing it as it arrives will spread out the computational resources of the cluster better. Second, MapReduce systems typically depend on a relatively large block size to reduce the overhead of distributed computation. When data is streaming in, it comes in record by record. These hurdles make processing streaming data difficult with MapReduce.

As in the previous section about large media files, this gap is likely to be filled by a combination of two things: new patterns and new systems. Some new operational patterns for storing data of this nature might crop up as users take this problem more seriously in production. New patterns for doing streaming-like analysis in the framework of batch MapReduce will mature. Novel systems that deal with streaming data in Hadoop have cropped up, most notably the commercial product HStreaming and the open-source Storm platform, recently released by Twitter.

The authors actually considered some "streaming patterns" to be put into this book, but none of them were anywhere near mature enough or vetted enough to be officially documented.

The first is an exotic `RecordReader`. The map task starts up and streams data into the `RecordReader` instead of loading already existing data from a file. This has significant operational concerns that make it difficult to implement.

The second is splitting up the job into several one-map task jobs that get fired off every time some data comes in. The output is partitioned into k bins for future "reducers." Every now and then, a map-only job with k mappers starts up and plays the role of the reducer.

The Effects of YARN

YARN (Yet Another Resource Negotiator) is a high-visibility advancement of Hadoop MapReduce that is currently in version 0.23 and will eventually make it into the current stable release. Many in the Hadoop community cannot wait for it to mature, as it fills a number of gaps. At a high level, YARN splits the responsibilities of the JobTracker and TaskTrackers into a single ResourceManager, one NodeManager per node, and one ApplicationMaster per application or job. The ResourceManager and NodeManagers abstract away computational resources from the current map-and-reduce slot paradigm and allow arbitrary computation. Each ApplicationMaster handles a framework-specific model of computation that breaks down a job into resource allocation requests, which is in turn handled by the ResourceManager and the NodeManagers.

What this does is separate the computation framework from the resource management. In this model, MapReduce is just another framework and doesn't look any more special than a custom frameworks such as MPI, streaming, commercial products, or who knows what.

MapReduce design patterns will not change in and of themselves, because MapReduce will still exist. However, now that users can build their own distributed application frameworks or use other frameworks with YARN, some of the more intricate solutions to problems may be more natural to solve in another framework. We'll see some design patterns that will still exist but just aren't used very much anymore, since the natural solution lies in another distributed framework. We will likely eventually see ApplicationMaster patterns for building completely new frameworks for solving a type of problem.

Patterns as a Library or Component

Over time, as patterns get more and more use, someone may decide to componentize that pattern as a built-in utility class in a library. This type of progression is seen in traditional design patterns, as well, in which the library parameterizes the pattern and you just interact with it, instead of reimplementing the pattern. This is seen with several of the custom Hadoop MapReduce pieces that exist in the core Hadoop libraries, such as `TotalOrderPartitioner`, `ChainReducer`, and `MultipleOutputs`.

This is very natural from a standpoint of code reuse. The patterns in this book are presented to help you start solving a problem from scratch. By adding a layer of indirection, modules that set up the job for you and offer several parameters as points of customization can be helpful in the long run.

How You Can Help

If you think you've developed a novel MapReduce pattern that you haven't seen before and you are feeling generous, you should definitely go through the motions of documenting it and sharing it with the world.

There are a number of questions you should try to answer. These were some of the questions we considered when choosing the patterns for this book.

Is the problem you are trying to solve similar to another pattern's target problem?
Identifying this is important for preventing any sort of confusion. Chapter 5, in particular, takes this question seriously.

What is at the root of this pattern?
You probably developed the pattern to solve a very specific problem and have custom code interspersed throughout. Developers will be smart enough to tailor a pattern to their own problem or mix patterns to solve their more complicated problems. Tear down the code and only have the pattern left.

What is the performance profile?
Understanding what kinds of resources a pattern will use is important for gauging how many reducers will be needed and in general how expensive this operation will be. For example, some people may be surprised how resource intensive sorting is in a distributed system.

How might have you solved this problem otherwise?
Finding some examples outside of a MapReduce context (such as we did with SQL and Pig) is useful as a metaphor that helps conceptually bridge to a MapReduce-specific solution.

Bloom Filters

Overview

Conceived by Burton Howard Bloom in 1970, a Bloom filter is a probabilistic data structure used to test whether a member is an element of a set. Bloom filters have a strong space advantage over other data structures such as a Java Set, in that each element uses the same amount of space, no matter its actual size. For example, a string of 32 characters takes up the same amount of memory in a Bloom filter as a string of 1024 characters, which is drastically different than other data structures. Bloom filters are introduced as part of a pattern in "Bloom Filtering" on page 47.

While the data structure itself has vast memory advantages, it is not always 100% accurate. While false positives are possible, false negatives are not. This means the result of each test is either a definitive "no" or "maybe." You will never get a definitive "yes." With a traditional Bloom filter, elements can be added to the set, but not removed. There are a number of Bloom filter implementations that address this limitation, such as a Counting Bloom Filter, but they typically require more memory. As more elements are added to the set, the probability of false positives increases. Bloom filters cannot be resized like other data structures. Once they have been sized and trained, they cannot be reverse-engineered to achieve the original set nor resized and still maintain the same data set representation.

The following variables are used in the more detailed explanation of a Bloom filter below:

m

The number of bits in the filter

n

The number of members in the set

p

The desired false positive rate

k

The number of different hash functions used to map some element to one of the *m* bits with a uniform random distribution.

A Bloom filter is represented by a continuous string of *m* bits initialized to zero. For each element in *n*, *k* hash function values are taken modulo *m* to achieve an index from zero to *m* - *1*. The bits of the Bloom filter at the resulting indices are set to one. This operation is often called *training* a Bloom filter. As elements are added to the Bloom filter, some bits may already be set to one from previous elements in the set. When testing whether a member is an element of the set, the same hash functions are used to check the bits of the array. If a single bit of all the hashes is set to zero, the test returns "no." If all the bits are turned on, the test returns "maybe." If the member was used to train the filter, the *k* hashs would have set all the bits to one.

The result of the test cannot be a definitive "yes" because the bits may have been turned on by a combination of other elements. If the test returns "maybe" but should have been "no," this is known as a *false positive*. Thankfully, the false positive rate can be controlled if *n* is known ahead of time, or at least an approximation of *n*.

The following sections describe a number of common use cases for Bloom filters, the limitations of Bloom filters and a means to tweak your Bloom filter to get the lowest false positive rate. A code example of training and using a Hadoop Bloom filter can be found in "Bloom filter training" on page 51.

Use Cases

This section lists a number of common use cases for Bloom filters. In any application that can benefit from a Boolean test prior to some sort of expensive operation, a Bloom filter can most likely be utilized to reduce a large number of unneeded operations.

Representing a Data Set

One of the most basic uses of a Bloom filter is to represent very large data sets in applications. A data set with millions of elements can take up gigabytes of memory, as well as the expensive I/O required simply to pull the data set off disk. A Bloom filter can drastically reduce the number of bytes required to represent this data set, allowing it to fit in memory and decrease the amount of time required to read. The obvious downside to representing a large data set with a Bloom filter is the false positives. Whether or not this is a big deal varies from one use case to another, but there are ways to get a 100% validation of each test. A post-process join operation on the actual data set can be executed, or querying an external database is also a good option.

Reduce Queries to External Database

One very common use case of Bloom filters is to reduce the number of queries to databases that are bound to return many empty or negative results. By doing an initial test using a Bloom filter, an application can throw away a large number of negative results before ever querying the database. If latency is not much of a concern, the positive Bloom filter tests can be stored into a temporary buffer. Once a certain limit is hit, the buffer can then be iterated through to perform a bulk query against the database. This will reduce the load on the system and keep it more stable. This method is exceptionally useful if a large number of the queries are bound to return negative results. If most results are positive answers, then a Bloom filter may just be a waste of precious memory.

Google BigTable

Google's BigTable design uses Bloom filters to reduce the need to read a file for nonexistent data. By keeping a Bloom filter for each block in memory, the service can do an initial check to determine whether it is worthwhile to read the file. If the test returns a negative value, the service can return immediately. Positive tests result in the service opening the file to validate whether the data exists or not. By filtering out negative queries, the performance of this database increases drastically.

Downsides

The false positive rate is the largest downside to using a Bloom filter. Even with a Bloom filter large enough to have a 1% false positive rate, if you have ten million tests that should result in a negative result, then about a hundred thousand of those tests are going to return positive results. Whether or not this is a real issue depends largely on the use case.

Traditionally, you cannot remove elements from a Bloom filter set after training the elements. Removing an element would require bits to be set to zero, but it is extremely likely that more than one element hashed to a particular bit. Setting it to zero would destroy any future tests of other elements. One way around this limitation is called a *Counting Bloom Filter*, which keeps an integer at each index of the array. When training a Bloom filter, instead of setting a bit to zero, the integers are increased by one. When an element is removed, the integer is decreased by one. This requires much more memory than using a string of bits, and also lends itself to having overflow errors with large data sets. That is, adding one to the maximum allowed integer will result in a negative value (or zero, if using unsigned integers) and cause problems when executing tests over the filter and removing elements.

When using a Bloom filter in a distributed application like MapReduce, it is difficult to actively train a Bloom filter in the sense of a database. After a Bloom filter is trained and serialized to HDFS, it can easily be read and used by other applications. However, further training of the Bloom filter would require expensive I/O operations, whether it be sending messages to every other process using the Bloom filter or implementing some sort of locking mechanism. At this point, an external database might as well be used.

Tweaking Your Bloom Filter

Before training a Bloom filter with the elements of a set, it can be very beneficial to know an approximation of the number of elements. If you know this ahead of time, a Bloom filter can be sized appropriately to have a hand-picked false positive rate. The lower the false positive rate, the more bits required for the Bloom filter's array. Figure A-1 shows how to calculate the size of a Bloom filter with an optimal-k.

$$m = \frac{-n \cdot ln(p)}{ln(2)^2}$$

Figure A-1. Optimal size of a Bloom filter with an optimal-k

The following Java helper function calculates the optimal m.

```
/**
 * Gets the optimal Bloom filter sized based on the input parameters and the
 * optimal number of hash functions.
 *
 * @param numElements
 *            The number of elements used to train the set.
 * @param falsePosRate
 *            The desired false positive rate.
 * @return The optimal Bloom filter size.
 */
public static int getOptimalBloomFilterSize(int numElements,
        float falsePosRate) {
    return (int) (-numElements * (float) Math.log(falsePosRate)
            / Math.pow(Math.log(2), 2));
}
```

The optimal-k is defined as the number of hash functions that should be used for the Bloom filter. With a Hadoop Bloom filter implementation, the size of the Bloom filter and the number of hash functions to use are given when the object is constructed. Using the previous formula to find the appropriate size of the Bloom filter assumes the optimal-k is used.

Figure A-2 shows how the optimal-*k* is based solely on the size of the Bloom filter and the number of elements used to train the filter.

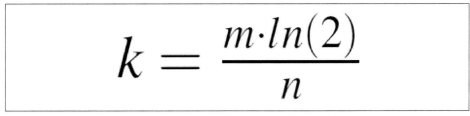

$$k = \frac{m \cdot ln(2)}{n}$$

Figure A-2. Optimal-k of a Bloom filter

The following helper function calculates the optimal-*k*.

```
/**
 * Gets the optimal-k value based on the input parameters.
 *
 * @param numElements
 *           The number of elements used to train the set.
 * @param vectorSize
 *           The size of the Bloom filter.
 * @return The optimal-k value, rounded to the closest integer.
 */
public static int getOptimalK(float numElements, float vectorSize) {
    return (int) Math.round(vectorSize * Math.log(2) / numElements);
}
```

About the Authors

Donald Miner serves as a solutions architect at EMC Greenplum, advising and helping customers implement and use Greenplum's big data systems. Prior to working with Greenplum, Dr. Miner architected several large-scale and mission-critical Hadoop deployments with the U.S. government as a contractor. He is also involved in teaching, having previously instructed industry classes on Hadoop and a variety of artificial intelligence courses at the University of Maryland, Baltimore County (UMBC). Dr. Miner received his PhD from UMBC in Computer Science, where he focused on Machine Learning and Multi-Agent Systems in his dissertation.

Adam Shook is a software engineer at ClearEdge IT Solutions, LLC, working with a number of big data technologies such as Hadoop, Accumulo, Pig, and ZooKeeper. Shook graduated with a BS in Computer Science from the University of Maryland, Baltimore County (UMBC), and took a job building a new high-performance graphics engine for a game studio. Seeking new challenges, he enrolled in the graduate program at UMBC with a focus on distributed computing technologies. He quickly found development work as a U.S. government contractor on a large-scale Hadoop deployment. Shook is involved in developing and instructing training curriculum for both Hadoop and Pig. He spends what little free time he has working on side projects and playing video games.

Colophon

The animal on the cover of *MapReduce Design Patterns* is Père David's deer (*Elaphurus davidianus*). It is originally from China, and in the 19th century the Emperor of China kept all Père David's deer in special hunting grounds. However, at the turn of the century, the remaining population of the deer was killed and eaten in a number of natural and man-made events, making the deer extinct in China. Since Père David, a zoologist and botanist, spirited a few away during the 19th century for study, the deer survives today in numbers of over 2,000.

Père David's deer grow up to be a little over 2 meters in length, and grow to be 1.2 meters tall. Its coat ranges from reddish in the summer to grey in the winter. Père David's deer is considered a semiaquatic animal and tends to enjoy swimming. The deer eats grass and aquatic plants.

In China this deer is sometimes known as sibuxiang or "like none of the four" because it has characteristics of four animals and yet it seems not to be those animals. Many remark that it has the tail of a donkey, the hoofs of a cow, the neck of a camel, and the antlers of a deer.

The cover image is from Cassell's *Natural History*. The cover font is Adobe ITC Garamond. The text font is Linotype Birka; the heading font is Adobe Myriad Condensed; and the code font is LucasFont's TheSansMonoCondensed.

GREENPLUM
UNIFIED ANALYTICS PLATFORM
FOR BIG DATA

FOR ALL OF YOUR DATA, TOOLS AND PEOPLE

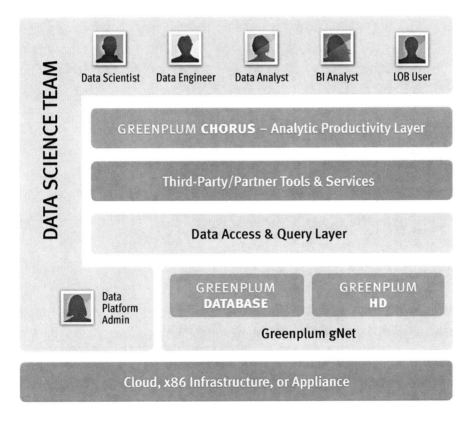

FOR MORE INFO, VISIT WWW.GREENPLUM.COM

CPSIA information can be obtained at www.ICGtesting.com
Printed in the USA
BVOW061309121012

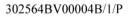